The Complete Idiot's Guide® to Writing a Novel

Second Edition

by Tom Monteleone

ALPHA

A member of Penguin Group (USA) Inc.

This one is for all my new friends, who will read this book and go on to create great novels. It's been fun …. Keep it that way.

ALPHA BOOKS

Published by the Penguin Group

Penguin Group (USA) Inc., 375 Hudson Street, New York, New York 10014, USA

Penguin Group (Canada), 90 Eglinton Avenue East, Suite 700, Toronto, Ontario M4P 2Y3, Canada (a division of Pearson Penguin Canada Inc.)

Penguin Books Ltd., 80 Strand, London WC2R 0RL, England

Penguin Ireland, 25 St. Stephen's Green, Dublin 2, Ireland (a division of Penguin Books Ltd.)

Penguin Group (Australia), 250 Camberwell Road, Camberwell, Victoria 3124, Australia (a division of Pearson Australia Group Pty. Ltd.)

Penguin Books India Pvt. Ltd., 11 Community Centre, Panchsheel Park, New Delhi—110 017, India

Penguin Group (NZ), 67 Apollo Drive, Rosedale, North Shore, Auckland 1311, New Zealand (a division of Pearson New Zealand Ltd.)

Penguin Books (South Africa) (Pty.) Ltd., 24 Sturdee Avenue, Rosebank, Johannesburg 2196, South Africa

Penguin Books Ltd., Registered Offices: 80 Strand, London WC2R 0RL, England

Copyright © 2010 by Thomas F. Monteleone

International Standard Book Number: 978-1-61564-033-1

Library of Congress Catalog Card Number: 2009941623

12 11 10   8 7 6 5 4 3 2 1

Interpretation of the printing code: The rightmost number of the first series of numbers is the year of the book's printing; the rightmost number of the second series of numbers is the number of the book's printing. For example, a printing code of 10-1 shows that the first printing occurred in 2010.

Printed in the United States of America

Most Alpha books are available at special quantity discounts for bulk purchases for sales promotions, premiums, fund-raising, or educational use. Special books, or book excerpts, can also be created to fit specific needs.

For details, write: Special Markets, Alpha Books, 375 Hudson Street, New York, NY 10014.

Publisher: *Marie Butler-Knight*

Associate Publisher: *Mike Sanders*

Senior Managing Editor: *Billy Fields*

Senior Acquisitions Editor: *Paul Dinas*

Senior Production Editor: *Megan Douglass*

Cover Designer: *William Thomas*

Book Designers: *William Thomas, Rebecca Batchelor*

Indexer: *Brad Herriman*

Layout: *Brian Massey*

Proofreader: *Laura Caddell*

Contents

Introduction

Who am I?

And why should you listen to me?

Listen, I'm just a guy who likes to write and has written *a lot of stuff ... including 27 novels.*

I've spent most of my adult life writing and avoiding what I call the "grown-up-people" jobs. During that stretch of time, I've learned a lot of things—mostly self-taught—that helped me get better at what I do. Self-taught means a lot of rumblin'-stumblin'-fumblin' my way through the world of writing and publishing. It means trial and error, frustration, and rejection.

I hope I can help you avoid much of that sort of thing. In fact, I'm going to make you a promise to be informative and entertaining. If you want to spend your time writing a novel, I believe it should be *fun*, not work. If you want *work*, go get a gig in a pie factory or selling vacuum cleaners door-to-door.

I want you to move through this book with a growing confidence that will come from familiarity with me and a belief in your own abilities. There's no magic or secret knowledge to writing a novel. There *are* techniques, guidelines, and even a few tricks to make it a rewarding endeavor; but you'll see, as we move from topic to topic, it's not much harder than making a 6-foot model of the Statue of Liberty out of little LEGO blocks.

Just different.

Anyway, before we get started, a little more about me, which should help you believe what I'll be telling you, and a few words of coach-in-the-locker-room inspiration before we go rushing to our keyboards to kick serious butt. I figure the easiest way to get started is tell a little story, so here goes ....

Picture this: I'm at a party—a barbecue, a wedding, or just about any other kind of social gathering—and I'm meeting people for the first time. As is the custom of most people, they will, soon after meeting you, ask what you "do." Meaning: how do you make your money? Inevitably, when I tell them I'm a writer, they ask what I've come to call the *Three Dumb Questions* and, thus, give me a chance to have a little fun at their expense.

Dumb Question No. 1: "You're a writer?—Oh, have you ever had anything published?"

People are surrounded by the printed word every day, but apparently it never occurs to them that someone actually must *write* the words before they can be put into print. No one, it seems, has ever met anyone who is a *real* writer—at least that's how everybody acts around me.

Anyway, I usually answer with a smile and a question of my own.

"Hey, come on ...," I say. "If I told you I was an astronomer, would you ask me if I've ever used a telescope?" (And following that logic, I'm reluctant to imagine what question a proctologist should get.)

Most people chuckle when I offer the astronomer analogy. And then I follow up with a thumbnail of my extensive and not-too-shabby bibliography. (You can check for yourself by looking at the inside back cover of this book. Go ahead, I'll wait.)

Finished? Okay, so I tell them I've been a professional writer for more than 30 years, and that I've written and published a variety of novels that have fallen into categories such as science fiction, horror, suspense, thrillers, and everything in between.

That usually prompts ...

Dumb Question No. 2: "Wow, that's really somethin' ... uh, do you use your real name?"

Now you know why they ask this "real name" business, don't you? Because they find themselves standing jaw-to-jaw with a *real writer*, someone who *writes books*, ... and they have *never heard of me*. They never admit this fact, of course, but they're thinking it, and they figure the only reason they don't recognize me is because I *gotta* be using a fake name.

So I tell them I love to see my "real" name on my books, and always make sure it works out that way. I tell them I'm like most writers, which means a lot egotistical and a little crazy. This usually satisfies them, but after a little pondering, many of them wheel out the single question all writers hear more than any other:

Dumb Question No. 3: "Wow, that's really neat, ya know—but ya gotta tell me, where do you guys get all your crazy ideas?"

Yeah. And even though I *know* it's coming, even though I've heard it literally *hundreds* of times, I'm still a little amazed that people are so perplexed when confronted with the concept of having original ideas. Now just so you know, most writers I've met have evolved and perfected their own wise-guy response to Question No. 3, and here's mine: "I subscribe to an Idea Service—and for only $9.95, they send me *10* new ideas each and every month."

I usually get a smile or a laugh, and everybody knows I'm kidding around, and then I explain my "crazy ideas" come from the molten core of my imagination, from the pit of my fears and the heights of my dreams, from the very stuff and fabric of life, that they come from *everywhere* around and within all of us, and that one only need be watching and listening to the world around him to gather up some ideas of his or her own.

It's usually cool after that, except when somebody pulls out a notepad and asks me (just to be on the safe side, mind you) if I could give them the address of that service ….

Actually, I'm lying. It usually doesn't end here.

Most of the times, least one person tells me he's lived the absolutely most *incredible* life and his experiences are just *so unbelievable*, so great, they are simply crying out to be chronicled in a book. At this point I can pretty much count on this guy to make me what most writers know as the "Standard Offer," which is: he'll tell me his life story, *I* get to then *write* it, and we split the money 50-50.

You can imagine how the rest of that conversation unwinds.

But the point of this story (and I *was* going to make one) is that people are fascinated with the idea of storytelling and writing a novel. It's been said that everybody has at least one novel in them, and maybe it's true. But some of you *also* have this burning drive to let that novel out, to actually sit down and spend the time you need to get it *written*.

If you're that person, I am here to help you.

When I was first starting out, I made all the mistakes you could make, and I sought help from people I met at conventions and workshops. People like Ted White and Damon Knight took the time to show me what I was doing wrong. They taught me how to eat criticism for breakfast and go back to the typewriter and write some more. They both told me that if I was any good, I'd make it; and I had to work to *make* myself good. And if I made it, then on a farther away "someday," I would be asked to help out a new writer or two, or hundreds ….

They were *correctimento* on all counts, friends.

And here we are, with me being asked to help you get that novel written.

If you picked up this book to browse around or if you've actually paid good old American Federal Reserve Notes for it, you are, in some way, like me—you want to be a writer of novels.

Well, you've come to the right place, because I know how to write novels. And when you finish this book, you will, too.

But in addition to the things I will teach you, it will be to your benefit if you have the following items:

- *The support and belief of those close to you.* I speak from experience, having been blessed to have my wife, Elizabeth, always in my corner. She has been my best editor, adviser, publicist, proofreader, and critic, and has made my work all the better for her efforts. You should be so lucky. And no, you can't have her.

- *Time.* If you have a full-time job or other obligations that don't allow you a sizable block of daily hours when you can be alone, then writing will be difficult.

- *Talent.* This is one of those nebulous things that can only be determined by spending a lot of time on writing, and writing, and then writing some *more*. Your talent will eventually find itself and develop in its own unique way.

These are three things I cannot provide, but you and your circle *can*.

Now we're almost ready to start. Here's a little heads-up on what's coming:

Part 1, An Overview, explains in general terms what it's going to be like and what you need to become a writer and, more specifically, a novelist. I give you the inside look at creative, economic, and plain old business requirements of writing a novel. We also spend a little time figuring out what novels are, why people like to read them, and what preparation you're going to need before you actually start pounding out the pages every day.

Part 2, The Elements of Writing a Novel, is when we go out to the workshop, roll up our sleeves, and open the big writer's toolbox. That's where we're going to find everything we need to write your book. We talk plot, characters, setting, dialogue, and all the other stuff that makes a good book.

Part 3, The Process of Writing a Novel, gets you comfortable with the more subtle parts of writing. Look on this part as the point where we start fine-tuning the things you learned in Part 2—from the simplest ideas of format and presentation through the weird and illogical worlds of grammar and style to the concept of discipline and how to use your time efficiently.

Part 4, Revisions and Beyond, centers on that part of the project many people don't think about—what do you do after you've finished the first draft? The answer is: you do a lot, because you're *not* finished yet.

And in the appendixes, you'll find a big, comprehensive glossary to help you keep up with the language of writing a novel. After that, I've given you a big appendix full of interviews with best-selling writers. This appendix gives you a chance to see what other successful novelists have to say about how they got started, how they work, and other insights into their craft.

Extras

In addition to all the other great information in this book, I also provide a number of sidebars, which give you lots of cool stuff to think about, remember, and utilize.

TRADE TALK

These boxes include terms and phrases that are part of the language of publishing.

A LIKELY STORY

These idea-prompts appear every now and then to give your imagination a little jolt.

TOM'S TIPS

These boxes contain lots of little tricks and things to remember to make your writing easier and even fun!

WORDS OF WISDOM

These are strategically placed quotes by writers about writing that will have some relevance to the issue at hand.

So let's get started, okay?

Acknowledgments

This project came together very quickly, but it would have never happened without the belief, support, and outright assistance from some very special people. Huge thanks and appreciation to Matt Bialer, Gary Goldstein, Ginny Bess, Bill Blatty, Janet Evanovich, Heather Graham, Stephen Hunter, Dean Koontz, Kat Martin, Richard Matheson, David Morrell, Peter Straub, and Whitley Strieber. And special thanks to my editor, Paul Dinas!

And especially my wife, Elizabeth, who is tireless in her hours of reading, editing, and proofing my efforts to inform and entertain you. It couldn't happen without her hand, heart, and mind in the mix.

Trademarks

All terms mentioned in this book that are known to be or are suspected of being trademarks or service marks have been appropriately capitalized. Alpha Books and Penguin Group (USA) Inc. cannot attest to the accuracy of this information. Use of a term in this book should not be regarded as affecting the validity of any trademark or service mark.

An Overview

We—meaning you and me—are going to use this first part of the book to get you up to speed on the entire "world" of writing. Despite the shopworn saying that writing is essentially sitting in a chair that happens to be in front of a keyboard, in the following pages, you'll discover that there's a lot more to it than that.

We're going to look at the basic personal attributes many writers share. We're going to think about talent, ability, and that elusive thing called *creativity*. We're going to find out how to develop, nurture, and unleash your own creativity. You will also be reminded to check the weekly and monthly lists of best-selling novels so you can see if you're writing a book people will want to read. Then we analyze the various types of popular fiction. We also discover the value of being a reader before being a writer.

So You Want to Be a Writer

In This Chapter

- Do you have a basic ability?
- Telling stories
- You gotta be tough
- Asking the next question
- Remembering to have fun
- A little help from your friends

Lots of people think it would be very cool to be a writer. What they don't know (but probably suspect) is that not everybody *can* be a writer. You need a certain number of skills and attributes, and in this first chapter, I'm going to talk about them and provide a little analysis and advice.

As we work our way through the list, I want you to think about these attributes and how they might apply to you. A fair amount of honest self-assessment is needed at this initial stage. Look at yourself in terms of these characteristics, so you can see what's usually necessary to be a writer. You'll need to decide which ones you already possess and which ones you don't.

When you've figured that out, you have to decide which ones you have in sufficient quantity and quality, and which ones you can develop and improve.

The Write Stuff

In no particular order of importance (because they are *all* important), let's talk about the following attributes of having the "write stuff":

- Basic writing ability

- Natural storytelling talent

- The right temperament

- A natural and abiding curiosity

- A sense of humor

- A support group

Let's take a look at each one in a little more detail.

A Basic Writing Ability

And here I mean *very basic*. You should have at least an elementary grasp of how sentences are constructed as well as an idea of what grammar is (without necessarily being an English teacher or a grammarian) and how it can be employed to make sense to anyone who is reading what you write.

This goes far beyond knowing which end of the sentence gets the period, okay? What I mean is a good understanding of the basics of composition and exposition we're supposed to be taught by the eighth grade. You should be able to write clear, simple sentences that say what you mean.

Later on, we spend plenty of time and space checking and ensuring that your basic writing skills are up to speed and then making them even better. But there's no substitute for understanding grammar as the foundation upon which everything else is built. You have to know the rules in order to break them and be so familiar with good grammar that you understand it intuitively. This is not as daunting as it may seem.

WORDS OF WISDOM

I don't know anything but the simplest rules of English grammar, and I seldom consciously apply them. Nevertheless, I instinctively write correctly and, I like to think, in an interesting fashion. I know when something sounds right and when it doesn't, and I can tell the difference without hesitation, even when writing at breakneck speed. How do I do this? I haven't the faintest idea.

—Isaac Asimov

A Natural Storytelling Talent

People who fit this mold can usually be pegged very early on in their lives. Most of my friends are writers, and they almost universally relate stories about their child-hoods when relatives and friends noticed a particular tendency to spin tales out of nothing. This ability usually took its earliest shape when we came up with a plausible explanation for how or why we did *not* do something that got us into Big Trouble. Some kids are marvelously inventive when it comes to making up stories, so try to remember if you were like that, or ask someone who can remind you.

I can personally vouch that a knack for storytelling emerges early. I liked to draw pictures, but my pictures weren't like the other kids'. I would draw a series of pictures all on the same subject or scene. After a typical session with the crayon box, I would have a stack of papers that told simple stories: of battles across the sky, landscapes in which armies and planes would progressively get knocked around, and monsters from dark forests that would wade into towns and cities to spread their mayhem. The interesting thing is that, even at the age of 6 or 7, I was doing what the Hollywooders call *story-boarding*, which means mapping out your story in visual blocks, almost like a cartoon.

My favorite kids' TV show was *Winky Dink*, which was 40 years ahead of its time as an "interactive" program. With the help of a "magic screen" and a washable marker, I was able to create parts of the cartoon that would help Winky get through his weekly adventure.

As I grew a little older and learned how to write, I started writing down simple stories. I had become addicted to comic books early on, and the first stories I wrote were basically just rip-offs of what I'd seen in a particular comic and couldn't get out of my head. That was just fine; at least I was writing.

When I was in the Cub Scouts, I was always the one to come up with a ghost story when it was time to sit around the campfire. I was the one who had to make up a name for our team, club, pets, secret hideout, or even the games we would invent in that wonderfully free-form way kids have a talent for.

One day, after I turned 12 or so, I realized that all the stuff I liked to read had been written by people. I'd known it before on a less conscious level, but suddenly it hit me hard, and I knew in one Zen moment why I'd always liked drawing and writing—because I wanted to be a writer. I bought my first typewriter soon after that.

Now at the risk of saying some people are just "born" storytellers, I'm left with the conclusion that maybe some of us are—myself included. If that's true, then it's up for discussion whether this particular trait can be trained or taught. In Appendix B, the interviews with best-selling writers, I ask them about this very thing.

The idea of a story can certainly be imparted to every one of you: the concepts of hero, antihero, villain, moral, resolution, and all that good stuff that was established way back with the creation of the Greek dramas. What might be harder to define and nurture is that inner drive, that thrumming turbine in the imagination's engine room that just makes some of us *need* to tell stories.

That's the part that gets really interesting. And that's where *you* come in. You need to develop the ability to peer down deep inside yourself (I know, I know, it's dark in there!) and see what's pushing you, what's making you want to be a writer, and more specifically, a novelist.

WORDS OF WISDOM

I think you must remember that a writer is a simple-minded person to begin with and go on that basis. He's not a great mind, he's not a great thinker, he's not a great philosopher, he's a storyteller.

—Erskine Caldwell

The Right Temperament

This can be called temperament, spirit, or constitution. When you distill all the unnecessary elements of a writer's personality and you see what's left in the collecting jar, you find massive quantities of toughness, resilience, and ego. It's important stuff, and we need to examine these aspects of a writer's makeup thoroughly.

A writer has to be tough—especially a writer of novels—because of the sheer amount of time they need to invest in creating a manuscript of such length. The average novel can be from 300 to 600 pages long, and some may end up more than 1,000. It takes great inner strength to spend the time and energy, to outlast the pressure to simply stop, to keep on pushing even when you don't feel like it, when you'd rather be doing anything but writing. At those times, you need to be tough on yourself.

But even greater toughness is necessary when you face rejection in the marketplace. Get used to this idea: being a writer means you will face a lot of rejection. What makes a story or a novel "good" is highly subjective, and some people are going to really like what you write, while others are probably not going to like it very much at all. It is a simple fact of life, so cut it into the wall of your writing compound in big, block letters: *rejection comes with the territory.* You have to learn to eat it for breakfast and go on to the business at hand, which is writing your story or your book.

> **TOM'S TIPS**
>
> *Never doubt you will finish what you set out to do.* Writing a novel is a long process requiring your persistence, a few pages a day, and about 6 months.

When I was first getting started—seriously writing every day and sending my stories out to every market I could find—I was only a few months out of college. I would finish a short story; send it out with an SASE (self-addressed, stamped envelope) to a mystery, science fiction (SF), horror, or adventure magazine; and start on another one. After some time, I probably had 15 or 20 stories circulating among all the possible markets. And every few weeks, I'd get one of them back with a form letter or notepad-size rejection paper-clipped to the first page.

I would then do what any real writer does: I yanked off the rejection slip, put the story in a new envelope with a new SASE, and sent it off again. It's the only thing you can do. Never take it personally. Never get mad. Just tell yourself you will eventually show them the error in their judgment of your work.

I sent off stories and harvested rejection slips—close to 200 of them—for about $2\frac{1}{2}$ years. But I never gave up. I told myself I would simply keep writing. I told myself I would eventually start selling my stories. And I did. But the reason I was able to do it is because I was mentally tough. I always had enough inside to bounce back from yet another failure in the marketplace, and I had a big enough ego to not only absorb the impacts, but also to believe I would make it someday.

So the simple line here is *never* take no for your final answer. Always recover from rejection with a renewed will. If you can do that—no matter how long it takes—you will succeed.

A Natural and Abiding Curiosity

This is a no-brainer, really. It helps if you're the type who goes out to the backyard after nightfall every once in a while, looks up at the endless scatter of stars, and is struck by the sheer immensity and wonder of it all. Or how about this one: you're watching The History Channel or The Discovery Channel and something makes you wonder *Wow, what if …?*

These are just two examples of how your imagination should be working if you want to write novels. You have to be like a sentinel on the watchtower. Your mission, if you choose to accept it, is to be ever vigilant and totally plugged into the world around you.

That means you are not like most people. You are immediately curious when you hear a neighbor mention a weird noise or a strange light, or when you read an article that notes an increase in hung juries, or you see a wacko-looking character running the Tilt-A-Whirl at the summer carnival on the outskirts of your town, or …. You fill in the blanks. It doesn't matter what fires your curiosity and gets your imagination burning like a coal furnace into which somebody tossed a bucket of paint thinner. What matters is that *something* does.

There's an old axiom among SF writers: you need to have what they call a "sense of wonder" to write science fiction. I'd extrapolate on that sentiment and say you need it to write *anything*. The world around you has got to strike you as interesting as hell, even if you live in a farmhouse in Indiana and the empty land around you is as plain and featureless as a freshly sanded tabletop.

When my parents, in their infinite wisdom, decided to send me to a Jesuit high school in Baltimore, I entered a world of disciplined learning. The curriculum was tough—4 years of Latin, 2 years of French or German, 1 year of Greek, 4 years of English grammar and composition, algebra and calculus, plus all the sciences, history, theology, philosophy, and music. In addition, you had to try out for at least one varsity team, participate in a dramatic production, and take a course called Elocution.

WORDS OF WISDOM

Rejected by 121 publishing houses before its publication in 1974, *Zen and the Art of Motorcycle Maintenance* thrust Robert M. Pirsig into stardom, selling more than three million copies in paperback alone.

—*The New York Times*

Yes, I learned a lot. Among the most important things was one of those little techniques the Jesuits have become infamous for among their more staid and traditional colleagues in the Church. More than one of them in the course of their lectures and lessons warned us: "Always ask the next question."

Think about it. Never be satisfied with anything you hear, see, or read. That's the secret of not only being an informed human being, but also a good writer. I've always tried to use that advice, to look at things from every aspect by turning, twisting, stretching, and squeezing. Never satisfied with just a single answer, I always bug and noodge my sources to share everything they know.

This is where your imagination kicks in. This is where your idea-engine and your mind's plot-machine get their fuel when you have them chugging and clanking through the long hours of the night.

Another thing I should mention in this section is something lots of writers rely on (even if they have no idea of what it is or how it works). It's that strange, vaguely understood part of our minds the psychiatrists call the *subconscious.*

Not everybody is on the same page when it comes down to the subconscious. Plenty of people will swear the subconscious mind doesn't even exist, much less help you be a great writer. But you'll find a lot more writers who swear by it.

It works something like this: you're writing your novel, and you're having problems figuring out a plot complication or how to explain a character's motivation for doing something you just made him do. You have a problem, and you have no clue how to solve it, explain it, or fix it. So what do you do?

If you're stalled, sometimes the best thing to do is drop it for a day or so. Leave it alone and work on something else: some other scene, a new chapter, maybe even an idea for a short story. The cool thing is, even though you don't think you're working on solving your creativity problem, believe me, you are. A part of you is doing it, and that part is your subconscious mind. It's the part that doesn't need to pay attention when you're eating, breathing, mowing the lawn, driving the car, sorting out the junk mail, and all the other stuff you do. For people who aren't creative types, that part of their mind has very little to do except crank up some hellaciously weird and detailed dreams. But for you, it's the part that's been working on your novel's problems.

So you learn to trust your subconscious. It's strange, because when you least expect to find the answer to a troublesome character or a needed twist in the plot, it will jump up and startle you with its freshness and utter applicability. I can't explain it any better than that, but if any of you have been in positions that required analysis and problem-solving, you've probably already experienced the power of the subconscious. Some people even have dreams in which they see themselves figuring out the answer, while others just wake up in the middle of the night, and *wham!*—they've got something totally worked out.

If any of this has happened to you, you know what I'm talking about. The rest of you? Until you feel it firsthand, you're going to have to trust me.

WORDS OF WISDOM

We write to expose the unexposed. If there is one door in the castle you have been told not to go through, you must. Otherwise, you're just re-arranging the furniture in the rooms you've already been in. Most human beings are dedicated to keeping that one door shut. But the writer's job is to see what's behind it, to see the bleak, unspeakable stuff, and to turn the unspeakable into words.

—Anne Lamott

A Sense of Humor

A sense of humor is important in ways you may not suspect. I don't primarily mean you should be thinking "funny" when you write, although a little levity can often push your material to places it wouldn't otherwise go. What I'm suggesting here: Don't take yourself or your work too seriously.

To be a good writer, you have to like writing. There has to be some part of the process you enjoy. In other words, writing has to be fun.

Over the years, I've met plenty of struggling novelists, and one of the prime reasons many of them have not yet succeeded is their insistence on making the writing of their novel a grim task, like a forced march through a scorched battlefield. In many instances, these would-be novelists have been poisoned by the largely pedantic attitude that writing a novel is such a noble and intellectually tedious struggle, it should be regarded as a labor—and most definitely not a joy.

Friends, I can tell you that this kind of attitude ultimately saps away a writer's lifeblood better than any B-movie vampire. Over the years, I've attended many conventions and workshops full of writers and editors, and I've been invited to my share of seminars and symposia in the groves of academia. When I speak to groups about writing, I let them know in a nice, casual style how much fun I'm having when I sit down to write. I tell them writing a novel has to be fun, or otherwise it would be too damned hard to do.

You'd be amazed at the reaction my attitude elicits from the professorial types in the audience. Many of them see me as a "commercial" writer (which I am, of course), and that is, in many English departments, a bad thing. Many Ph.D.s believe writing purchased in any quantity by the public must be, by its very nature, inferior and common when contrasted to what they've decided is Literature.

They tend to get a little cranky, as you might expect, when I talk about novels and writing without a lot of phony pomp and circumstance. I have, on some occasions, been accused by such doyens of not taking my work "seriously," of having far too cavalier an attitude to be able to produce work of merit or staying power. I'm cool with that.

Don't get seduced by that kind of thinking. There's something ultimately silly and funny about making up stories and getting *paid* for doing it. If you never discover that simple kernel of humor about writing, you're in for a long, arduous journey.

The longer you remain in the world of writing, the more publishing people you're going to meet. And if any of them ever starts to paint that silly portrait of the writer as a struggling, tortured soul, tell them you know better. Or as they used to say in the really old novels: *Claptrap!* Or how about: *Balderdash!*

 WORDS OF WISDOM

Writing's not terrible, it's wonderful. I keep my own hours, do what I please. When I want to travel, I can. But mainly, I'm doing what I most wanted to do all my life. I'm not into the agonies of creation.

—Raymond Carver

A Support Group

At first glance, a support group may not seem all that necessary because you, like most people, may imagine that writing is pretty much a solitary task. You do it alone. You don't need a lot of people around while you're doing it, and it's not much of a stretch to figure you're more comfortable when you're just hanging out with your best friend—yourself.

Actually, the exact opposite is usually the case. You'll find you spend so much time alone that, when you're *not* writing, it does your soul a lot of good to be around other people. The trick is to surround yourself with the *right* people. And that means people who understand your desire, need, and intention to write your novel and who are not going to give you a hard time about it. Let's take a look at who these people might be and how to deal with each of them.

Your Immediate Family

Number one in the group of your immediate family is usually your spouse, or what the politically correct crowd has decreed we should call your "significant other." And I'm going to tell you right now, if this person is not in your corner regarding your novel, then you're up a fairly famous creek without that equally famous paddle. I say this because your spouse/significant other is the one who's going to be with you the most and who is going to have to readjust his or her schedule and thinking more than anyone else with whom you're in contact.

> **TOM'S TIPS**
>
> When people see you at home, sitting in an easy chair with a notebook computer across your lap, their first impression is that you're not really working, that you're not doing honest labor. It will be your job to convince them otherwise.

Everyone will need to respect your need for privacy and a modicum of quiet (unless you like to write with a lot of music on). They will have to realize they will probably be the first person (and for a while, the *only* person) reading your chapters as they come whispering out of the printer. And going along with this, they'll have to learn how to be honest with you regarding your work. They need to be able to tell you when it's bad as well as when it's good, and it would help if they could tell you why. They also need to understand that, when you're sitting at your keyboard, typewriter, or notepad, it's probably not a good time to ask you to switch the clothes from the washer to the dryer or feed the dog.

Some couples have more trouble with getting this riff down than others. Lots of factors are involved here: education, the amount of reading they do, the amount of time spent alone, jealousy, the lack of respect, … you can fill in the blanks. If people are involved, the dynamic can create problems and stresses even I may not be able to foresee.

Your Friends

Your friends are your inner circle of associates ranging from your best friend all the way down to the distant neighbor you wave at across the hedges and talk lawn-stuff. Lots of factors only you know will determine how much of your dreams and actual writing you share with this group. If you trust their opinions and knowledge of what makes a "good read," then you might chivvy them up for honest criticism. If they really like you, they might be reluctant to tell you they don't like your writing, which might be noble and heartfelt, but not the real feedback you need.

So be sure you select those among your friends who, again, understand what you're trying to do and why. Impress upon them that you need them to believe in you, but you also need them to be honest. Also be aware that the potential jealousy, education, and the rest of the spousal concerns also apply here.

Academics

What I mean by this is basically anyone you may know from a college English department, the local high school teacher, or even people who teach floating writers' workshops. (We're going to spend more time on the whole workshop thing later.) This is a good pool from which you can drag some very supportive people.

Many college professors "have been working on a novel" for many, many years (which means they haven't been working very hard because you're going to write your novel in 6 months, but that's another story), and they may be able to give the standard grad-school tap-dance on the structure and purpose of the novel, which may or may not appeal to you. Local teachers and workshop mentors are also helpful for getting your manuscript edited and critiqued.

The important thing to look for in all these folks is that they're all in synch with what you want to do. They are all most likely active readers who wouldn't mind having a few publications listed in their resumés as well. They are, in that sense, *with you*.

So inform them of your project, and take what they tell you with a grain of salt and the Real Wisdom you're getting from me right here.

Other Writers

These people are theoretically the most important support group you can assemble, for obvious reasons. These are the guys and girls who have walked in your shoes. They shared the same dreams, the same rejections and harsh criticisms, and maybe even similar successes.

How do you meet other writers?

It depends on a lot of factors: the size of your town, your circle of friends, your profession, and your own interest in finding them. Some clubs advertise in libraries;

look at ads in the back of writers' magazines; and go online, where you can find just about anything, anywhere. Finding writers who want to talk about writing should be a piece of cake.

> **WORDS OF WISDOM**
>
> The complete novelist would come into the world with a catalog of qualities something like this. He would own the concentration of a Trappist monk, the organizational ability of a Prussian field marshall, the insight into human relations of a Viennese psychiatrist, the discipline of a man who prints the Lord's Prayer on the head of a pin, the exquisite sense of timing of an Olympic gymnast, and by the way, a natural instinct and flair for exceptional use of language.
>
> —Leon Uris

But here's the neat part: if you stay in the writing game, you'll meet writers without even trying. You'll meet editors at your publishing house. Editors mostly know other writers. You'll meet them, trust me. If you decide to get an agent, you'll meet the agent's other clients. You'll correspond with other writers, and you'll like it. It's just one of those processes that happens.

You may even join a writers' "group" that meets every once in a while to do writer-stuff such as readings, critiques, workshops, cookouts, library benefits, or whatever.

Try it. You'll dig it.

The Least You Need to Know

- Understand that being a writer requires that you assess yourself honestly.
- Spend the time to make a mental or real checklist of your writing assets and your liabilities. Then start doing whatever it takes to prepare yourself for the job.
- Never forget that writing a novel, if you're doing it right, is a lot of fun. It's a journey through the landscape of your mind, and it should be an enjoyable ride. This doesn't mean it won't be difficult. Everything that's worth anything is hard.
- Surround yourself with positive energy and positive people who believe in what you're doing as much as you do. If people in your life make noises of discouragement, derision, or other kinds of venality, you must distance your work from all of them.

Creativity and Talent

In This Chapter

- What is creativity?
- Talent and how you get better
- Evaluating yourself
- Staying in shape, talent-wise

The funny thing about creativity and talent—some people tend to worry way too much about whether or not they have any, while others never give it a second thought.

As we shall see, both approaches carry their own advantages and pitfalls. This chapter gives you a chance to assess how important creativity and talent are in your novel-writing adventure. Both concepts can be very slippery in terms of defining them and understanding how they relate to you.

I don't want to belabor a subject that's largely subjective—something on the abstract side of our learning experience. Subjective concepts tend to be warped by the attitudes, perceptions, and experiences of everyone involved, and they tend to make for tiresome discourse. This is something I want to not only avoid in the book, but also run away from screaming.

Why Analyze Creativity?

The only reason for examining nebulous things like creativity and her red-haired stepbrother, talent, is to be aware of their place in the whole process of writing a novel. The plain truth is, you need both of them in the largest quantities you can serve up.

I'm going to assume that, because you've kept reading this far, you are interested in writing a book. It's also a safe bet that you are a "creative person" and you're brimming over with talent like a fresh cup of coffee from one of those silver urns at The Plaza Hotel.

And that's great.

In fact, that's exactly how you *should* feel. Now let's lift up the hood and see what's in here, okay?

The Nature of the Beast

Recall the introduction to this book, in which I talk about the *Three Dumb Questions*. Also recall the last question: where do you get your ideas? Well, I have a confession to make—it's not at all a dumb question, and I guess I just like being a wise guy.

Because getting "good" or "crazy" or "wild" ideas is part of what creativity and being creative are all about. I think you'll have more ideas (probably more than you have time in your life to write about) if you learn to nurture your natural creative urges and feel good about unleashing them on the world without fear or regret.

So how do you go about this? By keeping a few basic tenets in mind. Now let's talk about them.

Fear Is the Killer

This is as good a time as any to bring up the notion that a lot of people seem to be plain *afraid* to be creative … or worse, let anyone see that they've already made an attempt to be so. To some of you, this must sound crazy, but to others, it might be touching an exposed nerve.

WORDS OF WISDOM

Hide not your talents, they for use were made. What's a sun-dial in the shade?

—Benjamin Franklin

Let me tell you a little story.

Back when I was in graduate school, I worked part time at the university library putting books away in the "stacks." The guy who ran the department was a kindly, older man, who'd come to the United States from Hungary when he was a young student.

I liked him, and so did all the other guys under his supervision. One night, he invited a few of us to his apartment just off-campus for dinner. It was a very interesting, very European evening—from the topics discussed to the style and presentation of the ethnic dishes. His wife was demure, gracious, and sweet, and she helped make the whole experience doubly charming as well as very different from the average college kid's night out.

The conversation eventually drifted into the realm of books, publishing, and writing. When I mentioned I'd like to be a full-time writer someday (and that I'd been sending out stories for a year or so with nothing in return but rejection slips), our host brightened for an instant as he told us that he also dreamed of being a professional writer. His wife whispered something to him in Hungarian, and although I couldn't understand what she said, I could detect a mildly reproachful tone. Our host suddenly looked a bit humbled.

I ignored their interchange and asked what he liked to write. After some prodding, he admitted he'd been writing novels. More prodding and he said he'd been writing them for 38 years (!). I asked him if I could read one, and he again brightened, then asked me if I was serious, if I really meant it.

When I insisted, he led me from the table and down the hall to a room assigned as a "guest bedroom," where he opened a closet that had been lined with shelves. Each one crammed with cardboard boxes, the kind used to hold reams of bond paper. He pulled one down, opened it, and pulled out a thick stack of typescript pages. I looked at it and then back up at the wall of boxes.

"Are they *all* your novels?" I asked, even though I knew the answer.

The gentleman nodded his head with an almost embarrassed expression on his face. He told me he'd written 26 novels, and he had never sent even *one* of them to an editor!

Why?

He admitted he'd always been afraid that the publishers wouldn't like what he had done.

 TOM'S TIPS

Don't try to be creative and critical at the same time when creating a story, character, plot, etc. Just let it flow! Let it fly! The time to tear it down and see how it works is later—it's called editing or revision.

I can't tell you how utterly sad I felt for him then, and still do as I write this. His fear had paralyzed him. His lack of belief in his own talent had stifled what might have been a wonderful career living out his dream. I couldn't figure out how he could have done that to himself, but I stood there and made a promise to myself I would never do the same.

So please stop worrying about what people might think of you when they find out you've been thinking lofty thoughts, when they realize you want to be more than a drone like so many others have chosen to do.

Creativity Is All About Your Ideas

One point about creativity is really obvious when you think about it. If you're going to be a writer, you are essentially recognizing and positing intriguing ideas and situations and then working them out on paper. If your ideas are extremely clever and insightful, people will say you're very "creative."

See what I mean?

So that's the secret—have good ideas. And you're sitting there thinking, *Right. Easy for him to say. He's already had a bunch of great ideas.* Well, that's true, I have; but now I'm going to show you some sources and techniques for finding and developing your own ideas so you, too, can bask in the radiation of a High-Creativity Quotient.

So what are some ways to develop your creativity? I'm glad you asked.

Dreams. This is one of the most obvious sources of ideas, and for a good reason. If you are one of those people who's able to recall much of their dreams, you're already aware of how unbelievably detailed dreams can be. This is the mark of a mind (yours) working very hard at figuring out things you fear or look forward to. Freud was a big believer in dreams being a key to what was truly important in our lives.

> **TOM'S TIPS**
>
> Always keep a small notebook and pen on a nightstand near your bed, or even a voice-activated digital mini-recorder. I know plenty of writers who've jotted down ideas they *knew* were simply wonderful but could not read their half-asleep handwriting the next morning. You want to get those images and impressions from your dreams while they are still immediate and fully realized—and be able to decipher what they are the next day! And now that most cell phones and MP3 players have "record" functions, you can also use them to save great ideas whenever and wherever you are.

Remember when I mentioned the subconscious mind? Well, this is where that part of your brain is *always* on the job. If you will begin to pay more attention to your dreams, you will discover a hidden wealth of cues, triggers, and ideas from which you can extrapolate and then combine into a great, original novel. (By the way, *The Complete Idiot's Guide to Interpreting Your Dreams* [Alpha Books, 2004] agrees with me on this one. Check it out as a more extensive source of using your dreams creatively.)

Travel. Always look for reasons to get yourself to a city or even a country you've never visited. New locales often stimulate us in ways that would otherwise never happen. When I was in Palermo, Sicily, and saw the Capuchin catacombs, I came up with ideas that spawned several stories and a novel. You'll find that you gain a different perspective on even the most common aspects of your life when you see them re-focused through the lens of an unfamiliar culture.

WORDS OF WISDOM

What is important are ideas. If you have ideas, you have the main asset you need, and there isn't any limit to what you can do with your business and your life.

—Harvey Firestone

Other novels. The more you write, the more you will learn to be keenly aware of what you're reading in the works of others. And every once in a while, a passage in another novel will somehow "speak" to you—as if it were written for you alone. And usually it will be something the other novelist glossed over or included in passing without intending to make it all that important. But for you, the passage made you pause, imagine, ask the next question, and suddenly realize you've chanced upon a great idea for a new story or novel.

Your own life. So many people think everyone else would be fascinated by reading their life stories. While I have my doubts about this, I do have a feeling that most of us, running the gamut of opportunity for an infinite range of experiences, have events in our lives that would provide fertile material for stories and novels. If you've worked in a particularly unique profession, or lived in an exotic location, or were part of a noteworthy event, you will certainly have experiences that can be teased into story ideas.

Mythology and history. You don't have to be writing a historical romance or a heroic fantasy to use the rich and textured events found in the myths of countless countries and cultures. Many myths are instructive tales of morality or caution, and if you take the time to examine what they are telling us, you'll find a deeper layer of meaning you can apply to characters and events far removed from ancient texts and oral histories.

And speaking of history, if you spend some of your time reading about it, you will learn some incredible stories about fascinating characters and events. In many cases, you'll discover that truth is far stranger than fiction, and you'll know you have another boundless source of ideas, situations, and templates for your stories and novels. William Styron's *Confessions of Matt Turner* is a great example of this.

Brainstorms. This one is a little harder to make happen because it normally requires more than one person and assumes you have access to a bunch of like-minded people—all of whom are very interested in, if not driven to, getting their novels written. It usually involves sitting around with a few drinks (or at least coffees) and just letting the ideas fly around the ether with little or no regard to what makes perfect sense and what is patent nonsense.

When I was just getting started, I was part of a writers' group that would meet on a fairly regular basis and brainstorm ideas for stories and books. It was fun and always inspiring. The best thing about brainstorming is that it didn't matter if 95 percent of the stuff everybody came up with was bilge … as long as the other 5 percent was pure gold.

Try new things. This isn't as hard as it sounds. Just tell yourself you're going to make an effort to expand your opportunities for new input because that equals new ideas. Read a book you *never* imagined reading. Try a new recipe. Talk to someone you normally would ignore. You never know where your next great idea can come from. But always give it a chance to come from as many sources as possible.

A LIKELY STORY

What would happen if a cheesy, lounge-act stage magician suddenly discovered one night that he was performing *real* magic?

Talent: Putting Your Ideas to Work

There isn't a lot to figure out when it comes to talent, and again, it's not something you should worry about. Just like you have to trust the ideas to "come to you," you have to do the same thing with the way you put your ideas to use.

Trust your instincts and see where they take you. If you think you have a "big enough" idea to carry a novel, you'll know sooner rather than later. The thing to keep in mind here is to *stop worrying* about whether or not you have any talent. If you believe you do, then you most likely have plenty.

The good news: your talent can be sharpened and improved. It gets better the same way you get better at shooting baskets at the foul line, or flipping cards into a hat, or walking a tightrope—with practice, practice, practice.

All that means to a writer is to keep on writing. If you have the main idea for your novel already worked out, you need to start making decisions about how you will tell your story. When we get to Parts 2 and 3 in the book, where we examine the elements and processes of writing, you will see how to make good decisions.

By the way, if you already have a bunch of great ideas for novels, you're very fortunate, and you probably don't need some of the things I'm going to suggest in this next section. But for the rest of you, I have a few things that will help keep you on your imaginative toes.

Ways to Stay Ahead of the Curve

If you can get in the habit of doing some of the things suggested in this section, you can be assured of never feeling like you've "run out of things to say" or "don't have any good ideas."

And the other thing to remember is repetition. The more you do some of these things, the easier they get, and the more they become habits you don't want to break.

Keep a journal. This is like the old diary idea, but you need to layer and texture the entries to include not only what you did the day before, but also anything you witnessed or heard about that struck you as singular, odd, interesting, scary, challenging, inspiring, and so on. You also want to include dreams, problems to solve, and people who affected you. This isn't as easy as it sounds. You need to save time every day to allow you to get this done. Count on 20 to 30 minutes … get used to it … and do it.

TOM'S TIPS

Think young! Imagination rules in the minds of children. Don't ever believe the deadly advice lurking beneath the surface of the old saying "act your age!" Growing up should not mean we let our imaginations atrophy. Good writers know this.

Carry a notepad. This should be small and unobtrusive in a pocket or purse. It could also be a personal digital assistant (PDA), smartphone, or whatever you have with you most of the time. The idea is to use it to jot down fragments of ideas, impressions, or weird questions you hear or that occur to you during the day. You'll be amazed how many ideas will pile up—some you may eventually be able to use. More than once, I've turned a simple one-line phrase from my notepad into an entire novel. I know it sounds daunting and crazy, but trust me, it's not.

One more thing: if you do use a digital recorder or something otherwise technical instead of the old-fashioned notepad, just remember that you'll eventually have to transfer your ideas to something you can peruse at your leisure.

Idea boosters. A number of books, games, and software packages claim to be able to stimulate your creativity and make deposits in your idea bank. The rate of their efficacy and success depends on very subjective factors neither you nor I can predict. So if you want to, go check out some of this stuff or do some research about them online. If nothing else, some of these products are at least good amusement.

Music. Pay more attention to the lyrics in the music you hear. Avoid music videos, where everything is already provided. Listen to the music through headphones with your eyes closed, and see what takes shape in the "theater of the mind." This is a very good technique for opening the idea floodgates. Many writers find that music and lyrics really get their imaginations running at higher gears.

New stuff. Don't let your life get into a rut. Make room for new experiences. New input from activities and cultural stuff you don't normally indulge in mean new ideas and new ways of seeing things. I mentioned this in one of Tom's Tips, but it bears repeating. (In fact, you may notice as we go through this book that some things are repeated … and it will usually be for a good reason: they're important.)

Read more carefully. This one is a lot more intuitive and sounds simpler than it really is. When you are doing your normal reading during the day, try to remind yourself you're reading something someone else had to think up and write down! Try to be very aware of every word the writer chose, and make an effort to understand the choices.

Analyze the passage for tone, style, attitude, and intent, and ask yourself if there are unspoken questions or assumptions waiting "in between the lines" of what you're reading. Whenever I go to a concert with a friend of mine who's a serious musician, I notice he hears things I totally miss. He's listening with musician's ears. You need to learn how to read with writer's eyes.

The Least You Need to Know

- Trust in your instincts and your ability. Believe you have what it takes.
- Tell yourself there's nothing to be afraid of.
- Cultivate sources for good ideas, and make a habit of always being ready to recognize one when it presents itself.
- Create new habits that will keep the ideas coming. Experiment with a whole range of "tricks"; keep the ones that work for you, and forget about the rest.

Looking at "The List"

In This Chapter

- The List as we know it
- How The List works and where it came from
- Examples to learn from
- Getting there and staying there

Everybody's heard of it, most people have probably seen it, and plenty have actually read it and plan their own reading according to its dictates. In the world of publishing, it's usually called The List, and it has historically meant The Best-Seller List. It has been divided up, for your convenience and reading pleasure, into both fiction and nonfiction, hardcover and soft.

If a book appears on the best-seller list, it becomes something of a self-fulfilling prophecy. People see the title and start buying the book, which fuels the buying frenzy in geometric progressions.

The History of the Best-Seller List

The history of the best-seller list is amply recorded in articles and even a few books, but I should at least sketch in a few facts. A man named Harvey Thurston Peck published the first-ever best-seller list in a publication called *Bookman* in 1895. It was concerned only with fiction, and it derived its information from a few scattered sources around New York. In 1912, *Publishers Weekly* was the first to issue a best-selling tabulation of nonfiction books.

> **WORDS OF WISDOM**
>
> A best-seller was a book which somehow sold well simply because it was selling sell.
>
> —Daniel J. Boorstin

From those beginnings, an attempt to chronicle literary success at the cash register has been an ongoing weekly tradition. And it wasn't too long afterward that one compiler of best-sellers stood head and shoulders above the rest—*The New York Times*.

The One and Only

For a very long time, there was only one best-seller list (that actually mattered)—and it was touted and ballyhooed and treated with great adoration and respect—*The New York Times* Bestseller List. Perhaps you've heard of it? But things have changed in the last decade or so, and these changes have affected the way the book-buying public selects its reading material.

The New York Times Bestseller List is compiled by a process long believed to be complex and more than a little arcane. The story circulated by the insiders along "publishers' row" in Manhattan goes something like this: a group of bookstores throughout New York and a handful of other major cities around the country have been recruited (and presumably paid) by *The New York Times* to keep very extensive records of the books they sell each week and send their numbers to *The Times'* book editor every 7 days.

The selection of bookstores and vendors represented, claimed *The Times*, a very accurate picture of what titles were popular on a weekly and, therefore, timely, basis. Adding to the "lore of the list" was the oft-heard refrain that the identity and location of the "target bookstores" was the Holy Grail of the publishing industry. Practically no one knew exactly what book vendors were responsible for the numbers that created the weekly lists of best-selling books. Book people in New York still say it's one of *The Times'* most closely guarded secrets.

The Man with a Plan

However, an apocryphal story has been circulating in Manhattan for a long time about a writer who somehow discovered the names and addresses of the bookstores that reported their sales to the editor of the list. This young writer, who recently had a book published, was totally unknown and unheralded, but he devised a bold stratagem.

He took his entire advance, dispersed it to an army of friends and cohorts, and sent them off to all the "target" bookstores. Every day, at each location, some of the writer's legion would buy his book from the "right" stores. He spent all his money buying his own book, which caused it to be reported as an extremely hot-selling title, and so it ended up on the list. That caused all the people who buy only the books on the list to buy his book and further propel it up the ladder.

Once he'd fueled the fire, it raged on its own, and his novel enjoyed a good few months on the best-seller list, making him more than 100 times the money he spent to put it there.

Did it really happen? I have no idea. But it certainly could have worked, given the mechanism that had been in place for so many decades. It was the only way to get a feel for what was going on in "real time" because sales figures were kept in the time-honored fashion of ledgers and paid invoice receipts, and publishers couldn't compile and release those for many months after a book had ceased its popular run.

The Effects of the Information Age

In the days before the computer, and all the ways of tracking data on an instantaneous basis, this system appeared to have worked very well. But the blossoming of the information age has allowed more people to be involved in the traffic and sales of books. The involvement isn't restricted to a secret cabal of booksellers in secret locations.

There are now more lists people can consult when trying to figure out what they should read next. The daily national paper *USA Today* publishes a "top 150" best-selling book list, which they claim is based on nationwide, computerized sales numbers compiled by a vast network of wholesalers and retailers who have digital information updated per minute. *Publishers Weekly*, the trade magazine of the publishing industry, also claims to have established a similar computer-assisted data stream.

But perhaps the most interesting and totally immediate way of tracking book sales has been the advent of online bookselling through outlets such as amazon.com and barnesandnoble.com. Potential buyers and readers can now simply log on and check up-to-the-second book sales records. They can even read sample chapters and reviews by other readers like themselves (as opposed to a small clique of professional "critics").

The current state of what and how we perceive a best-selling book seems to be fairly positive. We're getting figures that are more immediate and more real in terms of consulting a source that's actually connected to the widest, deepest data pool.

This does not, however, get into the philosophical question of whether or not we *need* a best-seller list. I figure it's a great target to aim for. If your novel gets on it, you can be assured of making some serious money, and there's nothing wrong with that.

The List Pulls the Train

Big publishers definitely need the list because they need best-sellers (to fund other, less-profitable publishing ventures), especially because many publishing companies have been devoured by huge, diversified corporations. A profit-driven mentality has slowly overwhelmed the older, more patient methods of running a publishing house. Now for many imprints, the number of copies of a book being sold is no different from the number of bags of potato chips being sold by another division of the same company.

WORDS OF WISDOM

The writing of a best-seller represents only a fraction of the total effort required to create one.

—Ted Nicholas

What a lot of these mega-corporations don't immediately get is that publishing involves quite a bit of risk. Unless your publisher already has a stable of well-known, "brand-name" authors, it's taking a chance with every title it prints … every month. If enough readers aren't willing to try a new writer they've never heard of (in other words, a writer they've never seen on any best-seller lists), the publisher is going to lose big-time.

The reality of modern publishing is simple when you boil it all down and flense the meat off of its bones: Every successful publisher has a few brand-name authors who make them the hundreds of millions it needs not only to stay in business, but also to fund the hundreds of other books in its catalogs that may not be making *any* money at all.

Most writers haven't thought about things like this, but you will see as we work our way through this book that many aspects of writing and publishing are interconnected and interdependent in ways not initially obvious. It's my job to not only make you aware of this stuff, but teach you how to use the awareness to your advantage.

So some of you may be thinking, *If publishers have a few writers making them all that money, why do they even bother publishing any new, or high-risk, books and writers?* That's a good question, and it deserves a good and thoughtful answer. Without going too deeply into the core essentials of how good capitalism is based on forecasted unlimited growth and all that cool stuff, I think a few points can be made to convince new novelists that there is a real need for their books.

The most glaring fact new writers forget is that best-selling writers usually started out from the same place as any new writer—unknown and with little or no sales potential.

The word we need to key on is *potential*. Editors (and their publisher-bosses) are always looking for new writers who have the potential to be the next best-seller, the next brand name to occupy the list. Editors do this because they're operating in an economic and esthetic continuum where writers grow old and weary and eventually stop writing, die, or worse—stop writing well. Editors need to have ready and able replacements to fill the ultimately vacant keyboards, so they spend a lot of time taking risks with unknown writers who display some spark or sign of the talent needed to "hit the list."

In publishing, it's okay if you have 20 failures as long as you have 1 success. It's that kind of business ….

Don't Know Much About History

Some writers I've known have tried to "predict" what kind of novel is going to be the "next best-seller," and more than a few have had some success at it. If you've been around long enough to pay attention and listen to the stories of the guys who've been around even longer than you have, you can get a feel for the somewhat cyclic nature of the publishing industry.

A LIKELY STORY

Novels about artists and writers have been surprisingly popular. There's a story about a writer of science fiction/espionage novels who is visited by government agents because he has inadvertently written about a *real* "secret weapon" (which he had just dreamed up on his own). The agents think he's a spy and go after him.

Peoples' tastes change and are influenced by a variety of cultural, tidal forces. The variations are mirrored in our home décors, our clothes, our cars, the kind of art we admire, the books we read, etc. Academics and scholars will tell you that the politics, economics, and psychology of any particular era are reflected and also embedded in the culture of that era. Everything from architecture to music and fashion reveal how people were thinking about themselves and their immediate world.

If you look at the best-seller lists from decade to decade, you can track the concerns and escapes of the public with a fair degree of accuracy. Unfortunately, as intriguing as this might sound, we don't have the room or the time for it in these pages. Besides, plenty of books on popular culture do a good job of breaking it all down. If you're interested in it, you have plenty of available material for further research.

For our purposes, let's take a quick look back at the list—a couple years during the last full decade and most of the next will be more than enough to illustrate the points I want to make. It will be a loose, unscientific, generational portrait of reader preferences.

We're doing this for several reasons—the main one is to get you focused on exactly *what* your potential audience likes to read. You should fully comprehend the preferences of your readers because your job is to write a novel that will touch them, involve them, and leave them wanting more—from you.

Becoming a Brand Name

Take a look at *The New York Times* Bestseller List, fiction category, from 1991:

1. *Scarlett* by Alexandra Ripley

2. *The Sum of All Fears* by Tom Clancy

3. *Needful Things* by Stephen King

4. *No Greater Love* by Danielle Steel

5. *Heartbeat* by Danielle Steel

6. *The Doomsday Conspiracy* by Sidney Sheldon

7. *The Firm* by John Grisham

8. *Night Over Water* by Ken Follett

9. *Remember* by Barbara Taylor Bradford

10. *Loves Music, Loves to Dance* by Mary Higgins Clark

11. *Cold Fire* by Dean Koontz

12. *The Kitchen God's Wife* by Amy Tan

13. *Star Wars: Heir to the Empire* by Timothy Zahn

14. *WLT: A Radio Romance* by Garrison Keillor

15. *Sleeping Beauty* by Judith Michael

Even a cursory glance should bring you to some obvious conclusions right away. The following sections discuss some of these conclusions.

The Name Game

Note that more than 80 percent of the writers on this list are some of the Biggest-of-the-Big, Brand-Name, Guaranteed-to-Sell *NAMES* of the early 1990s. Millions of people—who not only don't read their books, but don't read anything!—know the names of these authors.

And if you think about it, achieving this kind of name recognition is a huge accomplishment. I mean, how many times have people told you about this great book they're reading but they can't remember the author's name?

But even the great unwashed throngs of citizens who haven't read a book since they graduated high school 20 years ago can tell you who Stephen King or Tom Clancy or Danielle Steel is. And that tells you a lot about the brand-name recognition game.

Longevity

Most of the names on the list are *still* big names, and some continued to appear on the list with a numbing regularity 10 years later. What does that tell us? Well, simply put, it underscores the importance of having a best-seller. If you have what it takes to get on the list (as many of these writers have demonstrated), you can usually *stay* there by continuing to do what you do.

A corollary to this fact is not as cheerful: it's difficult to get on the list, especially if it means knocking off one of the big names that seem to live there month in and month out, year after year. But that's what makes America such a great country, right? Long live competition—it makes us all better.

Variety

No one, single type of novel dominates this list. In fact, I'm very impressed and heartened by the wide spectrum of genres, or publishing categories, represented. Other than the one-shot silliness of Ripley's sequel to *Gone with the Wind*, we see science fiction (Zahn), spy/thriller (Clancy and Koontz), historical thriller (Follett), horror/suspense (King), romance (Bradford and Steel), and mystery/crime (Clark).

And how could I forget? There is also the appearance of a book that signaled one of the hottest "new" genres of the entire decade—the legal thriller—marked by the publication of John Grisham's *The Firm*.

What you should retain from this nonscientific study is that no matter what you may want to write about, no matter what category your novel may fall into, you have a shot at appealing to and capturing a very large audience. So don't be afraid to write the kind of book you like to read—chances are, a lot of other people out there like to read the same kinds of books.

You should also take heart that even if you don't have a novel that fits conveniently into an existing market niche, you may be able to start your own new one—like Grisham did with all his legal thrillers and the hordes of imitators who followed.

I did it myself on a smaller scale with the publication of my novel *The Blood of the Lamb*, which the reviewers dubbed a "religious thriller." It cashed in on the then-approaching millennium and all the cultural and metaphysical trappings that went along with it. My novel did very, very well, spawning a sequel, staying in print for more than a decade, and garnering an endlessly renewed film option.

And I did it about 10 years before anyone had ever put the words *code* and *da Vinci* in the same sentence.

> **TOM'S TIPS**
>
> If you have a burning desire to be on the best-seller list (and most novelists should), my best advice is to think High Concept. Even though your cursory examination of the front flap copy of most of whatever is on the best-seller table at Borders this week may sound ordinary and familiar, don't let that sway you from your mission—come up with a *Big! New! Idea!* You don't have the big-name thing going for you, so your novel needs a big idea. And I know, I know—they don't come to us every day. So pay attention to *everything* going on in the world and all around you. The ideas are there; you just need to recognize one and turn it into a story.

Be innovative, visionary, and smart about the kind of novel you construct. Timing can be everything, and if your story parallels events or cultural psychology of the moment, you may be able to take advantage of it.

Staying Power

Now let's take a look at fiction again, this time for 1999:

1. *The Testament* by John Grisham

2. *Hannibal* by Thomas Harris

3. *Assassins* by Jerry B. Jenkins

4. *Star Wars: The Phantom Menace* by Terry Brooks

5. *Timeline* by Michael Crichton

6. *Hearts in Atlantis* by Stephen King

7. *Apollyon* by Jerry B. Jenkins

8. *The Girl Who Loved Tom Gordon* by Stephen King

9. *Irresistible Forces* by Danielle Steel

10. *Tara Road* by Maeve Binchy

11. *White Oleander* by Janet Fitch

12. *A Walk to Remember* by Nicholas Sparks

13. *Pop Goes the Weasel* by James Patterson

14. *Black Notice* by Patricia Cornwell

15. *Granny Dan* by Danielle Steel

Again, this is a very interesting list, wouldn't you say? Nearly a decade separates the two lists we've looked at, but we see many of the same names dominating the group. (And if you sneak a peak back one more year, we would see the 1998 list includes more old pals from 1991—Sidney Sheldon, Tom Clancy, and Mary Higgins Clark.) This supports my belief that when you make the best-seller list, the odds are very good you can stay there … if you keep writing and keep delivering the goods.

And what about the categories? Let's take a look: science fiction (Brooks and Crichton); horror/suspense (King and Harris); romance (Steel and Binchy); mystery/crime (Cornwell and Patterson); legal thriller (Grisham); and (hey!) religious thriller (Jenkins).

This is no accident. The genres that appear on the best-seller list are very popular. People seem to have an unending fascination with certain topics and themes. Many genre novels share a common thread—they tell stories about our odd capacity to inflict harm on our fellow humans. Physical, emotional, or psychological harm are all major concerns of most of the fiction on the previous lists.

Flaubert said, "When we are at out worst … we are also at our most interesting." Is that the secret of the best-selling novel? That's for you to decide.

One More Time …

Now because this is the second edition of my book, and we are preparing to lurch and stumble forward into the *second* decade of the twenty-first century, I think we should take a look at The List today—as I am writing these words in the autumn of 2009. In the 10 years since we did this kind of analysis—What's different? What's the same?

Fiction, 2009:

1. *The Lost Symbol* by Dan Brown
2. *An Echo in the Bone* by Diana Gabaldon
3. *The Last Song* by Nicholas Sparks
4. *The Help* by Kathryn Stockett
5. *The Associate* by John Grisham
6. *Hothouse Orchid* by Stuart Woods
7. *South of Broad* by Pat Conroy
8. *Alex Cross's Trial* by James Patterson and Richard DiLallo
9. *The Year of the Flood* by Margaret Atwood
10. *Hardball* by Sara Paretsky
11. *Spartan Gold* by Clive Cussler
12. *A Change in Altitude* by Anita Shreve
13. *Scarpetta* by Patricia Cornwell
14. *A Good Woman* by Danielle Steel
15. *Twilight* by Stephanie Meyer

Okay, this is pretty interesting stuff. Once again, my contention of staying power is supported with *five* writers from the 1999 list—John Grisham, Danielle Steel, Nicholas Sparks, James Patterson, and Patricia Cornwell.

In the previous few weeks, The List had also seen work by perennial favorites such as Stephen King, Dean Koontz, Michael Connelly, and Nora Roberts. Even though they weren't part of my random week selection, their continued presence supports my repeated contention that once you make The List, you have a decent shot of remaining in the neighborhood—if you can keep churning out the books.

Categories of all stripes continue to be well-represented—science fiction (Atwood), horror/dark fantasy (Meyer), crime suspense (Patterson, Paretsky, Cornwell, Woods), romance (Steel and Shreve), thriller (Brown, Cussler), and contemporary (Conroy, Gabaldon, and Stockett). This is a good sign that no matter what type of fiction you like to read (and, therefore, write), plenty of readers are out there, waiting for your fresh ideas and delivery.

So what does all this mean?

It means you should carefully examine the kind of story you want to tell, checking to see if it fits comfortably into any of the most popular categories. This will give you a pretty good idea if you have an audience who would be receptive to your type of story.

However, I say this with the following caveat: there are always exceptions to the general knowledge and expectations of editors and readers. Sometimes a book that fits no known genre or category comes along and catches fire. That is called the X-factor, and it's like that mutant gene no one can predict or anticipate.

That's just another way of saying your novel may not be a good fit for any of the well-known categories, but it could still be a monster hit.

And I'll leave you with this, which is the main point I wanted to make here: if you're ever fortunate enough to land on The List, you need to have a plan that will ensure you stay there.

The Least You Need to Know

- Millions of books are sold (or not sold) because of best-seller lists.
- Because of modern technology, the way best-sellers are tabulated has changed. Today, you can get up-to-the-minute information on the hottest sellers.
- Best-sellers can come from any category or genre.
- If a writer writes a best-selling book and gets on The List, he or she has a very good chance of remaining on The List.

Genres and the Mainstream

In This Chapter

- Genres in general
- Are genres good or bad?
- Genres in detail
- Above and beyond genres

When I first started writing at the age of 12, I wrote science fiction stories. Although I didn't know it at the time, I was writing genre fiction. I think many young writers are the same way. And in the long run, it's the *best* way to write—without any awareness of conforming to a narrative template or a set of market expectations.

But as nice as that sentiment might sound, I should also tell you it's probably impossible in the contemporary publishing arena.

Now wait a minute, you may be thinking, *I've been pretty much with this guy until now, but what exactly does he mean by templates and expectations?* I was hoping you'd ask, because this idea of novels being placed into specific slots or categories is important.

In Chapter 3, I touched on genres and how they appear on the best-seller list at any given time with stunning regularity. Now it's time we looked at the topic in some detail.

What the Professor Said

Let me interject an anecdote here, which should add a little perspective to our study. Back when I was in graduate school (working on a Master's degree I never used), I was also sending out short stories to magazines at a pretty good rate.

My first sale was to a science fiction magazine called *Amazing Stories,* and when the issue finally appeared with my story inside and my name on the cover, I was bursting with joy and a profound sense of accomplishment.

I remember the day I brought the magazine into the offices of the University of Maryland English Department and showed it to my fellow students and graduate assistants. In the middle of the glad-handing and smiling, one of the department's professors entered the foyer where we had gathered and asked what all the "hub-bub" was about. A buddy of mine held up the magazine and said: "Monteleone got one of his stories published!"

The professor arched his eyebrows, approached us, and delicately held the magazine between his thumb and index finger as if it were a stinking and very dead fish. After looking at it with obvious disapproval, he nodded gravely and handed it back before it could contaminate him. "Oh," he said primly. "*Commercial* fiction ..."

And with that, he turned away and headed toward his office without another word. My story and I had been summarily *dismissed.* Because my work had appeared in a digest-size magazine with a lurid cover, it was somehow not worthy of further notice or comment, as if there was something wrong with having someone actually *pay* you for your writing and then go out and sell your story to others who might want to read it.

Before that moment, I'd always figured genre fiction didn't enjoy the highest respect of the academic and literary types. Now that the professor had put me in my proper place, there was no room for doubt.

The moral of the story is that although some people might not like it very much, genre novels are wildly popular and make up the majority of fiction currently being published. In fact, many of today's best-selling and most widely admired writers got started writing category fiction and continued to write genre novels after hitting The List. The only difference is that their books are now placed on the general "fiction" tables in bookstores instead of the ones with specific labels. Insiders call such non-genre books "mainstream" fiction.

TOM'S TIPS

Go back and reread a "favorite" novel from your youth or childhood. See if it holds up as an influential book for you. Try to identify what elements captured your attention and made you remember it with such fondness and then make a conscious effort to re-create that intensity and appeal in your *own* writing.

Why do the sales figures of a novel somehow change how publishers perceive it and how the booksellers market it? I'm not sure, but there's definitely an unspoken bias against genre fiction. There is a longstanding belief that it cannot be real literature if it's clearly a category novel.

WORDS OF WISDOM

Frankly, I am not one of those college professors who coyly boasts of enjoying detective stories—they are too badly written for my taste and bore me to death.

—Vladimir Nabokov

That's just silly. Readers, the people who buy books, don't make their purchases based on whether or not a book passes the "literary certification test." They buy books because they want to be entertained. They want to read a good story. Whether it's a mystery, or a romance, or a contemporary coming-of-age story, it's all fine with them. But it's not to say they don't have their favorites, and that's what genres are all about.

The Nature of All the Beasts

Years ago, a well-respected writer (I think it was John Gardner) called the commercial novel "drugstore fiction." He meant a few different things in applying this term, and I have my suspicions he was trying to be a bit snide and elitist.

For one thing, if he were describing novels you could find in a drugstore, I have to assume they would be mostly in paperback, featuring eye-catching covers with splashy color and foil and slick illustration. The word *drugstore* could also suggest easily accessible (because you can find just about *anything* in a Rite Aid), or worse, it could suggest *common* or *cheap*.

Or here's a thought—maybe Gardner was referring to those spinning wire racks that held hundreds of paperbacks. When those books first became popular, they were also called *pocket books*, but the industry term is *mass-market paperback*—as opposed to the larger paperback approximating the dimensions of a hardcover—the *trade paperback*.

Many genres have enjoyed a healthy lifespan appearing only in the mass-market format. Many books appear only in this format, never having enjoyed the quasi-permanence of hardcover publication.

Genre fiction has also been called "category" fiction or "formula" fiction, and neither of those labels sound all that good to me. Whether or not genre fiction follows strict formulas is something we need to look at. I don't think it's all that accurate unless we want to admit that *all* fiction conforms to certain formulae of structure and resolution.

Regardless of what the professors and the critics might imply, there's no question that publishers, booksellers, and reviewers all have a penchant for dividing fiction into neat little compartments. They do it right from the start of a book's life when it's submitted to publishing houses—editors specialize in just about every genre imaginable, and they consider themselves experts in each of their fields. It's unimaginable that a romance editor would know a good mystery from a bad one, and a mystery editor presumably has no ability to recognize a really compelling science fiction novel.

At least that's what they tell you.

A Very Important Warning

Regardless of what genre you think your novel may be, you must adhere to one simple truth: do not attempt to write a genre novel if you are not already a "fan" of that genre. In order to write a credible science fiction novel or any other genre novel, you need to know at least as much as the serious fan of that particular genre. If you know *more*, consider that a huge bonus.

You have to trust me on this one. If you try to write a romance novel and you've never even read one, you will be exposed as a fraud instantly by any editor worth his or her weight in dog food. This means you would have zero chance of seeing your book published, but even if the miracle happened or you committed the disastrous mistake of self-publishing the book, your readers would know you were trying to fake it by the end of Chapter 1.

Pushing it, I think a genre writer needs to have been a genre *fan* as well. Let me clarify this. Merely reading a couple mysteries does not necessarily qualify you to be able to sit down and spin out riveting tales of deduction and discovery. I think the writers who are successful in their chosen genres most likely grew up not only reading, but *steeped* in the said genre.

I say this from experience. I know writers in most of the major genres, and they all tell me the same thing—they've always loved reading the types of books they eventually started to write and sell. See, I'm not making this up!

Truth in Labeling

Okay, it's time to take a closer look at the wide range of novel "types." This is going to help you in several ways:

- You'll be able to see if the story you want to tell fits comfortably into an established genre.

- You'll have a good, basic understanding of what each genre needs in order to be successful.

- You'll start thinking about how comfortable you might be writing "similar" material book after book.

 A LIKELY STORY

It's quite possible that all the advances and miracles of modern medicine have weakened the human gene pool to such an extent that our species may be doomed to extinction. What about a story about a group of people who attempt to do something about it? What they do is up to you.

I'm going to investigate the most popular fiction categories alphabetically because I don't want to even *imply* any one of them is any more significant or important than any other.

Be warned: many genres enjoy "boom and bust" cycles during which they sell better or worse than the average category. Publishing is a trendy kind of business, and the successful genre writer usually has been the person who can "catch the wave" and ride it to a good living. But each genre enjoys its own enduring, dedicated group of readers who *never* go away; and that's why genre fiction remains the backbone of every big publisher's annual list of new titles.

Action/Adventure

This is one of the lesser-known genres in terms of name recognition, but nonetheless, it has maintained an enduring popularity among its core audience. It's also gained a reputation as being the male counterpart to the (female) romance novel. Critics are particularly unkind to this genre, claiming even the lead characters are heavy-handed, predictable, and not very likable.

Action/adventure novels tend to be very straightforward, shoot-from-the-hip kind of stories, told in a straight, linear fashion, with a clean, no-bull style. They rarely have many subplots, and they are pure escape fantasies, which appeal to men in much the same way romantic tales appeal to women. And I say this with no snideness. Just the facts, Jack.

If you want to write action/adventure, you need a hero who is a John Rambo–type guy; a rogue, ex–special ops man or a soldier of fortune; or maybe a paramilitary commander. Many times, these heroes are working under cover, just barely on the right side of the law, and have a very keen sense of justice. They do the right thing— even when it may require violence … a *lot* of violence.

The heroes battle (and vanquish) bad guys of every stripe—drug runners, street gangs, terrorists, extremists, rogue government dictators, and any other bad guy you can dream up. They whup up on these types, and they do it with a lot of panache.

The plots are similar and, yeah, they follow a fairly recognizable formula. The hero is drawn to the problem either by association with a group or a friend, he vows revenge, and he makes elaborate plans to defeat the enemy. Sometimes he goes solo; sometimes he gathers a team, and we have some fun meeting the variety of eccentric "specialists" he needs for the job. Usually, he engages the bad guy(s), suffers a few setbacks, and finally overcomes heavy odds to be victorious.

A friend of mine pointed out the backbone of most action/adventure novels, which is that they are essentially a template of *heroic myth*, and I agree with him. If you think about it, you'll see how it's a surefire storytelling model, which has built-in cultural appeal. And you have the added incentive and advantage of looking to the daily news and the vast stage of geopolitical maneuverings from which to draw events and scenarios. That's the making for stories that "could happen."

TRADE TALK

A **heroic myth** is a reference to some of civilization's earliest examples of epic storytelling. The heroes in these tales—such as Hercules, Gilgamesh, Ulysses, or Aeneas—encountered great challenges and hardships in a seemingly unending number and overcame them all.

If you're drawn to this kind of novel, there's an additional benefit: if you create a clever, adept, and popular hero character, you and your editor can easily create a *series*, a string of novels based on your protagonist and his supporting characters. If you sell the first one, be sure you tell your editor you envision a long line of novels in which the adventure continues from one exotic locale and tough situation to the next. A series provides nice steady income, and there's always the possibility of selling the film rights.

Fantasy

This is probably one of the oldest categories if you look at it in terms of its blatant elements of myth and legend. Fantasy tales are concerned with things like magic, imaginary creatures (elves, fairies, dragons, and so on), ancient civilizations, and very clear delineations of Good and Evil.

Many examples of fantasy employ the standard formula, which involves a long, harrowing, and ultimately character-building quest. The object of the quest can be any number of objects, persons, or secrets. What matters is that something needs to be found, and your hero is just the person for the gig.

Depending on your own preferences, you can actually write in several subcategories:

- *Light* fantasy is populated by magicians, elves, and spells

- *Heroic* fantasy employs larger-than-life warrior-types like Conan and Kane (This is also sometimes called Sword and Sorcery.)

- There's even a whole sub-subcategory of *Arthurian fantasy*, which rings endlessly inventive changes on the world of legend's most famous king

Whatever type of fantasy you want to write, you'll have to make decisions about your setting, your characters, and the rules you're going to play by. Fantasy novel readers are imaginative and usually open to whatever otherworldly trappings you want to offer them, but they are also intelligent and will require that you don't ignore the internal logic of your story or "change the rules" for the purpose of getting yourself out of a difficult plot complication. If your magic spell won't work during an electrical storm, you can't change your mind later.

Fantasy novels are also good candidates for series material. In fact, because of J. R. R. Tolkien's influence, many fantasy readers almost *expect* their stories to come in groups of at least three novels. These fans enjoy the epic, sweeping scale of this genre and tend to be patient with a long-winded never-ending yarn. The plots of many of these novels might seem similar, but as a writer, your challenge is to invent characters who come to life and rise above all that may be familiar.

Horror

The horror novel has been with us for centuries and represents our unending interest in the supernatural, our darker philosophical musings about the nature of Evil. Some of our most enduring and popular writers wrote horror novels and stories—Mary Shelley, Bram Stoker, Edgar Allan Poe, Ambrose Bierce, and Nathaniel Hawthorne, among others.

Because of this heritage, dark fantasy/horror has always enjoyed a bit more literary respectability than other category fiction, but in its modern attire, I think we're safe calling it a regular old genre. And like most genres, it falls in and out of favor with the reading public.

I've always had a gleeful fascination with this genre, which I can trace back to my childhood when the EC line of comics was at its peak with titles like *Tales from the Crypt* and *Vault of Horror* and *Shock Suspense*. I loved the lurid covers and the grisly stories, and I'd like to think those early comics warped me forever. I discovered Poe in high school, and I read a lot of paperback anthologies of classic horror. It became one of my favorite kinds of fiction to read, as well as write.

I can remember the late 1970s, when the novels of Stephen King became the hottest books in the industry, and for the next 15 years, horror was easily the most popular genre in publishing. As a reader and writer, I was in my glory.

The elements of the horror novel all center around one basic emotion—fear. Horror stories investigate the things that scare us, and the good ones try to offer explanations *why*. The subject of horror novels can be very traditional *icons* such as ghosts, vampires, mythical creatures, demons, ghouls, and zombies, or they may deal with more contemporary monsters such as the serial killer and range off into areas far more imaginative and disturbing.

> **TRADE TALK**
>
> In publishing, an **icon** (or a *trope*) refers to something that's been used so much it's instantly recognizable and has become part of the genre culture. Think of the tall, dark stranger in romance; the vampire in horror; the wizard in fantasy; etc.

An interesting sidebar on the subject is the cyclic popularity of some of this genre's staple icons. Vampires were number one for more than a decade and then after a brief flirtation with werewolves, the zombie (as popularized by the George Romero films, not the old voodoo stuff) became the *au courant* boogeyman. However, the keyword here is *cyclic*, and you can expect all of this to roll in and out of fashion without cease.

My wife, Elizabeth, and I have been editing an anthology series called *Borderlands* for many years now, and the basic premise of which is to explore new territories for the tale of horror and dark suspense. The challenge to writers is to find new images, new sources of our basic fears, and new ways to scare us. No vampires, ghosts, or zombies need apply.

Unfortunately, the influence of the film industry and its insistence on promoting an unending parade of "slasher" or "torture" films as *horror* has given many potential readers a very wrong impression of how rich and provocative the genre can be. Many of the worst horror clichés (werewolves, vampires, Jason, and others) must be blamed on the nitwits in Hollywood who continue to roll out one bad film after another and call it horror with a very small *h*.

Good horror novels are about what truly scares us, psychologically as well as physically. They are novels of characters placed in situations where choices between Good and Evil must be made—and consequences faced. Horror novels are successful when you tell your story in the most familiar of places and circumstances, where everything appears to be safely moored to the pillars of the "real" world, and suddenly something unexpected and unexplained destroys the illusion of safety and normality.

The truly great horror novel tells us that danger and death lurk *everywhere*, they are largely inescapable, and they may present themselves at any moment. What your character does at those crucial moments is the stuff of your stories.

The horror genre will always be around because it deals extensively with one of our elemental fears—the fear of the unknown and, by ultimate extension, *death*. Horror has a hardcore following who not only continue to read just about everything published, but they also support an impressive number of small presses that produce short-run and limited editions of popular, collectible authors.

Mystery/Crime

Along with horror, this one gets my vote as one of the oldest genres. Many claim Edgar Allan Poe created the mystery story with his detective, Auguste Dupin, who solved "The Murders in the Rue Morgue." One of the vernacular terms for a mystery novel is "the whodunit," and that does distill it to its most basic component.

A mystery novel is basically a puzzle to be solved, and the puzzle is a crime—more likely than not, a murder. The classic requirement of a good mystery novel is that the detective or protagonist and the reader both be given the same clues, placing the reader in competition with the hero to solve the crime. How difficult the writer wants to make it is all part of the fun.

It's generally agreed that the mystery genre is comprised of several main branches and a few subdivisions beyond them:

- The cozy

- The private eye (or detective)

- The police procedural

The cozy has historically been the most popular, but I'm not sure why. This type of mystery features an investigator who is not a professional but happens to be very, very good at figuring things out. Priests, writers, horticulturalists, and jockeys have all proven to be popular and effective crime-solvers. They are all amateur detectives, if you will, and therein lies the appeal—everyone who reads mysteries probably figures they would make great detectives themselves.

This type of mystery features hardly any graphic violence, a lot of serious Q&A and logical deduction, and a final scene during which the detective explains how he or she figured it out. It helps to involve police who are totally baffled and in no way able to solve the mystery without the usually unwanted intervention of the amateur *sleuth*. (I love that word and have been waiting all these pages to finally employ it.)

The private eye is the professional investigator, the "P.I." who earns a tough living by being at the wrong place at the right time. These mysteries are often called "hard-boiled"; they're not afraid of some in-your-face violence and usually feature urban, contemporary, and culturally hip settings. They are distinctly different from the previous type. Creating a likable but scarily capable hero is part of the challenge of writing this kind of mystery. And again, the film and TV businesses are responsible for offering up some lasting clichés to be avoided.

TOM'S TIPS

In the mystery genre, you have to be clever. And there's one crime you can never commit yourself: you cannot allow the reader to think he or she is smarter than your detective. If that happens, you've lost game, set, match, and a reader.

The P.I. protagonist knows "the street" and is usually sardonic, very intelligent, cynical, and physically tough. The characters he deals with can be found among the lower links of the society's food chain—hustlers, petty thieves, gamblers, low-lifers, and their ilk—people who have access to the kind of information our hero might need. You usually need a cop who knows our detective and isn't terribly fond of him; this kind of tension makes things interesting and helps reveal clues when necessary.

The procedural is probably the most demanding kind of mystery to tell because readers are expecting to find the hard, polished edge of realism in this kind of novel. The protagonist is a cop, and unlike the cozy cops, your procedural hero is a top-notch crime-solver. You usually need a fairly good-size supporting cast in procedurals because police work is team-oriented.

In addition, you need to know more than a little bit about how bureaucracy and city government work. Also, there's been a dramatic increase in the amount of forensic science being applied to police work, so your procedural novel will need lots of authenticity along those lines as well.

Another admonition: don't rely on the information and "insider" stuff you may have read in other writers' novels about police procedure. There's no guarantee it's all correct or still in effect. You have an obligation *not* to rely on what's already been written—or worse, been portrayed on television. Do your research and talk to real cops and detectives and forensic types. Absorb as much as you can about their daily world.

Romance

Another mainstay of genre publishing is the romance novel. Over the years, several requirements or conventions have evolved to which most romances adhere. However, several subcategories have huge audiences. Within the last decade, this genre has enjoyed tremendous expansion and success.

The heroine of all romance novels must be bright, headstrong, and adventurous, but above all, she must be beautiful and brimming over with passion—but only for the right man. She is usually alone, although not by choice—a family tragedy, an abduction, lost on a journey, etc. The hero in a good romance is usually a little older than the protagonist and attractive, and it doesn't hurt if he's rich and powerful. He should also be headstrong and not afraid to take matters into his own hands—the law or social convention be damned. The entire novel centers around the relationship between these two people, with plenty of distractions and obstacles along the way, including some stormy points when they *really* irritate each other.

If this sounds more than a bit like Scarlet and Rhett … well, make what you will of it.

Now let's look a little closer at the subcategories, starting with historicals, which are very popular, and they allow you to place your story on just about any stage you want. The important things here are setting, culture, and of course, the flow of the *events* of the particular time period that influence and affect the lives of your characters. Research is vital, and you will be expected to show off your knowledge about the historical era you've selected. Some readers like to learn their history in this context, while others like to see if your historical expertise is a match for their own.

There are also sub-subcategories, such as one covering the days of American western expansion (they used to be called "Indian romances," but with the PC thought-police roaming the cultural streets, I'm not sure about the health of these books …). Another is the Regency romance, which highlights English history from 1811 to 1820. Again, attention to detail is important in these books. Editors tell me their readers are *very* familiar with the trappings and chronicle of events in that tiny period, so if you don't know what musicians or writers were popular at that time, you will be much the less for it. And your readers will catch you.

The gothic is probably the oldest romance template. For sheer formula, I don't think anything even comes *close* to the gothic. In their paperback heyday, even all the covers of the gothics were essentially *identical*—they always featured a large house, castle, fortress, mansion, estate in the background (usually storm-lashed); descending from it was a winding path or steps cut into a cliff; and fleeing downward on these steps was a young woman, always looking back at the massive structure above and behind her. One other element was always present—*one* light in *one* window, through which a silhouette of a lean male figure could be seen.

TOM'S TIPS

The primary message about genre novels is simple: readers know what they like, and if they like what *you* give them, they will come back for more. If you plan to write more than just one novel, you must understand this point.

The plot was even more locked in—a young woman protagonist arrives at the house/ castle/mansion/estate because she's a recently orphaned niece/housekeeper/governess/ secretary. She is disturbed by a tall, dark, and mysterious male presence in the house, who at first seems evil but is eventually revealed to be good, and who not only vanquishes the *true* evil in the house, but in the end marries the beautiful young woman.

This is formula writing taken to its highest exponent. Why did it work so well? Good question, and it's my point in bringing all this to your attention: many genre fiction readers who keep returning to the same kinds of stories do so because they feel comfortable knowing they already understand the book before they really start reading it. I'm not sure I fully understand that kind of reading, but I can accept it as a valid path of entertainment. Some people choose the familiar over the strange because it provides them with a kind of security.

Next is the *contemporary romance*, obviously set in the present, and normally in the world of "the beautiful people"—big business, fashion, the arts, and entertainment. These are sometimes called "glitter" or "glitz" novels. The men in these novels are brokers of power and influence, but they always display a reckless, carefree, and dashingly impulsive side of their nature—sometimes even dangerous or malevolent. The same plot structure we've already looked at applies here, and the large audience for this kind of book knows what it wants.

Variations on the basic theme include something called *romantic suspense* and the *paranormal romance*, which are "hybrid" genres. The former adds elements of the mystery to the regular formula, while the latter borrows from horror and dark fantasy. Both began making inroads into the standard romance territory around the second decade of this new century, and are more than worth considering as a hot genre.

Another hybrid adds a science fiction riff to the formula—time travel—in which either the male or female lead meets their counterpart from a totally different era. Jack Finney's great novel, *Somewhere in Time*, is the archetype for this tale.

There's a lot of experimentation going on here. If your tastes run in this direction, you'll have plenty of space to work out something original, yet comfortable for the reader.

That reminds me: genre readers seem to exhibit habits as distinct as the genres themselves. Horror and mystery readers seem open to new authors because they consider the essence of the stories they like more important than *who* wrote them. (I say this as a dangerous generality because readers will always have favorite writers, and these are the familiar names on The List.) Romance and paranormal suspense readers tend to be female, *and* they tend to buy more books per visit to the bookstore. The reports I get from editors and store managers is that women often buy their favorite genres in *bunches*.

Science Fiction

Although the general media dub this genre "sci fi," its writers and fans prefer "SF" or "speculative fiction." With its roots in the pulp magazines of the early twentieth century and the associations of space ships, robots, and aliens, many readers assume most SF is hardware-oriented and full of the "hard" sciences like physics, astronomy, chemistry, biology, etc. But that's just one avenue of speculation in what may be the most textured and variegated of all fiction categories.

> **WORDS OF WISDOM**
>
> A good science fiction story is a story with a human problem, and a human solution, which would not have happened without its science content.
>
> —Theodore Sturgeon

As with many of the other genres, this one can easily be subdivided into a variety of more specialized types. Stories that deal with how technology impinges upon culture and society involve the "softer" sciences of anthropology, psychology, sociology, and others. SF can be contemporary, far-future, or time-traveling. Locales can be earthbound, intergalactic, or transdimensional. There's a freedom to examine and explore the limits of your imagination that doesn't really exist on such a scale in the other genres.

In fact, a major characteristic separating SF from the rest of the genres is a distinct *lack* of a single formula the audience expects to follow. Readers of science fiction don't really want the familiar, comfortable structure of some of the other genres. They want *Gosh! Gee! Wow!* Your SF fans want to be challenged, enriched, educated, and surprised by the novels they read. They want to have their imaginations stretched and expanded. They don't read SF for the same-old, same-old.

I grew up reading SF, in both comic and book form. I watched all the classic films, and I even attended some of the conventions that celebrate the genre in a different city somewhere around the country on an almost weekly basis.

Remember what I said about being a genre fan first? This truth is probably most paramount in science fiction—unless you've immersed yourself in the literature of SF, it's going to be *very* tough to write it. Shopworn clichés abound, and uninitiated writers tend to wheel them out for one last performance and then are roundly rejected by wizened SF editors.

Suspense/Thriller

Although related to mysteries, the *thriller* is definitely a distinct genre. While the plot usually centers around something Alfred Hitchcock called "the McGuffin" (the thing everybody wants, needs, is looking for at *all* costs), there must be layers of complication, subplot, and exotic characters.

Most thrillers are fairly long books (500 to 600 pages) and are told in multiple viewpoints, which means your reader will learn the story as it filters through the perceptions of more than one character. The scale of your average thriller is large rather than small, and having actions take place all around the globe simultaneously is not at all unusual. Attention to details regarding foreign cities, contemporary geopolitical tensions, industrial and government technologies, and a general knowledge of the espionage game must be in your thriller-writer's toolbox.

There are many types of thrillers, which continue to do well, despite the ever-changing political climate on the world stage.

Techno-thrillers popularized by writers such as Tom Clancy and Dale Brown have enjoyed enduring popularity. Historical thrillers like those written by Ken Follett and Jack Higgins also have a wide enthusiastic audience. A subcategory of thrillers about the Third Reich has had a truly unbelievably long and successful lifespan. There's something chillingly fascinating about the Nazi brand of evil that has never faded.

Espionage thrillers took a big hit when the Soviet "evil empire" fizzled away like a cheap balloon losing air, but they still have a pulse. The challenge is for you to find *new* bad guys the reader can cheer against with the same relish they had for the Commies. I bet you probably can think of a few nominees for the position.

Medical thrillers have carved out a special niche in this genre, although the ones I've read tend to be very formulaic, and ultimately predictable. They generally require that a lone hero discover something awful going on at a hospital, medical center, hospital, bio-research center, hospital, government laboratory, or ... hey, did I mention *hospital?* The "something awful" is usually a riff on using hapless patients as some sort of guinea pigs.

The main thing you need to have in the thriller is a high concept or a Big Problem that's going to have Big Consequences ... no matter how it's resolved. You need a plot with enough complications to spin out a suspenseful discovery of all the clues and an unwinding of the facts that demands the turning of pages.

Western

Yes, this is still a viable genre. Just because you don't see it around as much you used to doesn't mean it's not an important segment of the book-reading marketplace. At one time, the Western was one of the top-selling genres in the business, and some of its writers like Louis L'Amour and Zane Grey were enormously popular, best-selling writers.

The Western is probably the most straightforward of all genres because it centers on a fairly small stretch of time and territory: west of the Mississippi during the post–Civil War years up into the 1880s. The stories deal with clearly delineated characters who are either good guys or bad guys, and the reader always knows for whom to cheer.

As with many other genres that depend on historical underpinnings, it's very important you have extensive knowledge of the period in which you place your stories. The geography, economy, culture, politics, social norms, and especially the weapons of the times are all very important aspects you can't ignore because your readers *definitely* know all that stuff, and if they catch you napping, your credibility—and, therefore, your sales—are in trouble.

Great Wheel Keeps on Turnin'

To wrap this up, I need to leave you with a few final observations I've probably mentioned before. However, their utter importance forces me to repeat them.

Very crucial: genres tend to have groups of dedicated readers who frequent the bookstores on a regular basis looking for new titles. This means they buy up the new mysteries, the new romances, or the new thrillers *regardless of who wrote them.*

This is very good news for new novelists. While the hardcore genre audience may have favorite writers, they are much more willing to read a new writer (like *you*) than the people who tend to read *only* what's on the best-seller list. So if you want to break in as a novelist, writing genre fiction isn't a bad idea.

Also, I think it would be very difficult, if not downright *impossible*, to write a good genre novel if you've never read an example of the type you're trying to create. You need to know what preceded you and what contributed to the current template of your genre of choice. Better that you've read *extensively* in a genre before you can write it well. And it would help if you've grown up thoroughly immersed in the kind of books you want to write. That's especially the case with SF and horror writers I've known over the years—and I've known a *lot* of them.

Lastly, keep in mind that most genres have cyclic periods of booms and lulls, when, for some reason or another, a particular category's afterburner kicks in, and it takes off into the upper layers of the sales atmosphere. And then, after a hot run, the genre takes a slow slide downward. There are probably a lot of sophisticated socioeconomic theories bouncing around to tell you why these cycles occur, but we really don't need to know them.

All you need to know is that they *do* happen. So whatever genres interest you, feel good knowing there will always be an audience for your kind of book—if you write it *well*.

The Least You Need to Know

- The vast array of genre titles published every month are the backbone of the publishing industry.
- Each genre has a loyal and dependable core audience.
- Many genre novels are published as paperback originals (often called "mass-market editions").
- Successful genre authors are also enthusiastic readers of the categories in which they write—and probably have been since they were kids.

Reading to Write

In This Chapter

- Why you read
- What you should have read
- What you should be reading now
- Reading as instruction

> You can't be a writer if you're not a reader.

This is probably the most obvious, simplest truth in this entire book. I say that with confidence. So much so, I'll lay you some huge, Vegas odds you'll *never* find a writer who does not flat-out love to read. Read a thousand interviews with writers, and the majority will tell you they became totally hooked on the written word when they were very little.

We're going to see why being an avid reader is absolutely essential to being a writer. If you want to write novels, you need to *read* novels.

That Magic Moment

Something happens to some of us when we're being taught how to read ... or maybe even a lot farther back than that. There was a single, special time when one of your parents put you on his or her lap, wiped the drool off your cute little mug, and held a book up in front of you for the first time. Sure, it was most likely a picture book with all the bright colors and fuzzy animals the child development folks like to tell you are so important.

WORDS OF WISDOM

Books are a delightful society. If you go into a room filled with books, even without taking them down from the shelves, they seem to speak to you, to welcome you.

—William E. Gladstone

But there was something else going on for some of us, something more elemental and unanticipated. There was a subconscious recognition in our baby-toddler minds that the picture book we just saw was really a door, a gateway to endless numbers of worlds, times, people, and … *stories*. I know, it sounds silly. But you'd better believe it. Somehow, some of us, when we were babies, instantly connected to the whole book experience in a way most others never do.

Writers like books. They like them so much they live in places where you can't walk into a room without seeing a bunch of books. Look around your own living space. If you don't have shelves, boxes, and horizontal planes stacked and jammed with books … well, then maybe you should be thinking about picking up *The Complete Idiot's Guide to Vegetable Gardening* instead of this one. (But hey! That's a book, too! See, you can't get away from it, friends.)

Something Missing

Okay, time for another anecdote. Years ago, when I was first getting started as a full-time writer, the checks came in very erratically, so I used to fill in the cracks with a variety of part-time jobs that would still allow for my allotted daily number of hours devoted to writing.

The best imaginable gig I ever found was selling cable TV hook-ups to new subscribers. The hours were perfect—6 P.M. to 9 P.M., five nights a week—because you needed to catch potential customers at home when they were settling down to watch some tube. On any given evening, I would talk to 15 to 25 people on average, which meant I probably saw (minimum) the interiors of at least 100 houses per week. One hundred houses that represented the average citizen in your average big-city suburb.

Over months and months, it was probably a fair enough sample to provide a decent "snapshot" of what most folks' habitats are like. In addition, I was often given little "tours" of the customers' houses because they'd want to show me the rooms where their televisions were located because they liked to ask me how the cable was going to penetrate the walls to reach their inner sanctums.

The upshot was this: I saw pretty much of *everything* in everyone's homes. I could assess their taste in artwork, interior design, home appliances, toys and gadgets, their hobbies, and just about anything else you can think of. As a writer, I was always paying attention, always looking for details and data that might be material or detail for a story.

After a few weeks, I had to admit a terrible truth. In 98 percent of the homes I entered, I never saw even *one* book. No kidding. I saw plenty of kids with school textbooks, but that was it—not even a paperback laying around. And there were certainly *no* bookcases or rooms that could be called studies or libraries. In fact, in most homes, I hardly ever even saw a magazine, unless it was *TV Guide* or *Soap Opera Digest*.

The word *pitiful* comes to mind, but even that one doesn't describe the situation.

The Rest of Us

But don't be too distressed. It's always been an axiom of the publishing industry that 10 percent of the population buys 90 percent of the books. I'd heard it before, but when I went out there hawking cable TV, I actually saw the truth of it.

So *what* if most people don't love books the way you do? Most people, after getting out of high school (or even college), don't even *think* of reading books. The point remains: you need to read every book you can get your hands on if you want to be a writer.

That's what we're going to talk about here:

- The kinds of books you already should have read.
- The books you should be reading now.
- The books you're going to need to read for the rest of your life as a writer.

You're also going to learn how to evaluate what you read by looking for things in books most people don't bother with, or are unequipped to notice. You might be thinking you already know how to read, but I'm here to tell you you don't know everything … yet.

What Has Gone Before

I've always believed writers are people who shouldn't know a little bit about everything—they should know a *lot* about everything. Because knowledge is power; power is the word; and the word is only *everything*.

But let's take it one step at a time. The way you get to a point in your life where you at least know a little bit about everything is for you to read lots of stuff about, well, lots of stuff.

Ideally, before you start writing, it would be great if you've already achieved what the academics call "cultural literacy." It's a scholarly buzz-phrase meaning what I said in the previous paragraphs. It's never too late to reach such a level of awareness, but if you've spent your life being curious and reading, you're probably well on your way. If, however, you've spent more hours watching ESPN and The Shopping Channel than even The Discovery Channel, you may be in a little trouble.

Okay, so how do you know if you're culturally literate? My initial, impulsive (and very Yodalike) reply would be: "Surely he is not ... who must ask." But I'm feeling really good today, even charitable, so let's just have a quiz!

Ten Easy(?) Pieces

1. Who wrote *1984?*

2. What was the "white man's burden"?

3. What is the Golden Fleece?

4. Who is Carl Jung?

5. What does *carpe diem* mean?

6. Who is George Frideric Handel?

7. Where is Chernobyl?

8. What is a light-year?

9. What is semantics?

10. Who is Frank Lloyd Wright?

That wasn't so bad, was it? If you got at least 5 right, I'd say you're in pretty good shape and on your way to being more "culturally literate" than 80 percent of the population. And you're certainly more than well-enough-equipped to be a decent writer. If you got them all right, then you need to tell me you know what *syzygy* means, as well as the identity of Laocoon, the location of Nan Madol, as well as the origin of the term "a slough of despond." And don't be looking for the answers at the end of this chapter or in any of the appendixes. And don't necessarily trust Wikipedia. Part of the joy of learning is the pursuit of the knowledge.

Throughout your life, you should have been reading in enough different disciplines to have a working knowledge of the world—its history, technology, geography, etc. I'm going to be a nice guy and assume you have. Now let's get on to what you should be reading *now*, and from now on.

Everybody Needs a Stack

Most writers I know have a pile of books they call their "To Read Next" stack. It can be on the nightstand, on the coffee table in the den, in the bathroom in a special wicker thingie; or, if they're slobs, even on the kitchen counter or the dining room table.

It doesn't matter where it is, really. What's important is that you have one. Now let's see what should be in it.

Your Favorite Writers

You have writers you really like. These are the writers whose new books always end up on your wish list and eventually in your stack. These are the writers who, if they aren't around to produce any new books anymore, still get an occasional re-read from you. These are the writers who inspired you to be a writer, who influenced your own writing.

Ray Bradbury and Loren Eiseley were two writers I admired greatly, and there's no doubt my early work reflected my desire to write like them. If you have favorites equally important to you, keep at least one of their books in your stack once or twice a year. But the next time you read one of their works, ask yourself what it is about their writing that captivates you.

Your Favorite Genre

Ideally, this genre should also be the one in which you want to write. At least for now. Plenty of seasoned pros out there rarely read in their published genre now that they're successful and have evolved their own voice and shtick and have carved out their own audience. But you're not there yet.

I talked about this in the previous chapter, but it bears a little repeating. If you want to break into a genre, you need to know who's writing in it with success, and what they're writing. You need to be on the leading edge of any new styles, directions, or trends that may be changing the basic anatomy of your fiction category. You also need to know what's already been examined, explored, exploited, or done to death. The last thing you want to do is spend time on a manuscript that's essentially yesterday's news. You want to ring some changes on what's been done before; you want to turn it inside out and make an old idea fresh and new.

TOM'S TIPS

These days just about every genre has fan clubs, professional organizations, and, most important, websites. You can keep your finger on the pulse of many genres by checking out their sites and exploring their link pages, chat rooms, and message boards. You'll be surprised how fast you'll catch buzzes on the hot books and writers, the trends, and the flops.

Other Genres

Even if you're waist-deep in hard-boiled detective fiction, you should read what the cozy and the police procedural writers are doing as well. (Remember those from Chapter 4?) You should also read some global thrillers, to get a feel for different ways to pace a story, and some historical romances, to learn how knowledge of location and detail can help create a more believable setting.

Besides, you never know, but you may get inspired and really catch a serious interest in another genre, which can be a good thing. There's nothing wrong with expanding your horizon. And lastly, some of the more interesting recent novels, even some recent best-sellers, have incorporated elements of one genre into another to create never-seen-before hybrids. The thing to keep in mind here is you can never predict or assume from where your next great idea for a novel might spring. Always do things that will leave the doors to your imagination open.

Another Country Heard from—Nonfiction

Nonfiction is a very important component of your stack. This is how you rev up the rpms on your cultural literacy engine. Nonfiction is a vast territory overflowing with information on topics as diverse as transgender politics to mountain climbing to disease-vector microbiology. Within this massive vault of data, you need to be a little selective. Read books on your areas of interest and also look for the odd book you wouldn't normally first grab off the new release shelf at your local bookshop.

I recently read a book about a hurricane that hit Galveston, Texas, almost a hundred years ago—precisely because I knew I had no salivating interest in any detail of the event. It was great grist for the mind-mill. I may never use any of the carefully chronicled information in the book, but it was extremely well researched and very well written. I was pulled in because the writer knew how to tell a good story, even though it was technically nonfiction. And don't ever forget that novels are all about storytelling. You never know where you're going to learn something valuable.

Reading nonfiction is not only a place to do your research, but also an inexhaustible supply of ideas for novels. What Will Durant used to call the "Lessons of History" are full of fabulous examples of how epic struggles grow from small, seemingly unrelated elements—pretty much the way a novel is plotted out. See what I mean? Science books on just about any discipline can spark your imagination to *ask the next question*, and you have a new techno-thriller taking shape. True crime chronicles can give you an invaluable look inside the mind and family history of a street hood or a full-blown psychopath.

WORDS OF WISDOM

I'd rather read a bloody train schedule than nothing at all.

—Somerset Maugham

I could go on for a long time with a parade of examples. But I can't stress enough how much nonfiction will improve your fiction.

Every Life Telling a Story

Characterization is a big piece of every successful novel, and you need to understand people to be able to create your own. One of the best ways to train for the job is to read biographies. If you haven't read many in the past, a whole shelf of recent material is easily accessible and written with style. And the nice thing about biographies is that you can usually find a person who was involved in a field or pursuit you're already interested in.

If you're into science, read a book about a scientist; if you like crime, read about a real criminologist; if you're into history, … well, I think you've got the idea.

I know a lot of writers who swear by the biography method of creating characters, and I can see why. When we bring in a new character, we don't include every detail about him or her you'd find in a formal biography, but by being biography-aware, you will unconsciously understand all the elements that influence a person and make him or her as complex and interesting as possible.

Reading as a Learning Experience

I discuss this in depth in another chapter, but it doesn't hurt to touch on the kinds of books available on the subject of writing, per se.

Reading About Writing

When I was first getting started as a professional writer—which meant writing every day, sending out queries, stories, proposals, and racking up the rejection slips—I also did a lot of reading about my craft and my intended career. A really nice guy and wonderful writer by the name of Roger Zelazny, whom I met in those days, told me that every once in a while I should read a biography or a novel about a writer. I remember him chuckling with wisdom as he said it would both inspire and depress me.

He was right. Many novels about writers are just brimming over with all that pseudo-romantic nonsense about having to be a miserable, suffering fool before you can write with any "feeling" or "soul." After you throw in liberal dollops of narcissism, arrogance, failed marriages, and substance abuse (alcohol seems to be the most popular poison-of-choice among writers), you've got all the ingredients for a sweeping saga of the terrible life of the artist. The funny thing is, when you're a young writer yourself, all full of hope and energy, you read those novels about desperate, brooding, and misunderstood artistic types, and you say, "Hey, that won't happen to me!"

A LIKELY STORY

A firefighter discovers a corpse in the debris of a burned-out building. The body is identified later as his wife's secret lover. Although innocent, the firefighter is arrested on suspicion of murder. What happens next?

Guess what? In most cases, you'll be right. Most of my friends and acquaintances are writers, and very few of them are all that miserable or unhappy. So go off and read a novel or a biography about a writer once in a while, and don't let it scare you. It tends to remind you of who you really are. And every now and then, the author will touch upon an experience or an observation that will resonate with you like a perfectly struck tuning fork, and you'll say "Wow, that's exactly what it was like for me, too!" Or you might think to yourself, *Yeah, I had the same thought!*

And that makes it all worthwhile—just knowing that other writers are traveling the same path, exploring the same desolate territories of the imagination. It feels good just knowing you're not alone out there, even if you rarely see those who are in the same situation as you.

However, you have to be careful when selecting novels with writers as protagonists because the whole story can get caught up in the "struggle" of creating a book, and usually that is flat-out boring. This "plot" is often found in what are called *literary novels*. They are filled with a lot of silly, fevered posturing, and I suggest you avoid them as much as possible. Other novels, where the main character just happens to be a writer but other events and characters shape the plot, tend to be far more interesting.

I often get requests from people asking me to recommend biographies and novels about writers, and you know what—that's not a bad idea. So here is a list of recommendations, in no particular order:

- *Martin Eden* by Jack London
- *Misery* by Stephen King
- *Hemingway* by Carlos Baker
- *Heartbreak Hotel* by Ann Rivers Siddon
- *Richard Wright: The Life and Times* by Hazel Rowley
- *Dean Koontz: A Writer's Biography* by Katherine M. Ramsland
- *A Portrait of the Artist as a Young Man* by James Joyce
- *Flannery O'Connor: A Life* by Jean W. Cash

And just for fun, I'm going to throw in my own collection of essays about a life of writing and publishing and popular culture called *The Mothers and Fathers Italian Association*, which you can get online at borderlandspress.com. Try it; you'll like it. (If you call and tell them you were referred by me, they'll give you a whopping big discount—trust me.)

There are tons of other novels and biographies, but these are some of the ones I've read myself and can recommend as worth your while. If none of these seems right, you might want to hit a few bookstores or libraries and stroll down the aisles to see what catches your eye.

Bad to the Bone

This is going to sound silly, but you're also going to need to read some *really bad* books.

WORDS OF WISDOM

A bad book is as much of a labour to write as a good one; it comes as sincerely from the author's soul.

—Aldous Huxley

Relax, there's a method to my madness.

In order to fully appreciate what will be expected of you and your manuscript, you need to have a sense of the range of quality of published material. Because, believe me, there *is* a range. There's a difference between R. L. Stine and Philip Pullman; between Jacqueline Susann and Flannery O'Connor. And yet, all of it gets published, which means there are levels ... and there are levels.

By good and bad, I don't mean the "classics" as opposed to "commercial" fiction. There are plenty of wretched classics (for my money, you couldn't find a worse stink-bomb than *The Bostonians* by Henry James unless it might be *O Pioneers!* by Willa Cather), and some commercial novels that are absolutely spectacular (*Shogun* and *Lonesome Dove*, for instance). So please, don't start making arbitrary distinctions based on labels or packaging.

Reading the truly awful stuff not only gives you perspective, but it also makes you appreciate really good writing all the more. At the risk of waxing like a Zen master, I submit there can be no mountains without valleys, no pleasure without pain to compare it with. The same holds true for reading. I think you'll appreciate just how lyrically Raymond Chandler can spin a mystery novel after reading the bland sausage links served up by the writer of the "alphabet" mysteries.

By the Guys Who Wanna Be Like You

The last type of reading we need to look at is literary criticism and book reviews. At first, you may think they're basically the same thing, just wearing different sets of clothes. And I don't blame you. They're close.

Literary criticism tends to originate from the groves of academe, spawned by a never-ending need to legitimize the existence of English professors. Having picked up a Master's degree in English myself, I know of what I speak. This kind of writing about writing tends to have a lot of footnotes because you are supposed to support everything you say about the book in question with similar opinions by other people.

It's an acquired taste, but if you can get a handle on it, reading formal literary criticism might be a helpful tool in the learning experience for you. I want to stress, however, that it's not for everybody. Some writers simply cannot stomach this kind of scholarly "deconstruction" of a novel—the accepted method of seeing what makes it tick. You need to decide for yourself.

WORDS OF WISDOM

Asking a writer what he thinks about critics is like asking a lamppost how it feels about dogs.

—John Osborne

Book reviews are usually more accessible and useful to an everyday novelist like you. They show up in the newspapers and magazines and on some websites instead of obscure periodicals like the staid and stiff-collared *Journal of English Literature* or the totally recondite publications such as *The Sewanee Review*. They are read by a much larger audience of book buyers all over the country, plus many of the librarians who are always selecting new titles for their collections.

The endnote on this one is for you to read reviews to find out what other writers are doing. This can be very important if you happen to think you have the Next Great Idea for a high-concept thriller. But if you don't keep up with what's being published, you might never realize someone beat you to it.

It happens more than you might think. Years ago, I came up with a great suspense/thriller called *Critical Condition* about a group of sophisticated thugs who take over the entire floor of a big-city hospital where a famous billionaire is being given a heart transplant. Tension, mayhem, daring escapes, and rescues—it had all sorts of fun stuff. I wrote the first 200 pages, plus a tight synopsis, and gave it to my agent. He looked at it and said, "This story is going to be published next week. It's called *The Hostage Heart.*" I was shocked. Some other writer had come up with almost the exact same book, beat for beat, and had written and sold it about 6 months ahead of me. Naturally, it hit the best-seller list, and I have my old manuscript moldering away in a file drawer like a mummy in an urn.

So pay attention, and like I said at the beginning of this chapter: read.

The Power of the Word

This one is so obvious I shouldn't even mention it, but because we're wrapping things up, I figured it can't hurt to just remind you.

> **TOM'S TIPS**
>
> When reading, always keep that little notepad (or if you're a techno-geek, your PDA or cell phone voice recorder) so you can preserve any new words you encounter. If you're near a dictionary, nail down the meaning right away. If not, at least capture the word and look up the definition at a more convenient time. And as I lurch fitfully through the twenty-first century, I should mention you can get a dictionary app for your PDA or smartphone. Whatever you do, always make the effort to learn new words and enrich your vocabulary. This is how you grow more powerful.

The last and final reason why writers must read is to constantly build and improve their vocabulary. It's like those commercials we've all heard on the radio: People judge you by the way you speak—yeah, well, they will also judge you by the way you write, and the words you employ.

There's nothing worse than a tired vocabulary. The dunderheads of the world don't see the need for a powerful arsenal of words to use whenever they need *just the right* one. They don't understand that words have shades of meaning, or even the meaning of the word *nuance.*

When I was in high school, the Jesuits made me take 4 years of Latin. I wasn't happy about it at first, but the longer I studied the language of the Romans, the more I understood it and its incredible power. Latin gave me the keys to understand just about any word I ever encountered. It's a good feeling. People who read my bimonthly column in a magazine called *Cemetery Dance* are frequently telling me how many times I make them go to the dictionary, amazed at the staggering number of unfamiliar words at my disposal. That's nice.

So read to improve your own vocabulary. When you hit a word you've never seen before, go look it up, write it down, and most importantly, remember it so you can use it. That way, you will never be accused of being circumambagious or arch, but … okay, maybe a little sesquipedalian.

The Least You Need to Know

- You must be a voracious reader to be a writer.
- You should read in your chosen genre.
- You should read nonfiction.
- Reading teaches technique and builds your vocabulary.

The Elements of Writing a Novel

Part 1 attempted to give you a good, basic overview of what writing involves. In Part 2, we're going to get into some coveralls, grab our toolbox, and look under the hood so we can examine the basic components necessary to make a novel run on all cylinders. (See how we said that metaphorically?)

When you finish Part 2, you'll have a working knowledge of plot, characters, setting, dialogue, and other important stuff.

Plot: Creating One and Making It Work

In This Chapter

- Telling yourself what happens next
- Different kinds of plot
- The elements of a plot
- What every plot requires

Okay, let's say you have this interesting bunch of characters, or you have this great idea no one's ever thought of before. What happens next?

That's a good question. Because that's what plot is all about—going from scene to scene, from what happens to what happens next. Having a fascinating protagonist and supporting cast, a clever premise, but no plot is like being dressed in designer attire, with plenty of bling in the old pocky, a limo at the curb, ... and no place to go.

This is why readers want to read a good book—they want to know what's going to happen next. A well-plotted novel keeps readers guessing but almost never allows them to be right. Calling a book a "page-turner" in the reviews means the plot gets into gear, and keeps shifting into higher and higher registers, literally yanking the reader along for the ride.

The best praise you can get for your novel is when people get angry with you—for keeping them up half the night. They started your novel just before bedtime, thinking they'd read a chapter or two, and they simply couldn't stop. Suddenly it's 3 A.M. and they gotta get up to go to work in a few hours. I hear that all the time whenever somebody's reading *The Blood of the Lamb*, *Night of Broken Souls*, or one of my other thrillers, and they send me an e-mail or call me to "complain."

Some writers don't seem to understand what a plot is and are, therefore, very poor at plotting out their novels. You tend to see this kind of plotless writing in the genres generously called *modern literary* novels or *contemporary fiction*. (These are not to be confused with the *classics*, which are also called "literary." The difference is simple: the classics *are* literary; the modern stuff is usually just boring.) These are just synonyms for novels in which very little happens other than a series of loosely connected sketches in which the protagonist, usually a young, alienated urbanite artist-poseur, struggles to find meaning in his or her life and the insensate universe at large.

Please, if you were planning to write that particular "story," don't. It is written thousands of times a year, and it seems as if several hundred of them manage to get published with every change of calendar. Most of them are hyped and reviewed with mention of their "dazzling prose" or "iconoclastic style," but rarely (try *never*) for their riveting storytelling.

The purpose of this chapter is to get you to understand how important plot is to your novel. Writing a story without a plot is like trying to walk around without your skeleton—not too likely to happen.

Plot-Engines

There's no mystery to this concept. A plot-engine is what gets the plot up and running and keeps it in motion. There are really only two kinds worth mentioning or remembering:

- Event-driven plots
- Character-driven plots

Event-driven plots advance because of a sequence of events that keep happening, one after the other, outside the protagonist and secondary characters' sphere of influence. These events change just about everything that can be included in your story—the settings, the action, the mood, the tone, and most importantly, your characters' reactions. The essential thing about event-driven plots is this: your protagonist and supporting cast don't need to undergo any drastic changes (in attitude, belief, motivation, spirituality, or whatever). They only need to react to all the events, and then deal with them or fail to deal with them, until the final event in your plot, which forces the resolution to your story.

An example of an event-driven plot is a group of characters trapped on an island where a volcano is beginning to erupt. All the subsequent events force each of the characters to react to the situations that unfold.

> **WORDS OF WISDOM**
>
> The first thing to consider when writing your novel is your story, and then your story, and then your story!
>
> —Ford Madox Ford

Now for character-driven plots. You might have figured this out because it's pretty much the obverse side of the coin on this issue. The events, which change and keep the plot moving and the reader wondering about what can possibly happen next, all spring from ongoing changes within your characters—the protagonist and everybody in the story. If your hero is driven to make things happen (by revenge, a sense of adventure, desperation, and so on), things will happen, believe me. An interesting aspect of this kind of a plot is that a crafty writer can sometimes allow the reader to see and understand the consequence of the protagonist's actions before the character does.

An example of a character-driven plot is a woman who grows up with a mission to find her mother who abandoned her at an orphanage when she was an infant. The protagonist and her quest drive the plot from place to place and person to person she encounters along the way. The story unfolds because of the main character's persistent actions and inner drive.

Plot Components

The components that go into making a plot have been with us for a very long time. They probably go back to the days when the idea of a nice home was defined by the size of the cave you crawled into. And then one night, when everybody was sitting around the fire, one guy decided to tell everybody else something that wasn't altogether true. Or maybe not?

You can pretty much bet that our first storyteller used a lot of the components we're going to look at now. He didn't think about them; he let it flow, relying on his instincts to hold everybody else's attention.

And that's what you need to do, too. Even though we're going to look at plot in fairly analytical terms, I don't want to suggest you do your plotting mechanically (as in following a formula). Even though you may employ something of a system, or a method, it's not like one of those paint-by-number sets. You still have to use the old noggin and plenty of imagination. (I mean, c'mon, does anybody *really* think those number-paintings actually look like a piece of art?)

Okay, back to the components of plot—problem, complication, and resolution. Let's have a look.

Houston, We Have a Problem

NASA may not want any problems, but if you want to tell a good story, your plot *must* have them. Your characters need to have questions to be answered, things to be found, and obstacles to be removed. This is fairly simple stuff, and new writers shouldn't worry so much about "coming up with a plot." If you stay with me in this chapter, everything will seem easy. Trust me.

Problems are best revealed through conflict. Following are the basic kinds of conflicts in fiction:

Man against society. These are the stories in which your protagonist is an individual who sees the world differently from those around him. Or he has willingly placed himself in a position to physically oppose the society in which he lives and works. For example, he has a new idea, like a steam engine or antiseptic surgery or radio waves, and everybody thinks he's a fool; he is a slave in an oppressive government and plots to make himself and his fellow slaves free; or he is wrongly accused of a terrible crime, and the entire community is out looking for him.

These are classic kinds of plots, which never fail to stir the audience into pulling for your hero, who is usually the archetypal underdog. This type of plot can usually write itself, but I'm going to tell you right here: *you* need to write it. The pitfall here is to unconsciously mimic a great book or a familiar movie. So be sure you're original.

Man against man. Another plot you recognize instantly is the tale of the two rivals. You create two dynamic characters, each one representing an antipodal (I'll wait while you look this up in your dictionary ... Ready? Okay.) army, philosophy, methodology, religion, scientific theory, political party, and so on. It can be the dramatic clash of famous generals glaring at each other across the battlefields of a world stage, or it can be as simple as the classic generational clash of the traditional beliefs versus the new ideas. Examples include father versus son or mother against daughter in the domestic confines of the suburban home.

The clash of two personalities, each delineated with enough differences to be apparent (but not so obvious as to be like a comic book), can be very volatile material. To make it even more fun, a skillful writer can make it a tough choice for the readers—which character will they ultimately cheer for?

Man against himself. This one is a little more complex and probably requires a fairly good understanding of human psychology and social behavior. These are the stories that focus on the inner struggles of a protagonist who must decide upon a particular path. It may be a moral choice between a political high road and one that leads to corruption, between marital fidelity and adultery, or between sparing another person's life and taking it.

This type of plot has produced some of the world's greatest literary treasures, but it is also a tricky assignment for young or unseasoned writers. The reason is the simple necessity of staging a lot of the conflict upon the internal landscape of the human psyche. Unlike this type of conflict, the previous two can easily be played out with plenty of external action, so be sure you understand your character before you try to tell this kind of story.

WORDS OF WISDOM

Story did not begin when the boy ran into the village and cried "Wolf!" and the wolf was chasing at his heels. Story began when the boy ran into the village and cried "Wolf!" ... and there *was* no wolf.

—Anonymous

Man against nature. This is perhaps the oldest of all plot types because it reflects upon our earliest evolutionary challenges and triumphs. This story is probably hard-wired into our genes because our ancestors repeatedly experienced such dramas to survive and make us the dominant, successful species. These are stories in which your protagonist attempts to climb the impossible peak; dive to the bottom of the Marianas Trench; defeat the bear, shark, or whatever; or withstand the oncoming hurricane, volcanic eruption, earthquake, meteor—you get the idea.

This type of conflict lends itself to high drama because you can always up the stakes and make things worse than anyone could have imagined.

All of the Above

The really great novels, the true classics, are probably the ones that combine elements of the conflict types discussed. So perhaps the protagonist is using the great white whale as a symbol for some deeply scarred aspect of his own soul. See? Did you ever think about that? Well, now you can.

Okay, let's move on from the specifics of conflict to a few generalities. I think you should know that the most successful plot conflict occurs when you can seamlessly combine external action and the inner conflict of a tortured soul.

Also, remember that conflict has more of a purpose than merely to create action. One of the most important functions of conflict is to create *changes* in your protagonist. He or she must learn from the experience of the conflict. Your characters must either become stronger or weaker (morally and physically), or they must become wiser or perhaps die in the effort because they cannot become wiser.

Why Does It Have to Be So Complicated?

Complication is what makes conflicts really interesting. It's not enough for your plot to merely state a problem and have your character fix it. No, no. Things have to get complicated. Things have to go wrong, and just when your character thinks he or she has it under control, something else has to go wrong, or the initial problem has to get worse.

When you think of complication, you're basically asking yourself, "Okay, what kinds of elements in my story can cause things to get worse?" Complication can stem from various sources—as long as they're believable.

You can have serious flaws in your characters—a nice date, but an alcoholic; would have loved to pilot the plane, but her glasses were broken; an evil mother has turned him into a psychopathic woman-hater; and so on. Or you can have someone or some agency make a terrible mistake—regarding identity, bureaucratic records, forgetting to make an appointment, or whatever makes sense. And of course, one of the best complicators is a character who is simply not a good guy—the villain or antagonist who always causes trouble.

WORDS OF WISDOM

Rules are a good point to build a story around. They are plain, solid, square foundation. If you stick to that foundation, you get a plain, solid, square build-ing. Nothing wrong with it, but nothing notable either. To make an interesting building, you've got to go beyond that foundation, ignoring it as much as you can without having the building fall apart. The bending of the rules until the story is ready to crumble is what makes a good story—interesting, intriguing, and plausible, but almost ready to burst.

—David "Pasha" Morrow

You should keep in mind two basic things about complication:

- Things must look as bad as they can possibly be and then get worse.

- Complication creates change—change in the character's feelings and actions plus change in the order or logic of future events and how they unfold in the plot—and that makes your story interesting.

Vive la Resolution!

The third and final plot component is the resolution—it's essentially the way you decide to wrap up your plot. Think about it: you've worked through problems and made things as messy as possible, and your characters have worked their way through the maze of obstacles. Now it's time to bring everything to a conclusion of some kind.

The type of conclusion you opt for defines your particular resolution. And as you might suspect, there are several basic types of resolutions:

Protagonist wins. This is the most simple, direct, and anticipated wrap for a story. Your main character is the one the audience has been pulling for throughout. She is the one the readers believe they know the best, and they want good things to happen for her. The corollary to this proposition is that the bad guy is going to lose, and the reader is going to derive great pleasure in seeing the villain get what he deserves.

So this ending has a double bonus pay-off, which rarely fails to satisfy your readers, who have "invested" time and emotion in your main characters.

Protagonist loses. This takes your plot in a completely different direction right at the end of your story, but it can also be very satisfying for your readers. When your hero loses, be sure the audience believes that, even in defeat, the protagonist has become a better person and has ended up in a better situation than before the story began. This final improvement can be physical (more money, a better house, improved health, and so on) but is more acceptable when the main character is better off spiritually and emotionally (true love, social acceptance, intellectual discovery, and so on).

This ending is a little trickier to write, but usually proves to be more powerful and more memorable because it is not the commonly predicted outcome.

Antagonist wins. You don't see this one all that often because it is, without question, the toughest resolution to carry off successfully. The audience is not going to accept the bad guy as the winner unless he undergoes some kind of transformation or revelation, finds the cause of his evil, and extricates it like the pulsing tumor that it is—or at least overcomes its influences. This is different from the protagonist loses in terms of how much emphasis you've given to deepening the character of the antagonist and how ambiguously appealing the antagonist may be.

If you choose to go this route, you must fully understand the concept of a character (even an antagonist) achieving what the "literary" critics call *transcendence*. This a state of self-awareness in which things happen that cause your character to suddenly understand herself in a more profound way. Writers who choose to handle their plots and characters like this would probably also enjoy trying to jump motorcycles over canyons.

Plot Requirements

Just as you need oxygen to keep the pulmonary exchange working, any good plot needs a few basics to keep it alive and fresh. Assuming you have your plot under control using the many pearls of wisdom you've picked up in the last few pages, you can now add the last few frills.

Direction

A plot needs to have a goal, a path the audience can somewhat perceive and anticipate. The usual direction of the plot of your mystery novel, for example, would be to unravel the clues and the process of whodunit. The expected direction of the paranoid suspense thriller is for the protagonist to search for his true identity and the reason why everyone else in the novel wants to kill him. You get the idea. Then just when the reader thinks they have the direction pinned down, you do what every good writer does—you change it.

Change Points

You employ change points to block out and pace your narrative. Think of them as mile-markers on the highway of your plot, and each one signals a point where you could change things up a bit. You do this with the following:

- *Reverses.* When the events suddenly seem to shift from really good to utterly awful.

- *Discovery.* When your characters stumble upon something totally unexpected.

- *Recognition.* When the protagonist reconsiders something or recalls something he should have comprehended earlier. (This can be something you laid out for the reader, and maybe the reader already knows it and is waiting with great anticipation to see if your hero will finally catch on.)

A LIKELY STORY

Your protagonist is a baseball pitcher, who suffers a terrible car accident and is in danger of losing his arm. He undergoes a series of operations and a long recovery. When he returns to the majors, he is practically unhittable. A female reporter suspects he has been given a robotic arm. What happens next?

Suspense

This is the final plot requirement, and also the most obvious. You need what's called *dramatic tension* to keep the reader wondering what could possibly happen next. You create suspense by keeping the reader off balance and by using tactics of deception, delay, and interruption.

How many times have you been reading a great story and, just when something alarming or exciting begins to happen, the chapter ends? And you flip the page excitedly to the next one … only to find that the writer has whisked you away to a completely new scene (and the alarming action you need to follow has been delayed).

Do you think the writer did that by accident? No, of course not. It's the essence of suspense. You've experienced it, and now you know how to create it.

A Few Words About Structure

Most basic classes on fiction composition tell you that your plot needs a basic framework. And you've all heard the old axiom about having a beginning, a middle, and an ending, right? Well, that's what plot structure is all about—very simple things that more experienced writers may seem to ignore, but upon a closer look, rarely do. The reason? Because the classic idea of how a story should hang together became classic for a reason. It has withstood the greatest test of all—the test of time.

The Beginning

Readers feel comfortable starting a story at the natural beginning of the tale. For that reason, the majority of young or new writers are most at home starting at the point where the real story begins. This is called *linear plotting*, and I recommend it for every one of you, until you get so good that you can start to experiment.

This is where you establish everything: your main characters, your setting and time, and most importantly, your problem (remember that one?). Do this correctly, and you've hooked your reader for the long haul.

The Middle

This is the part of the plot where you lay in all the information your readers will need, and where you start making things more complicated. You blend your action between internal and external stuff and establish the consequences of what might happen if your plot takes a variety of turns. The middle is basically a setup for the ending.

Your middle should wind down to what some writers call the *ignition point*, where alarm lights go off for the reader, who is now getting a "feeling" for the future developments of the plot—whether things will go well or not. Depending on your story, you can let that evolve the way you suggested it here, or you can serve up a sweeping curve ball and change everything again. This is your last chance to do that sort of thing because you're headed into the final turn.

The Ending

The ending is the place where you answer all the questions, tie up any dangling subplots, and allow your characters to face the consequences of their actions. This may also be the time when you factor in any inner resolutions or moments of understanding that layer the feelings of completeness the ending should suggest. How you handle the end of your plot determines whether the reader wants to return for a spin through your next novel.

Yes, as you might imagine, the ending is important.

Some Tricks

We're almost finished, but I thought I'd throw in a few plotting tricks, er, techniques. Not that you want to deceive your readers, but you do sometimes want to distract, mislead, or tantalize them.

Multiple Viewpoint

Multiple viewpoint means presenting the narrative through the perceptions of more than one viewpoint character. It's a good plot device because it allows you, under the pretense of needing to bring in another character for purposes of balance and pacing, to abruptly stop the action at a crucial moment. This makes the readers crazy, and it keeps them turning the page.

In Media Res

In media res is Latin for "in the middle of things," and it's the name of a nifty technique authors of spy thrillers and horror novels employ with great success. It means your book opens right *in the center* of some incredible action or predicament. The reader is yanked into the scene and doesn't get a chance to really come up for air, or understand what's going on, until later—and that's when you throw in a few chapters that back-fill the events leading up to the opening sequence.

Once you catch the reader up on what has happened previously, you move on with the middle of the story. This can be tricky and confusing for the reader if it remains equally so for the writer. So if you try this technique and you're not getting it, you can lay odds that your readers won't either. In that case, you want to call a cab, go home, and return to a more conventional, linear plot.

 WORDS OF WISDOM

The difference between reality and fiction? Fiction has to make sense.

—Tom Clancy

Logic and Nonsense

This seems almost silly to mention, but your plot has to make sense. What I'm talking about here is an elemental sense of cause and effect. Things must happen logically—if *this* takes place, then *that* surely will.

It's also called causality—the task of making one scene lead to another, either through direct action or implication. Believe it or not, this is one of the most common errors new novelists make. They devise wonderfully complicated plots but fail to construct a logical sequence of events.

There are three common crimes in plot logic:

The idiot plot. This is when everyone must act like a total idiot, or there would literally *be no plot.* The classic example is the dumb horror movie in which the band of friends split up and go their separate ways so the monster can pick them off, one by one.

Author convenience. This is when things happen in the plot for no reason other than the writer simply *needing* them to happen. This kind of silliness is usually explained away as "coincidence," but it's really just bad plotting. An example would be having a character arrive on the scene to keep the heroine from committing suicide without providing a reason for being right there at that crucial moment.

Rabbit out of hat. This is the red-haired stepbrother of the previous crime and is actually worse because it allows events to happen without even the convenience of "luck" or "serendipity." This is when things happen with *no* possible explanation. It's like the totally unexpected and unexplainable phenomenon of pulling a rabbit out of a hat. A particularly egregious commission of this crime is a plot that ends as "it was all a dream" when there has been utterly nothing in the preceding plot to rationally justify the ending or the entire story.

Having a good plot is crucial to telling your story. Now that you understand what makes it tick and what you should include and avoid, you're going to be able to craft your narrative more thoughtfully.

The Least You Need to Know

- Plots need conflict. When you create a problem, you need to have your characters go about the fascinating business of solving it.
- Complication improves a plot. Nothing is more nerve-wracking than thinking you have something under control, only to see it unravel and become worse.
- Plots need structure. The old wisdom about beginnings, middles, and endings will serve you well.
- Plots should be logical. If your story doesn't make sense, it can't hold up under careful analysis. Once your readers reject your logic, it's difficult to win them back.

Characters: Make 'Em Memorable

In This Chapter

- Why character is important
- Types of characters
- Aspects of character
- Bringing your characters to life

Why do people like to read novels? To some extent it depends on the genre. I think dyed-in-the-wool mystery readers enjoy solving puzzles, and science fiction readers want to be wowed by clever new concepts. But I think most of us enjoy novels because we like to identify with interesting characters. We get to play make-believe, on some largely unconscious level, and pretend we are someone else—usually someone who is living a far more adventurous and intriguing existence than we are.

That's why many writers argue the most important part of your novel is your characters. If your "peeps" aren't cool, your readers are going to lose interest fast.

Science fiction (SF) is the only genre in which you can get away with thin, one-dimensional characters. And I say this with no sneering or condescension because I broke in writing SF and soon realized the principle characters in most speculative fiction are the *ideas*, or the clever premises upon which the SF stories turn. The characters are often just necessary mouthpieces or vehicles that explain the idea. I've heard many SF writers reluctantly admit the premise is often the main character in a SF tale. I'm not saying this is okay; I mention it because readers of this genre tend to be more tolerant of characters who don't leap off the page.

But even if you're planning to write a science fiction novel, you should strive to make your characters as believable, original, and memorable as possible. If you combine good characters with a truly unique and innovative SF premise, your book will be that much better.

Make Them Care

You want to get your readers to connect with your characters. You want them to feel like they know your people, and most importantly, you want them to *care* about your characters.

And what does that mean? Well, for starters, you want your readers to invest the time to get to know your characters—you want them to keep reading long enough to become comfortable with your characters. Think of it as walking into a crowded room and meeting a lot of people for the first time. Your first impressions are usually important—this guy has an arrogant way of talking, that lady has a huge mole on her forehead, another dude is wearing a sport coat fashioned by Purina, the hostess has a habit of pursing her lips like she just tasted something nasty; and another woman looks elegant because of the single string of pearls around her neck.

So are you interested in any of them? Repelled? Intrigued? These are the concerns for readers when they first meet your characters, so you have to make them care from jump city—in other words, right away. How do you do it? I explain how in the following sections.

I Feel Your Pain

Introduce your characters (at least your principle characters) in ways that make the reader aware of feeling or experiencing something. This technique is very effective because it involves the reader in the character's inner workings almost instantly.

Your characters can be feeling any range of emotions or experiencing any number of things, but some are more effective than others. They can be deliriously happy, wistful, or nostalgic; but I would put fear up near the top, as well as paranoia, or even a distinct sense of unease or dread. Starting out with everything being copacetic might not be very arresting. If the reader can quickly recognize the sense of jeopardy your characters are sharing, you have a better chance of hooking your reader into caring about them.

WORDS OF WISDOM

That trite little whimsy about characters getting out of hand; it is as old as the quills. My characters are galley slaves.

—Vladimir Nabokov

Your characters can also be feeling that most reliable of dramatic elements—good old pain. It can be either physical or psychological. That's your choice, but introducing a character who is hurt by something or someone can quickly make readers very sympathetic.

By immediately giving your audience such an intimate look inside a character's soul, you're inviting them to share just about anything. And that makes your readers instantly more comfortable and willing to invest time and emotion in your make-believe people. It's quite a feat when you think about it.

Danger! Will Robinson!

Ah yes, this is a guaranteed grabber, isn't it? If your reader meets your main characters when they're in serious trouble, they are being "smoke-screened" just a little bit, but they don't usually care. If your readers buy into the immediate danger your character faces, they are willing to put off actually getting to know them, at least for a little while.

Sure, it's a bit of a trick, but if your protagonist just swam across a turbulent river with crocodiles snapping hungrily at his feet, the readers will feel somewhat of a bond with the character. They're willing to find out a little more about the person because they've been through a harrowing experience together.

The caution here is to not overdo or overuse this technique. If your novel is full of trumped-up introductions, in which everybody seems to have a knack for stumbling into potentially lethal situations just before the reader meets them, then you'll have a big problem with credibility. Edgar Rice Burroughs was guilty of this in his Tarzan and John Carter novels. Keep in mind that audiences are quickly bored by the familiar.

Larger Than Life

The third way to get your readers to care about your characters is to cast them as people who are special in some way. If your character is unique or extraordinary, you will grasp your reader's attention and their built-in willingness to learn more about the character.

Some of the most obvious examples are novels about famous and powerful people from history—presidents, generals, kings, assassins, corporate owners, movie producers, lawyers, and so on. But I'm sure you can come up with an entire cast of additional people who are intrinsically interesting by virtue of what they do or the amount of influence and power they wield.

You can also create characters who possess a singular skill or a striking appearance. The best way to portray these characteristics is by *showing* rather than telling your readers. If your protagonist is a great martial arts fighter, you'll do better matching him up against a master assassin than just listing his skill like a resumé credit. The same goes for that sexy lady in your novel—if you have other characters reacting to her alluring aspect, you're making a more convincing argument than just making a bland statement.

You're Not My Type

When we create and employ characters to help tell our stories, we're actually using what ancient Greece dramatists called *archetypes*—a cast of characters who are defined more by their dramatic and narrative function than their more obvious attributes. One guy may be the comic relief, another is the analyzer, another is the clumsy fool who complicates the plot by making mistakes, etc.

Being aware of the concept of archetypes will make your characters better. Your approach to matching up your characters to their most appropriate archetypes is best done in retrospect. After you've assembled your cast, see who serves each function so you can figure out who's missing, or who isn't necessary to the kind of story you're trying to tell.

Following are the basic archetypes:

Protagonist. This is the good guy we want to see win; the one who will make the most effort to prevail. However, the protagonist is not always the main character. (The main character is the one whom the story is really about—and that can be the villain.) In the novel *The Boys from Brazil*, the story is *about* Dr. Josef Mengele, but the protagonist is based on the real Nazi hunter, Simon Wiesenthal.

Antagonist. This is the character who acts against the needs and actions of the protagonist. He is the antipodal force that provides complication (see Chapter 6).

Conscience. This character is like a guardian angel or the little figure on the shoulder of characters in silly cartoons and commercials. He is the voice of "reason" and morality the protagonist can use to work out the problems of the story.

Tempter. This is the person who tries to distract the protagonist from his primary mission—either by harmless diversion or deliberate confusion motivated, for example, by jealousy, revenge, or something equally venal.

Buddy. Most novels employ this kind of sidekick character with great success—same or different sex as the protagonist, it doesn't matter. And the buddy works for the good guy or the bad guy just as well.

Skeptic. This is a different kind of character—because he or she tries to stay outside the conflict. He often believes in a third alternative and needs to be swayed to one side or another.

> **TOM'S TIPS**
>
> Be sure your novel has a good guy. Some modern novels are difficult to endure because no character turns out to be likeable enough to be the protagonist, or the one the reader wants to cheer for. A novel with an entire cast of nasty characters most likely won't be read all the way to the end.

Emotionalist. This is the character who responds to the story elements purely by gut reaction, or intuition. The emotionalist can give no reason why an issue receives or loses his support.

Rationalist. This is the opposite archetype to the emotionalist. This character only chooses a side of an issue or solution to a problem based on logic and reason.

Stereotypes

There's one more "type" we must examine, even if only to recognize and avoid it. In the strictest sense, a *stereotype* is a kind of shorthand sketch of the type of character who is so well known to be achingly trite. But the word has also come to carry far more negative freight. In this touchy-feely age, you have to be careful not to offend anyone.

If you're a fan of old movies, you've probably seen most of the more obvious stereotypes: the mother who likes to be a martyr, the ultrasweet and unreal girl-next-door, the misunderstood hooker with a "heart of gold," and the big lug of a hero who speaks in monosyllables.

The most egregious stereotypes are those that lean on ethnic or racial props. Even though most have some basis in historical fact, they have become tired symbols. Therefore, any writer who employs them is worse than lazy. Here I'm talking about the Southern waitress, Jewish lawyers, Italian thugs, Irish cops, Nebraska farm boys, etc. We've seen enough of these people, don't you think?

Character Attributes

This is pretty basic, but no discussion of characters is complete without at least noting the Things You Need to Know About Your Characters. These are the aspects of each character in your novel that will help you understand who they are and why they act the way they do. You can't expect your readers to know your characters unless you do. Here's what you need to know about your characters:

Physical appearance. This includes many attributes. Age is very important because it will determine whether your character looks young or old. You also need to decide if they are homely, handsome, or somewhere along the bell curve. Distinguishing marks such as moles, scars, and tattoos are always interesting. One that's often overlooked is speech habit—your character can be long-winded, terse, verbose, or can perhaps speak with a slight accent.

Psychological makeup. You don't need to have a complete neuropsychological work-up on each character, but some basic personality traits will get you started here. Is your character neat or sloppy? Moody or happy-go-lucky? Does he or she approach problems with a cold, analytical eye, or an effusive burst of feeling? Does paranoia fit the profile, or is he careless and trusting? What about the old smarts-scale: sparkling intelligence or a dullard?

Cultural influences. This one can be interesting and add a lot of color and spice to your character. Everyone has cultural roots. Casually exploring how families dress on Sundays, how the dinner table was "set," or the kind of music the family listened to can all add texture to your people. You're also providing extra opportunities for readers to identify with the characters.

Moral compass. At some point, fairly early, your readers like to know how your characters react to various societal issues, dilemmas, and demands of propriety and conduct. Religion is often a convenient handle for some of these attributes, but it can't be a catch-all. Characters can be uptight and timid; cautious and polite; hip, "free," and modern; or morally bankrupt and dangerous. Or they can be oil-and-water combinations of any of these, which can make them irritatingly complex.

TOM'S TIPS

When you describe your characters initially, don't unload all their attributes in the first paragraph like a dump truck operator. Drop them into the narrative slowly, and don't be afraid to repeat a major characteristic a few times over the course of the story. It's not obtrusive, and it helps to reinforce the readers' mental image of your people.

Social contacts. Do your characters come from large or small families? Happy, integrated ones, or the currently fashionable "dysfunctional" families? Married, single, divorced? Upper, lower, or middle class? And don't forget occupation, which is very important in defining and dictating many elements, such as abilities, experience, education, aspirations, and usefulness to other characters. Certain occupations lend themselves to mobility or travel and contact with specific groups. You should also know what kind of leisure interests shape your character's world—hobbies, sports, exercise, obsessions, etc.

When skillfully put into play, all these attributes conspire to create a richly textured portrait. Your job is to be sure you don't do it so clumsily that the reader becomes wise to your invention. Your characters should be like any other people your readers meet—they should be able to get to know your people gradually. And the more familiar they get, the more they'll want to know them, or get away from them. Just like in real life.

The main point is that the more we know them, the more interesting characters become. That way, when they inevitably change, the reader cares all the more.

The Name Game

One of the most essential parts of creating characters is giving them names. And it's more important than you might think. Names have all sorts of associative powers connected to them. If your hero's name is Glen, and one of your readers just got left at the altar by some mook with the same name, well … you've probably lost a reader. I'm not saying this to worry you; you're never going to please everybody. The real challenge would be to create such a dynamic guy named Glen that even the hypothetical jilted bride would find him appealing.

There's no surefire way to come up with perfect names for your characters. You have to employ some instinct and a little misdirection. Typical names like Rock and Dirk and Garth for tough-guy, commando-type heroes border on self-parody, so use good judgment and try to be original. The same holds true for all the typical "soap opera princess" names (like Marcella, Ashleigh, and Courtney) for your female characters. Even though you might really like the name, it just might not be appropriate.

The key word here is *association.* Even though it will be unavoidable to some degree, don't make it worse by picking a name with a high-recognition quotient for someone other than your character. Remember the *Seinfeld* episode when Elaine meets a new guy who has the same name as a famous serial killer? Well, even if you didn't, I've already given all you need to know about it and what a recipe for trouble it can be.

So where do you find all the names you're going to need, especially if you have a lot of characters? Even though it's an old saw, the phone book isn't bad. If you live in a small town, ask a friend or relative who lives in a big city to save you one of their old ones.

Your friends are another great source of names. I use my friends' names a lot, and they get a big kick out of it. Most people never expect to see their names in a book, so believe me, it's a pretty cool deal. The trick is not to link their names with anything close to their real identity in terms of occupation, age, or locale. If your poker-night buddy is a hardware store clerk, make him a Boston cop. You get the idea.

One of the more enjoyable name sources I've seen lately is a little website called the Random Name Generator (www.kleimo.com/random/name.cfm). It has an "obscurity" adjustment, so you can dial up either common or very uncommon names. It's a lot of fun and is guaranteed to amuse you, maybe even provide you with just the right name.

A LIKELY STORY

Two actors in a Broadway play begin to independently experience events in their real lives that mirror events in their play. It becomes evident that their characters are pulling them into an alternate reality. Can you create a novel that deals with this possibility?

Now before we leave this category, one last thing about names: don't pick names that are difficult to pronounce, or worse, have more than one pronunciation. I did this recently in a novel, and a reader wrote me an e-mail complaining that she never figured out whether one of my major characters named Streicher was pronounced *striker* or *streisher*, and it bugged her so much it became a major distraction. It was something that had never occurred to me, but I'll always remember it. The last thing you want to do is distract or irritate your readers.

Using Models

Some writers I know never bother to sit down with a legal pad or a PDA and consciously create their characters. They use a technique called *modeling*. Another word for it might be *stealing*. Basically, you use a real person as the template for your character. You use the person as completely as possible, capturing all the attributes and other things I've already mentioned. The idea is to place a familiar figure in new, invented situations (your plot), and extrapolate how that person would react.

Your model characters can come from several major sources:

People you know. These are the people you *really* know: your relatives, friends, enemies, co-workers. You can take the time to observe them closely and perform authentic analysis on their choices and all the things they do on a daily basis. Everything is available and is grist for your mill—how they dress, speak, laugh, and complain. You can learn a lot about human behavior by seriously studying the real characters in your life.

Historical and pop culture figures. These are some of those larger-than-life figures I mentioned previously. For example, if you're going to write a novel that features a powerful senator, why not study some powerful politicians and model your character after one of them? Seems like a reasonable plan, and for some writers I know, it works extremely well.

Remember when I talked about reading biographies? Here's where the practice will serve you well. Be a little more careful if you pattern a character after someone who is currently enjoying a high profile in popular culture. Readers may recognize your ploy and dismiss your character because he's not as interesting as the real person.

The roman à clef. Okay, this is a very special kind of template. It's not done very often, and I mention it only because I believe you should know about everything in this particular profession.

The literal translation of *roman à clef* means "novel with a key," but it really means a novel in which all the characters are real people and the story is an account of real events. Writers usually do this because using the actual people's names and real events would be explosive, scandalous, or libelous. So if the writer wants to tell the real story, he has no choice but to fictionalize actual events.

This is different from modeling several of your characters on real people because every character in this kind of a book is a real person with a fake name. Chances are, you won't be interested in this kind of a novel.

A Few Character-Creation Pointers

The process of creating characters involves maintaining a certain level of awareness of what makes people who they are and why they act the way they do. Keep the following ideas in mind when you are creating your characters.

Motivation is important. If you understand why your characters are driven to do specific things, you are tuned in to what's motivating them. And if you can successfully convey that understanding through the narrative, your readers will believe your characters.

As I've mentioned, you can't have things happen merely because you need them to. Your characters cannot appear to be marionettes being yanked around by strings. Motivation takes care of that. Characters and their actions make the most sense when they have goals or when they want something; the readers then understand their goals and desires. This understanding keeps your characters moving toward a resolution and keeps your readers reading.

The viewpoint character tells your story. Whether you realize it or not, one of your characters is going to be the one through which most of your novel unfolds for the reader. If you're writing a first-person P.I. novel, there's no choice involved. But if you're writing in the third person, you have plenty of choices.

 WORDS OF WISDOM

The legend that characters run away from their authors—taking up drugs, having sex operations, and becoming president—implies that the writer is a fool with no knowledge or mastery of his craft. The idea of authors running around helplessly behind their cretinous inventions is contemptible.

—John Cheever

The story can be told through the protagonist, or the main character (and we already now know they aren't necessarily the same person), or sometimes even through the experiences of the antagonist—the villain. I've seen some interesting stretches and variations on this choice. I remember one mystery novel in which the narrator is the victim—a dead person!

Who's in control? Sometimes I hear writers say they create certain characters who then "assume a mind of their own," or "take over the novel," and send it off in unexpected directions. This is usually a metaphorical explanation—or worse, an artsy-fartsy attempt to make characterization some sort of a mystical experience. I'm willing to admit that some characters don't turn out the way you originally intended, but I think good novels with good characters were usually written by good writers who had control of themselves and their sensibilities. I'm not flying solo with this contention—lots of writers I know agree with me.

Characters Under Construction

You should have a pretty solid idea of the function of character in your novel. You should know what kind of characters you're going to need and what attributes to give them. All that's left is an understanding of the various processes that will allow you to present and develop your cast.

Here are some ways to bring your characters to life:

Narration. You use the general tone and voice of the narration to introduce characters and describe them in the same way you describe action and setting. A formal narrative style supports more formal characters, while a breezy narration sets up more easy-going, accessible characters.

The best authority. This is the easiest way to reveal character, and it's perfectly acceptable for your first-person narrator to talk about himself. He can tell your readers all kinds of things about himself nobody else could possibly know.

Other characters. This is a nice, unobtrusive technique in which characters talk to each other about other characters. They argue with one another, accuse one another, suspect one another, and so on. The reader can learn incredible amounts about all the characters in your novel if you put everybody to work like they all write for gossip columns.

Actions speak loudest. Naturally, this is an effective way of giving your readers an accurate portrait of your characters. You can talk about them until you turn blue, but when the audience sees them in action and reaction, they will form their own opinions about what kind of people they are. Your job is to be sure your characters act logically, and they will do the rest of the convincing.

The power of the word. At first, many new writers don't realize how effective dialogue can be as a character-revealing tool. If a character uses a lot of flowery language or is prone to clipped, harsh commands and declarations, readers pick up on this and start making assumptions about the kind of person who talks like that. Tone and tempo of delivery can also contribute to character construction.

TOM'S TIPS

Even though I'm giving you all the ingredients you need to come up with interesting and dynamic characters, I don't want you to get the idea that you need to populate your novel by following an outline or a blueprint. You can't build characters like you lay bricks. Remember, you must inject abstract elements into the creation of the people in your novel—things like soul, intuition, and instinct. You must look at them with a cold eye and make them different. Turn them inside out, if that's what it takes.

The Least You Need to Know

- Your readers need to identify with your characters. If you make the audience care about the people in your novel, you're home free.
- A novel needs a variety of character types. Each type performs a different plot function.
- The success of well-realized characters lies in your ability to present a wide range of identifiable attributes.
- Characters become familiar to the audience through revelations from themselves, other characters, their words, and their actions.

Setting: Location Is Everything

In This Chapter

- The importance of setting
- Some general observations about setting
- Types of settings
- Setting tricks and techniques

It's funny, but when you ask writers to name the most important elements of a novel, you'd be surprised how many of them don't mention setting. The major reason, I think, is that most writers just take it for granted that a novel needs setting, and plenty of it. It would be like everybody listing "words" as one of the elements of a good novel.

Location, Location, Location

Setting is one of those components you cannot overlook just because you know you need it. Everybody knows they need yearly comprehensive physical exams, too, but very few people go through the bother and expense to make them happen. It's clearly not enough to tell yourself you'll pencil in plenty of settings in which to tell your story. Any good writer will tell you your knowledge of the places where the action happens is crucial to pulling off the entire illusion.

Setting essentially means information and details *about* the information. If you describe a neighborhood in the city of Buffalo, it's not enough to just baldly state your character's location. You're going to need to fill in some of the blanks to give the reader a few cues about what the place looks like, how it smells, and how it makes your characters feel. You have to determine whether it's day or night, present time or a hundred years ago.

It's crucial you get the details correct. If you don't, somebody will catch you. And if one person can catch you getting it wrong, you have to assume a lot more can do it. The important corollary to getting caught in a lie—you don't know anything about the city in which you set your action—can get you in trouble. Getting things wrong with your setting can be one of the fastest ways to lose your reader.

If a reader doesn't like your characters, your basic plot premise, or even your style, he's not going to realize that right away. The reader will give you time to develop interest in those elements of your story. But with setting, you have practically no time to get off on the wrong foot. You need to start convincing your reader immediately that your pirate ship, or your corporate skyscraper, or your desert town, or your Florida swamp is *real*. From page 1, you need to get your reader buying into the world you create.

Besides, I don't think there's anything worse than this experience with a book: you're reading along, you've plowed through several pages, and suddenly you realize the writer has lost you. You have no idea where the characters are … other than a vague suggestion of the setting. References are made to objects, items, and places that have no previous mention or grounding point, and you feel like you're getting more lost. You start asking yourself things like, *Where did that come from?* or *He picked up WHAT?*

I don't know about you, but that gets me thinking about softly closing the book before I throw it across the room. Novels that cannot successfully keep the reader firmly placed in the world of the story are penciled in for failure.

I'm going to assume I've convinced you how important setting is to your novel. In fact, when you decide what kind of story you want to tell, your setting should be one of the first decisions you make and feel comfortable with.

WORDS OF WISDOM

What you're trying to do when you write is crowd the reader out of his own space and occupy it with yours, in a good cause. You're trying to take over his sensibility and deliver an experience that moves from mere information.

—Robert Stone

For instance, a novel I recently finished has a German U-boat in 1945 as one of its settings. I knew right away when I began developing my story I was going to need to become pretty much of an expert on vintage submarines and underwater warfare. No problem; I prepared myself by doing the research. No way was I going to start the first chapter and realize I didn't know a ballast tank from a Biscay cross.

You need to make the same decisions. This chapter gives you a few pointers to help out.

Settings in General

Before we get into details, I'm going to give you a few general admonitions about setting. These are the things you should keep in mind most of the time.

Balance

One of the first things you usually do when you write your novel is establish the setting. There's some art and some craft to doing this without letting your reader realize what you're doing. When your story is up and running, it will be a lot easier to drop in additional details, new locations, and so on. But at the beginning, you have to put a lot of information into the reader's mind fairly quickly and efficiently.

The key to getting the right amount of information to the reader is *balance*. You want to strike equilibrium between the action and dialogue and your descriptive passages. That's what setting is all about—description, which inherently slows down the advance of the story itself. It's easy: mix your action, dialogue, and description of setting so you don't have any overly long sections of any of them.

The key thing to remember: use your descriptive passages to establish or reinforce setting as *instruments* of pacing. Use your scene-setting to break up long runs of dialogue or action. Then you can get creative and use your dialogue and action to set the scene. Everything starts to integrate and work together when you truly understand what you're doing and why you're doing it.

Personality Plus

If your setting or description of a scene can support and enhance your major characters' personalities, it will be a big plus all around. And this isn't as tough as it may sound.

When you start describing a setting, think carefully about the items and "props" you can mention, and decide whether or not they contribute to a fuller picture of the person or group who will be populating the scene. Let's take a room in a house, for example. If it's the main character's den or office, we can tell a lot about the guy just by running down a short inventory of the things in the room.

The presence of many bookcases and books means he's educated, erudite, and so on. The absence of books may indicate just the opposite. What about the pictures on the desk? Are they of family or a flouncy girlfriend? Either photo suggests a different kind of guy, right? What can you tell from the choice of décor in the carpeting, the drapes, the amount of light, etc.? How about the artwork? Does the person like landscape realism, pictures of nautical stuff, ducks, or something more abstract? Each choice tells you something different about the character. The same thing goes for the kind of car he drives or the places he goes to for recreation.

This Ain't No Travel Agency

There's no question that a book with a strong sense of place provides plenty of anchors for the reader. Knowing where you are is basic to a good story. But be careful. New novelists have a tendency to overwhelm the reader with everything they know about every new setting they introduce.

Too much detail becomes intrusive. The last thing you want is for big chunks of your novel to be nothing more than overcooked travel agency brochures. Remember, there's a big difference between subtle and obvious, and you always want to be leaning toward the former.

Research Versus Experience

Writers argue about this topic endlessly. Not as fiercely as the creationists and the evolutionaries maybe, but the debate has many proponents on both sides.

Some writers are very faithful to the old, hoary dictum: write what you know. They adhere to it so religiously that they wouldn't dream of setting a novel in a city or (the audacity!) another country they'd never seen. But there are a few basic problems with this philosophy, namely that some writers are (a) young and/or (b) untraveled, which means they haven't been around temporally or geographically enough to know much about anything. So that begs the question: should they be writing at all? And the answer is always a resounding yes.

You have to write about what you know because everyone has unique experiences that make each novel a singular piece of work. But you're also going to need to do research.

> **WORDS OF WISDOM**
>
> I didn't invent the world I write about—it's all true.
>
> —Graham Greene

If you've lived in the Midwest all your life and your main character needs to take a business jaunt to Manhattan, you're going to need to know enough about New York to convince your readers your character actually made the trip. New York is one of those cities that's so textured and so much its own differentiated town, no writer is going to try to fake it because most readers have been seeing it as a setting on countless TV programs all their lives. So if you set a scene or book in New York, be sure you know what you're talking about. Looking at city streets as background in cop shows is *not* research, okay?

The trick is to learn a lot more than you need to pull off the illusion, but not do a huge information-dump on the reader that makes it look as if you transferred a few pages from the encyclopedia into your narrative.

Kinds of Settings

When you work on setting, you're like an artist with a pretty big palette at hand. The components of a well-realized setting should blend in and out of each other and never fight for dominance. Aspects of setting are most conspicuous when they're totally absent, when the writer simply forgot to include them. If everything's there, working in a nice complementary balance, the reader absorbs the setting and doesn't even realize it happened.

That's the subtle effect you're looking for. So let's examine the kinds of settings you should always work on.

Place

This type of setting is the most obvious one. It's the basic stage where you will set every scene. Exteriors and interiors can be very different and will require different cues. Be mindful of architecture versus natural formations, colors and saturation points, comparisons and contrast to other known locations, and so on. Train yourself to observe every place you go to, and try to force yourself to notice things no one else is looking for. It doesn't matter if you're just doing the usual run to the grocery and Walmart. Keep your eyes open.

Places have other, less-obvious aspects, especially if they're historically significant; think about what they might be and how they will color your perceptions. I can remember visiting the Tower of London and experiencing several unexpected reactions because I had a subset of historical knowledge about the place that didn't always jibe with the physical facts.

> **TOM'S TIPS**
>
> An effective way to keep your story and your use of setting fresh is to turn things inside out. Take the most predictable situation or scene, and do the old switcheroo. Mix things up and see what kind of new, surprising variations you can achieve. Instead of a Scottish castle, see if a Malibu Canyon mansion might make things less recognizable.

Providing the reader with a solid sense of place is an ongoing exercise. As you proceed chapter by chapter, be mindful to include more and more detail each time you return to the same scene. That subtle layering effect reinforces the mental images the reader willingly constructs with just a little prodding. Just remember, it's more than just simple descriptive writing. You imbue a sense of place in the reader in an effort to achieve specific effects.

"Switching up" the expected or traditional settings can definitely bring some additional originality to your story. In an early horror novel of mine, *Night Things*, I deliberately went against type and set the story in the harsh, bright sunlight of an Arizona desert town instead of a cold, dank New England village somewhere in Maine or New Hampshire. I wanted to see if I could tell a small-town horror tale without the traditional tropes at work.

Time

Is your scene taking place during the day or night? Right there, your decision will bring an entire set of variables. Daylight suggests a certain openness, honesty, and an inability to hide. The dark of night ushers in caution, suspicion, and fear of what may be contained in shadow. Your use of sidereal time is clearly important to the general impression you want to convey.

Seasons also carry with them a whole list of impressions and cues. Summer is carefree and inviting, while winter is reclusive and foreboding. Spring is traditionally a time of rebirth and renewal, while autumn can be a metaphor for impending change or even death. Many writers set their novels in a specific season by design, not just convenience, to convey certain impressions.

You also want to be aware of the passage of time. This is a key element in the way you pace the action. Does the entire novel take place within a single day? A week? A year? These are decisions that, once made, will dictate how and how well you use the concept of time.

Mood

This aspect of setting is related to the tone and style of your novel, as well as the other aspects of setting. A mystery novel wants to establish a mood of caution and vigilance. A romance novel should strive for a sense of gentle adventure and hopefulness. A global thriller, on the other hand, is probably going to work best when the mood is more tersely urgent and full of paranoia.

A skillful writer can control mood by using the other elements of setting to suggest and imply rather than just flatly state what the reader should be feeling.

Atmosphere

Atmosphere is closely connected to the previous three components because they all contribute to create it. It's the most abstract part of a book's setting, and something you can't just describe or declare. It's more of a gradual compilation of details that build up to create the proper emotional and physical climate.

A novel like *Shogun* successfully creates an atmosphere of intrigue and a sense of the totally alien because its author is able to make us believe in his setting of feudal Japan. Slowly, the reader is introduced to a culture and a cast of unpredictable and inscrutable characters. The atmosphere is unsettling and wary, but the reader learns to not only accept this setting, but also enjoy it.

To best understand atmosphere, think of it as a part of the setting that makes your readers *feel* something—unease, fear, joy, curiosity, anger, etc.

Techniques for Creating Setting

Now that you have a handle on the variety of ways setting can be established and employed, I think we should spend a little time on the actual how-to end of creating believable settings that underscore the rest of your narrative.

Use of Detail

I hinted at use of detail previously when I asked you to keep your eyes open. What I meant was this: pay attention to the extra aspects of your environment.

When you're in a church whose walls have been decorated with thousands of tiny mosaic tiles, think about how long it may have taken a craftsman to lay in those tiles so perfectly. When you stop along a hiking trail, try to notice how insistent the voice of a distant waterfall or rapids-churning river may cut through the silence of the forest. Or reflect on the way a newly polished auto bends and reflects the light like a funhouse mirror.

Pay attention. Add details to your descriptions to enhance rather than dull your reader's perceptions. Don't use details just for the sake of piling up images. Be certain your details do their job.

Sense Impressions

I remember hearing a writer participating in a convention panel say he tried to include at least one sense impression per page of every novel he wrote. At the time, it struck me as a pretty tough self-assignment, and I didn't know how successful he was. But it also struck me as a good idea, and one that would surely enrich most novels— as long as the writer didn't become repetitive.

Many writers don't bother with the visuals: color, size, and comparisons with other objects. But you generally see even less use of smell and taste. The sense of smell can be very evocative, especially when you want to capture a memory from childhood. For instance, the smell of crayons and chalk erasers always make me think of the first day I walked into my first-grade classroom. The sense of taste is less easy to employ because you can't have your characters licking everything, but you should use it whenever feasible. It adds to the entire scenic experience.

The other sense impressions that are even less tapped include touch and the extrasensory areas. As part of your "paying attention" regimen, you have to notice the texture of objects and the way they resemble other, more familiar objects. Softness, hardness, appealing, and repugnant tactile sensations all add to the set.

And don't forget to use premonition, when a character gets a bad feeling about a future event, or a clairvoyant moment, when someone knows what's going on at a different location in the novel. I recall one of Trevanian's characters having a highly developed "proximity" sense that told him when someone was stealthily approaching. It was a fascinating little detail that increased suspense and mood.

Avoiding Clichés

The house was as quiet as the grave. The athlete was as quick as a cat. The wind howled through the dark and stormy night.

There are literally hundreds of examples of overused, overly familiar descriptive phrases, and I don't need to take up space with too many of them. You can recognize them as easily as I can when you read them in other books. The problem seems to "rear its ugly head" (hey, there's another one!) when writers use them in their own work and become suddenly blind to the offense.

The plain fact is, using clichéd language in setting a scene is just plain lazy. It sends the wrong message to your reader—that you're not interested in being fresh and original. And that's bad news for you. If you're a new novelist, you want to make the best possible first impression.

One of the most memorable opening sentences I've ever read was written by Joe Lansdale for his story "The Big Blow," which appeared in *Revelations*, an anthology edited by Douglas Winter. It set the scene in a wildly original manner, and I'll never forget it. I'm also not going to spoil it here. You'll have to find it in the library or on the Internet. Then let me know if you agree with me.

 A LIKELY STORY

Some fascinating and memorable novels have employed their settings as major characters in the narratives. You see it primarily in science fiction and historical thrillers. But what about a story in which the setting is the studio of a reality TV show where the participants have been "accidentally" locked in, with everything in the studio still running, after all the crew went home for the weekend? How much of what happens is controlled by this faceless character, the studio itself?

Character Perception

A very clever way to inject setting into your narrative is to filter the description through the viewpoint of several of your major characters. You can do this if you're writing a first-person narrative or a multiple viewpoint novel.

The nice thing about conveying detail through a particular character is that you give yourself a great opportunity to color those perceptions of the setting through your character's personality filter. By shading details through your protagonist's bag of bias, fears, preferences, and experiences, the reader gets to know him or her just a little better with every new opportunity to add to the setting.

Some Tricks to Creating Believable Settings

We've all read novels where the author has chosen just the right amount of detail to convince you he really knows what he's talking about. And when that happens, the reader is hooked for the whole ride. That's the kind of writing we all want to have working for us.

Writer Robert Ludlum used to do that consistently; he possessed an encyclopedic knowledge of European geography and an innate understanding of how contemporary history had shaped the geopolitical landscape of the late twentieth century. He had a way of dropping in a detail about a Zurich bank and the way the tellers addressed their clients, or the distinctive color of the water in a particular lake in Italy that told you this guy had the goods. You could believe him completely.

I can show you how to make your readers believe you, too. What follows are a few techniques guaranteed to make your settings as vibrant, original, and credible as the best of us.

Ask your friends. The longer you stay in the business of writing and publishing, the more conventions, panels, and seminars you'll attend. That means you'll be meeting writers who live in a lot of other places around the country. That's a good thing because you can call and ask them questions about their city or part of the country if you're setting a scene there, and that will make you look like an expert. You can get the name of the local supermarket chain, the best place to get a steak dinner, whether or not locals call it an ice-cream sundae or a frappé, and so on.

The result is a wonderful information network, and your readers will wonder how you can possibly know all those neat little convincing details. Hey, we'll never tell ....

Keep everything when you travel. I've been fortunate to do a lot of traveling over the years, both in the States and on several other continents. And whenever I do, I load up on maps, postcards, hotel and restaurant stationery and matchbooks, brochures on transportation services, unique brands of coffee, liquor, gasoline, and so on. I have file drawers and shelves full of travel information, which I often shuffle through to find that perfect Ludlum-esque detail that's going to seal the deal for me and my readers.

Timetables of history. If you're doing anything historical; employing a flashback; or needing details to enhance an old letter, manuscript, or anything else connected to the past, I have a great reference tool for you. It's a big paperback book (you can usually find it in used bookstores for less than $10) called *The Timetables of History*, edited by Bernard Grun.

This book is a record of human achievement, detailing who did what and when they did it, from 4500 B.C.E. to the present. Divided into seven major categories (history/politics; literature/theater; religion/philosophy/learning; visual arts; music; science/technology/growth; and daily life), the information is presented in easy-to-read columns and tables. In no time, you have a handle on everything that was going on at the time your characters were bopping around. How else are you going to know that the hit show on the London stage in 1728 was John Gay's *Beggar's Opera?* (Other than being as smart as me.)

Video rentals. I know I told you earlier that you're not going to get a good feel for a city by watching TV cop shows. But this is different. These days, just about every town in America has a video store, and if they're big enough, they have a "travel" section with tons of videos that provide a fairly complete picture of just about any city or country in the world.

If you have a big cable TV package, you probably have The Travel Channel (right alongside The Cooking Channel, The Garage Tool Channel, and so on), which is also a great resource for getting a quick distillation of faraway places you may never see in person, but that would make interesting settings for your novels. If all else fails, check the video collection at your local library.

Other Setting Considerations

Okay, I'm almost ready to put a lid on this one, but I have a few more points to make your awareness and use of setting even more effective. You've probably noticed that some of the topics I'm discussing are beginning to overlap; that's because so many elements of the novel depend on each other. Things like pacing and balance may also be examined later, but with a different perspective.

Pacing and Balance

I plan to get into this topic in Chapter 10, but for now, you should at least be aware of how the pacing of your novel can be controlled in part by your use of setting. *Pacing* is basically just you developing a sense of symmetry or balance as you lay out your story.

Try to keep too many scenes from taking place in the same setting. By changing the landscape or locale, or alternating the action among several major sets, you achieve a nice cinematic effect that keeps things moving.

Inside Out

Another thing to do is ask yourself if the settings you've chosen are too familiar. Is the desert highway truck stop in the Southwest really the best place to have your villain catch up with your heroine? Are you really going to wrap up the action with a big fight scene in yet another conveniently abandoned industrial complex of warehouses and assembly buildings?

A little self-critical analysis can go a long way. If your story really needs that familiar location, ask yourself if there's any way you can change things up. Reshuffle the deck and make your truck stop somehow different. (Hey, maybe it's one that's designed to attract women truckers?)

But be careful—don't turn things inside out if there's no logic behind your moves. Remember what I said about plot, which applies here equally: things have to make sense.

Place Names

If you're using fictional settings, pay attention to the names you give them. Just as names are important in characters, they can also carry extra freight in locale. In general, avoid town names like Newport, Middleton, Union City, and all the other bland, overly recognizable handles. Unless you have a distinct and meaningful reason for wanting to suggest a bland, nothing of a town, don't do it.

It's far better to be evocative, if possible, without being obvious or sophomoric. There's a difference between having your characters pulling up for gas in Calamity, Nevada, and having them attend Knucklehead High. Sometimes it's a thin line, but there is a difference.

Recurring Scenes

Sometimes you may come up with a setting that is so weird, so symbolic, you can use it for dramatic effect all on its own. In this instance, you can make a particularly unique setting more than just a location, but perhaps a powerful symbol. If you have a compelling setting, you can craft powerful scenes in which your characters are being drawn to it.

Stephen King's *Pet Sematary* is a great example of this because the pet "sematary" is so unique and strange—unlike anything you've ever seen before.

The Least You Need to Know

- Setting can be just as important to the success of your novel as your characters or your plot. Your readers must believe everything you tell them about your locations.
- Setting is not just place—it's also time, mood, and atmosphere. You need to establish awareness and control of all these elements.
- Use plenty of sense impressions to convey a total "feel" for your scenes and settings. It's important to place your characters and your reader in the midst of your sets.
- Avoid the overly familiar. Strive to be original in your inventions and borrowings. When you give readers more than they expect, they love you all the more.

Dialogue: You Gotta Have an Ear for It

In This Chapter

- Making dialogue work for you
- All kinds of ways to say it
- Style and execution
- Tricks, techniques, and things to avoid

Years ago, when I used to read the slush pile (an old term for unsolicited submissions) for a couple science fiction magazines, I learned a lot about what comprised good writing and bad writing and how to spot each quickly. One of the first red flags was incompetent dialogue. When a writer doesn't have his characters speaking in a convincing fashion, it sticks out like the hood ornament on a LaSalle.

So right about now, you might want to be saying: "Hey, c'mon, is dialogue really that important?"

"You betcha."

"Okay, so whaddya gonna tell me about it?"

"Plenty. So listen up …."

Generally Speaking

Good dialogue is absolutely essential in any fiction, but especially in the novel. A writer who handles his characters' conversations with skill and confidence will be very readable. Your audience will identify with people they can understand, and that's what writing dialogue is all about—connecting characters with readers.

Easy Reading

For one thing, dialogue looks inviting on the page. It is open, airy, with a lot of white space that connotes plenty of room for pause and thought. There's nothing more daunting than to flip through a book and see page after endless page of dense, thickly worded paragraphs with not much dialogue at all. I've noticed the novels of many contemporary South American writers have this general appearance. Novels like that don't look like a fun read. They suggest a slow, plodding effort that means real work.

As soon as it's introduced, dialogue makes a novel more accessible. Conversation and speech are universal to most of us, and we don't need to be schooled on it or prepared for it. Readers understand and accept it immediately and unconsciously. If it sounds right, they don't question it.

Keep It Moving

When you can integrate your dialogue into your narrative passages, you'll notice right away how much faster things seem to be going. There's a kind of kinetic energy of give-and-take in the conversation between characters that acts like the driving wheel on a big train engine, always moving forward.

You should use this innate characteristic, especially in your opening chapters, to pull your readers into the story and keep them there.

The Real World

Another aspect of good, effective dialogue is its proximity to the way people really talk. But it's a fine line to walk because if you attempt to re-create *in toto* the words of real people in their everyday exchanges, you will be dealing with a lot of quoted passages that are largely incomprehensible.

Real speech is often very fragmented. The next time you're out at a restaurant, a store, a subway, or anywhere else where people are interacting, do a little old-fashioned eavesdropping. Try to be subtle, and make believe you're doing something else, like reading or working a crossword puzzle, but zone-in on the conversations around you.

You'll notice pretty quickly that most of us tend to talk in a kind of verbal shorthand. It's very informal, and marked by pauses for breath, laughter, a lack of the correct term, the ever-present "uh," etc. People also tend to speak in the present, even if they're describing something that already happened ("… So my boss says: 'Okay, who left the lights on again in the copy room?' and I say: 'King Kong, you dummy!'").

You'll also notice a peppering of mild profanities, slang, contractions of words ending in *-ing*, and a distinct lack of the mention of names. This last one is interesting, because you'll often see characters named in written dialogue—writers think it's a slick trick for letting us know who's talking to whom, but it's not. And often sounds like lines from a soap opera script.

> **TOM'S TIPS**
>
> You need to have an ear for dialogue, of course. But you also want to develop an *eye* for it as well. Read a lot of plays, or at least enough to get you accustomed to the rigor of telling a story primarily through dialogue, which a play must do at its most basic level. Professional plays tend to contain dialogue that's economical and freighted with tension and power—all good things you should know how to employ when your characters open their mouths.

Hard-Working Words

Dialogue serves many functions in your novel, and most of them are things you probably never think about. That's because dialogue is such a natural and expected part of storytelling. You need to make yourself aware of the many tasks your dialogue can simplify for you.

Exposition

This is just a fancy way of saying that your characters' words can be a quick, efficient way to impart information about what's happened "offstage" or before the action of the novel commenced (sometimes called the *back story*), about any historical elements, and so on.

Setting the Mood

Each scene has its own mood and tone, or "feel," and you can use dialogue to help create this by having your characters talk about something that will evoke a particular mood. Mentioning an old spooky legend will set up feelings of fear or suspicion in the reader, just as the description of a handsome stranger could suggest starry-eyed romance and anticipation. Or what about an exchange of dialogue where the characters are insulting or threatening one another? That creates an immediate mood and tone that implies danger, trouble, or tension.

Revealing Character

I mentioned this before, but here it is again, exemplifying yet another point. Remember me saying how people can get an idea of who you are by noticing the words you employ? Good, because it applies to the current topic as well. Speech patterns, vocabulary, and grammar indicate a lot about a person, in a very short amount of time and space.

If your character is a construction worker, his dialogue should be different from that of the physician. Sometimes a character's occupation can be revealed and reinforced through dialogue. A career military man may have his speech colored by armed service phrases and buzzwords. A college professor may have a tendency to use words a little too lofty for everyday use.

Be aware of who your characters are, and listen to the words they use. Ask yourself, *Would they really talk like this?* If the answer is "Maybe not," you need to work on your dialogue.

WORDS OF WISDOM

I don't have a very clear idea of who the characters are until they start talking.

—Joan Didion

Individualizing

This is closely related to character and is a simple, effective way to make your character stand out from the crowd. Through dialogue, you can give him or her a habitual speech mannerism, or a favorite phrase, that becomes a familiar and comfortable identifier. Maybe the hero's sidekick always has a habit of saying "believe-you-me" when he wants to emphasize something. Or maybe the antagonist likes to describe troublesome things as "unsavory." You can also indicate attributes and "character type" by using terms that help root a character in a particular region of the country. A soft drink in Boston is called a "tonic," but it's a "soda" in the Carolinas. See how it works?

These are a few simple examples of the countless ways you can spice up your characters and make them less ordinary and more believable. Keep this function in mind, and your characters will thank you for it.

Tension

Dialogue tends to be most compelling when it conveys a sense that something is wrong. Think about it. If you overhear two people talking about something they both like, or discussing a topic they totally agree on, their conversation is usually nowhere near as intriguing as the dialogue between two people who disagree.

That's because disagreement suggests tension, or worse, conflict. If you've been reading these chapters consecutively, you'll remember that conflict is the essence of storytelling and the basis for most plots. So if you can arrange for your dialogue to convey some of that dramatic tension or outright conflict, you're deepening the texture of your narrative and pulling in the reader.

You can also use dialogue to increase tension and create suspense by foreshortening information one character may be telling another. Either by interruption or design, whatever your dialogue provides or withholds can torque up the tension in your story.

It Takes All Kinds

Although there aren't any hard-and-fast delineations of dialogue into formalized "types," I think it's worth looking at the variety of ways your characters can talk. And again, the method you choose should match the character's other traits.

Standard English

Your average character will be speaking standard English—the language and style we hear every day on radio, TV, and in the world of commerce and education. In that sense, it's a speaking style that becomes kind of "invisible" to us. We accept it as a conveyor of information, but it doesn't draw attention to itself.

This is the kind of dialogue we normally see employed in novels. If you learn how to write it well, no one will ever notice … and that's a good thing.

Dialects

A *dialect* is a variant of any language that's usually associated with geographic or socioeconomic factors. The first time I drove around the country, I remember stopping at a little gas station in Georgia where the attendant asked me if *th'all* was okay. I had no idea what he was talking about, and after a few minutes, I dumbly realized he was talking about "the oil," which a mid-Atlantic person pronounces *oy-uhl*.

This is dialect. It's difficult to capture in print unless you have a finely attuned ear for it and a knack for depicting it with phonetics that aren't conspicuous. If this sounds like I'm saying to use dialect sparingly, I guess I am. In other words, it's not for everybody. Some writers can pull it off, and some can't. My advice is to let your editor tell you if you're any good at it, and whether or not you need it to enhance a particular character.

And just in passing, even though it should be obvious, I should note there's also a distinct difference between the way English is spoken in the United States and the way it's spoken in the United Kingdom. During my first visit to London, I remember seeing a sign in a restaurant that said:

> *English Spoken Here. American Understood.*

That kind of says it all, don't you think?

Monologue

Monologue is another distinct type of dialogue that's really just one character talking—hence the prefix *mono-*. It occurs when one of your characters needs to make a speech, a proclamation, or that most literary of monologues, the soliloquy.

Be wary of this specialized dialogue. If too many of your characters are launching into long, singular passages of exposition, you run the risk of boring your reader. Even if you simply must have a scientist explain the plasma physics that's causing the molten core of the earth to suddenly solidify, it's probably a good idea to break up his delivery with the words of another character who either disagrees or doesn't comprehend. Long monologues tend to be speeches, and they just aren't very compelling in print.

If you need a soliloquy in which a character undergoes some self-analysis or introspection, it's probably a good idea to present it as a series of internal *thoughts*. If you have a character talking aloud to himself, it usually comes off as silly. So please avoid this. Believe me, it's the mark of the amateur.

Street Talk

This one is interesting because it's quite tempting and accessible. Modern novels tend to use less-formal and less-structured language than previous generations did, but without an overwhelming tendency to rely on colloquialism or slang. My point is, you need to establish some "rules" for yourself and your dialogue—mainly to be consistent. Be careful not to lapse in and then *out* of colloquial expression. If your character talks "street," be sure to keep it that way. But don't have everyone talking the same way.

It's a good idea to be attuned to contemporary speech patterns and mannerisms and employ them with control and judgment. If you listen to the way people speak, you'll probably notice that about half of them drop the *-ing* and replace it with *-in'*, and more than 90 percent use contractions resulting in *can't* and *didn't* rather than *cannot* and *did not*. In fact, many people only use the noncontracted versions when they want to express specific emphasis.

This is an example of language evolving. It's subtle and nonplanned. It's simply happening. Your job is to notice these changes and fold them into your writing—into your dialogue, more specifically.

You have to exercise a little caution, however, because in this high-tech, instant-information world, things have a way of changing quickly. What might be red-hot and super "in" when you typed "The End" on your novel's last page could be very old news when your book gets published less than a year later. This means that your use of trendy, pop culture phrases and terminology can heavily anchor your story to a narrow strip of time, thereby dating your material. This tends to be off-putting to some readers, who can't see past any universal and timeless truths you may be exploring because they don't see your novel as relevant.

TOM'S TIPS

One of the best ways to know whether your dialogue is working is to read it aloud. Sounds obvious, but many writers never try it or have never even thought of it. I discovered it very early on in my career, at a convention where readings had been scheduled for some of the guests. As I listened to some of the other writers reading their own work, I was frankly astounded by three things: most of them could not read well if their life depended on it, most of them had about as much personality as a newel post, and a lot of their dialogue sounded unnatural when spoken aloud. I knew I didn't want to be like them—I always read my work aloud.

Stylin'

Okay, let's see what we've learned. Now that you have a pretty good idea of what dialogue is and some of the jobs you need it to perform, let's take a closer look at the things that will make your dialogue soar above the ordinary.

Vocabulary

There's no substitute for having a wide-ranging vocabulary. I'm not talking about a huge arsenal of $50 words guaranteed to dazzle and confuse your readers. I mean having at your command an ample number of simple words that give your characters enough different ways to speak. You don't want to use the same words and phrases. Keep the writing fresh and interesting, and give your characters' dialogue individuality.

I can remember reading a mystery novel where all the characters kept referring to a part of the house as "the veranda," where a major scene had unfolded and people tended to gather. Everybody used this word so often that it started to look like a self-parody, and every time I encountered the word, I found myself yelling, "C'mon … *again* with the veranda?!" The writer should have thrown in a few patios, porches, decks, balconies, and even a few lanais instead of always relying on "the veranda."

It doesn't matter where you get your vocabulary, just that you have it at your disposal. At my Jesuit high school, I took 4 years of Latin, which pretty much ensured me a panoply of words for every occasion. But if you've got a nice big thesaurus (the ones in dictionary format are the best), or plugin software for your word-processing program, or a friend you call when you're stuck, you're in good shape. Whatever works for you is great. Just be sure it's working.

Rhythm and Cadence

This is one of the more subtle distinctions between good and outright clumsy dialogue. There's almost no way to describe it; this is the stuff you really need to have an "ear" for. Sometimes you have to listen to the way people talk rather than what they're saying.

Some people end most of their sentences with a question, or an implied question. Or they ask a question by making it sound like a declaration. Some people use very short, clipped sentences. They respond tersely and in ways that can be mistaken for rudeness. Others run on in flowery and effusive exclamations. That's cadence. Some people speak in a recognizable pattern of syllables, almost like the metered lines of a poem. Everything they say has a *da-da-dah-di-dah* sequence to it. That's a speech rhythm.

You don't need to try to re-create these patterns and mannerisms—just be aware of them. The words and the sequences you use when writing dialogue can contribute to unconscious perceptions of realistic versus phony. Your reader may not know why your dialogue isn't ringing true, other than thinking it just doesn't "sound right." Rhythm and cadence might be the issues.

Variation and Balance

There's more subtlety at work here. When you write your dialogue, pay attention to the length and intensity of what your characters are saying. Even if they have a fairly equal amount of information to impart, try to make their dialogue sufficiently different to keep it distinctive and always driving forward.

Having one character ask questions and another answer them sets up a nice balance that can carry things for a while. One-word replies should contrast nicely with those moments when you need lots of exposition. If you have both characters unloading long passages of spoken data-dumping, you may have a situation where people are no longer talking to one another—they're "speechifying," as I like to call it.

Brevity and Silence

These concepts are really refinements and enhancements to the previous variation and balance. Don't be afraid to have some of your characters actually say *less* than they should.

You've heard the expression that sometimes less is more, right? Well, it works well in dialogue, too. When a character is less than forthcoming with information, emotions, expectations, etc., it creates tension in the other characters and in your reader. And that's what you want.

When a character doesn't say anything, you can sometimes crank up suspense or frustration to an even higher notch. Even though you've probably never considered it, silence is a legitimate component of good dialogue.

Dialogue Tricks and Techniques

Okay, now I'm going to give you some clever ways to use your dialogue to accomplish specific goals or achieve desired effects.

Open With Dialogue

Early in my career, I remember listening to a panel on writing at a convention. One of the writers offered this tip: if you begin your story or novel with dialogue, you have immediate interest because people have to be talking about something and your reader's going to want to know what it is. Opening with dialogue that suggests an argument or a conflict is also effective.

Even better, open your story with one character asking somebody else a question—a question you may or may not answer. It's a natural hook that leaves the reader not only waiting for an answer, but also wanting to know who's doing the talking and who's doing the listening.

Use Humor

Dialogue is a natural way to inject humor into your story. By this, I don't mean having your characters tell jokes to each other (although I've seen it tried …). Humor can be wry and clever and suggest more than it reveals. In his *Spenser* novels, Robert Parker is extremely good at making the dialogue advance the plot in an entertaining fashion.

Humor can be sardonic or broad. However, I would avoid the use of the slapstick affectation of characters calling each other by silly names. Irony and satire are also subtle forms of humor that can be created through really good dialogue. You can't go wrong with less rather than more; subtle is almost always better than over-the-top.

Original Phrase

It's always fun and a bit challenging to come up with a catchphrase or sentence that can resonate through your novel and take on more and more meaning as the story inexorably unfolds. This is more difficult to do than I'm making it sound, but when it happens largely through good old serendipity, you should be ready for it and recognize it as an effective tool. Stephen King is good at this. Remember the janitor in *The Shining* telling Jack about the boiler thermostat, saying "It creeps …"? Great stuff.

I'm referring to double-meanings, ironic observations, words that eventually turn out to be code for something else, or a phrase whose meaning has been misapplied and suddenly made clear. This works well when you had a character saying it all along and nobody has caught on, even though they've been hearing it throughout the novel. In Ayn Rand's *Atlas Shrugged*, she includes numerous references to the rhetorical question: "Who's John Galt?" It's very clever how the tone, meaning, and answer to the question changes by the end of the novel.

Mannerisms can give your dialogue a little variety. Pay attention to the things people do when they talk—such as putting an index finger to their chin, talking out of one side of their mouth, licking their lips excessively, tsk-tsking, and so on. Describing the way people speak helps distinguish one speaker from the other and adds character.

A LIKELY STORY

Imagine a murder mystery in which the perpetrator is playing a game with the detective, daring him to pull together the clues that are deliberately being provided. In keeping with the theme of this chapter, let's say that all the clues are transcriptions of famous dialogue from plays, novels, and films. If the detective can assemble the "message" contained within all the words, he solves the crime. Your job is to decide what the clues are and how they tell the real story.

A Few Cautions

Even though I'm making this seem like writing dialogue is pretty easy, I have a few final warnings. Following are some simple mistakes and errors in judgment that can make your dialogue "less than smooth":

"As You Know ..."

I see this one in a lot of new writers' work. For some reason, they think it's a good idea to have their characters updating information or back-filling action that took place prior to the opening of the novel.

The problem with this is obvious: characters are telling other characters things *they already know*. And the only reason they're sharing the redundant information is because the writer needs his *reader* to know it, too. The only thing the characters leave out of their dialogue is the old prefatory "Well, as you know ...."

But that doesn't make it any less awkward. The best advice: keep that kind of exposition out of your character's mouths. Figure out other ways to tell your back story, even if you resort to omniscient narrative or one of your characters reflecting on past events or reliving them in a dream.

Long Speeches

This is an overuse of dialogue that has fallen out of favor, and for a good reason—it's boring. Nobody wants to be lectured to, not even college students; and *they* expect it. Long speeches feel too much like you're being reprimanded for not knowing something. A novel is supposed to be entertainment, remember?

I think the only novel I've read that employed the long speech with any success was *Atlas Shrugged* by Ayn Rand, and that was only because of the brilliant content of her speaker's words. But even then, the technique blew itself out like a tired storm because the unending torrent of words became too much of a good thing. At that point, it appeared the author didn't care if her readers knew they were getting a lecture.

I think you and I still need to care. So if you feel a speech coming on, keep it short and under control.

He Said/She Said

The use of *said* in dialogue is one of those necessary evils. New writers worry about overusing it, and if that includes you, here's my advice: don't worry about that. "He said/she said" is simply there when you write dialogue; try to think of it as punctuation. You have to believe that most readers just glide through the words as effortlessly as they do through periods and question marks. When you feel like you need to point out who's talking, use *said*.

But that doesn't mean you need to use *said* after every line of dialogue. Watch the exchange of lines, and get a feel for it. Use your judgment by throwing it in every time you think your readers might need another indicator as to who's doing the talking.

Nobody really notices "he said/she said." Trust me, okay? Going along with this as a kind of "copyeditor's war," *where* should *said* fall in the dialogue? Is it "said John" or "John said"? Whatever feels right is probably okay, and this depends on the rhythm of the sentence.

No Substitutes

Some writers take their apprehension of overusing *said* to a higher degree of paranoia. They decide it's a better idea to use just about any word in place of the offending *said*. So the reader is treated to an unending parade of sentences in which speakers never *say* anything. Instead, they *stammer*, *opine*, *declare*, *hedge*, and even *laugh out* their words.

Frankly, this is just plain awful. Half the time, the substitute is a word or word-sound that would preclude the speaker from actually producing speech. (Just exactly how would you *chortle* out a sentence?) I think you get the idea on this one, and it's easy to remember: said—*no substitutes*.

Adverbially Speaking

The last and final gaffe is yet another attempt by writers to do something with that darned *said*. They agree to use it, but they insist on dressing it up with an adverb, which, as Mark Twain once said, should be shot whenever we run into one.

So you have endless variations of "he said slyly," or "she said harshly," and so on. Again, the advice here is clean, simple, and to the point: avoid using such adverbs as much as possible. Every once in a while it seems unavoidable to add that one little extra piece of description to the dialogue, but keep it to a minimum.

The Least You Need to Know

- Good dialogue approximates the way people really speak. You can develop an "ear" for it if you make the effort.
- Dialogue is a powerful tool that can enhance the other elements of your novel. Characters can come to life and be distinctive through the dialogue you give them. Everyone should not sound the same. Dialogue can also advance your plot and create tension, conflict, and suspense.
- Understand the different kinds of dialogue, and learn to use them to create variety and originality. Be careful not to overdo dialect or colloquial speech. Good dialogue is all about balance and rhythm.
- Be aware of the amateur's concerns and common mistakes. Don't try to "disguise" the fact that you're writing dialogue. The word *said* is a perfectly fine word, so don't be afraid to use it whenever you need it.

Transition, Point of View, and Pacing

Chapter 10

In This Chapter

- Three necessary novel components
- Getting from here to there
- Who's telling your story?
- Speed limits

Our discussion and dissection of all the elements of writing a novel is almost complete. But we still have to examine three things that don't naturally occur to people when you ask them what they need to tell a good story—transition, point of view, and pacing.

All three elements are vital to the storytelling process, but when they're used properly, the reader never notices them. There's an art to creating things that, in order to be successful, must also be essentially invisible and undetectable.

It's like the secret of good book design, which is something typesetters and designers have known about for centuries: a book that is laid out well is easy to read. But if the margins are too small, the spacing too tight, or the font too ornate to be read without effort … well, the audience may not enjoy their reading experience. They tell themselves they're not liking the book, but they can't articulate why. Even though they're not familiar with the elements of book design, they know there's *something* about the book they don't like.

The "Little Big Three"

Novels with clunky or absent transitions become irritating because the reader feels like he's being yanked around and forced to make assumptions or leaps of faith with little or no warning or guidance.

The same goes for stories that aren't told consistently through the eyes of a single entity—the reader gets confused, or worse, disgusted with the writer's seeming indecision as to who's really telling the story.

And finally, trouble with the pacing, or the controlled flow of information, can also be distracting to the reader because there's no comforting sense of movement toward a goal; it's like a jerky ride that never settles into a groove. This kind of unconscious effect can bother the reader and make your novel an unpleasant read.

 WORDS OF WISDOM

Good work doesn't happen with inspiration. It comes from constant, often tedious and deliberate effort. If your vision of a writer involves sitting in a café, sipping an aperitif with one's fellow geniuses, become a drunk. It's easier and far less exhausting.

—William Heffernan

So let's take a look at each of these three elements under our microscope. When we finish, you're going to have plenty of tools and the instruction manuals for all of them.

It's almost time to get to work. But one more thing before we do: the smaller elements we're looking at now are just as important as the bigger ones we covered previously. The funny thing about writing a novel is that everything is equally important, and you must work hard at all the elements to make them come together and make sense.

Transitions

In case I haven't mentioned it yet, your novel is actually a large compilation of separate scenes. These can be actions, conversations, flashbacks, dreams, descriptions, transcriptions of letters, or anything that contributes to the telling of your story. These scenes need to be linked to one another in skillful, original ways.

The way to do it, of course, is with transitions. There's nothing complicated about them—they're connections between ideas, events, and every other kind of scene that keep your narrative from feeling choppy, or worse, lurching through a long series of starts and stops. If you understand transitions, you'll make it your business to create seamless ones, thereby moving the reader along from scene to scene with style and grace.

When you've reached a point in your story when there needs to be a change, you know you need a transition. I'm sure there are more types of change in your novel, but I'm going to cover four of the major ones. The idea is for you to get the feel for transitions and apply one every time you need them.

I'm not just talking about the changes from chapter to chapter, which are big, obvious, and hard to miss. There are also lots of scene changes within each chapter you need to handle with a deft keyboard. Here are four transitions you need to watch for:

Time. In addition to being the title of a great Pink Floyd song, it's also a major transition concern. Your novel is a story that moves along a timeline, so it's crucial that your readers always know where they are on that timeline. If you aren't aware of time, your readers may feel adrift and lose interest in what's happening.

Place. Your story will most likely have a variety of locations, and your characters and action will move from one place to another. If you don't provide the cues to these location changes, you will confuse and ultimately lose your readers.

Characters. Whether or not you need transitions between and among your characters depends on the point of view you choose for your narrative. I discuss this in depth later in this chapter.

Events. This one is important, especially when we're talking about changing from an action scene to dialogue, observation, or narration. Transitions are even more critical when you must switch back and forth between action and nonaction. You must keep your readers rooted in the sequence of the novel.

Transition Cues

Now that you know what kinds of transitions you can use, it's time to look at how to use them. Transitions are set in motion by a variety of what I call *cues.*

TRADE TALK

Transition **cues** are phrases or changes in your narrative that set up or prepare the readers for a transition.

These cues can be subtle or as obvious as an elephant in the corner of the room. Sometimes, depending on the mood or tone you've established, you're going to want a subtle change/cue. Other scenes may demand something more dramatic, suspenseful, or shocking. This depends on the nature of your story and the effect you need at the time.

Time Cues

Time cues can be inconspicuous or not, depending on how you introduce them. If your novel operates within a tight time frame, such as a single day or a week, you can use a "ticking clock," chapter headers, or in-text subheadings to indicate passing hours.

You can also use changes in the weather to mark the passage of time. For novels that span longer stretches of time, you can use changing seasons.

Communication Cues

You can move from scene to scene or chapter to chapter by introducing some form of communication, such as a phone call or a radio transmission, that will move or direct the action or focus to another location, character, or story complication. Receiving a letter or a telegram are older forms of this kind of transition cue. Other effective ones include having a nightmare or a vision, or receiving a prophecy or a strange package, etc.

You should have the general idea here: any kind of contact—that is, when a viewpoint character is touched or reached by an outside force or person you can arrange for a character or a scene—can thereby be used to move or change it to the next scene.

Motion Cues

Motion cues are a more obvious way of keeping your story moving from scene to scene. And you have a variety of devices to make it happen. I'm talking about cars, trains, buses, planes, bulldozers—you name it. Putting your characters into physical motion, from walking or climbing all the way up to warp-speed starships, provides almost automatic transitions, and the cues you use to employ them are also readily available—he keyed the ignition, ejected from the plane, jumped off the ship, got on the bus, and so on.

Your reader is so familiar with these kinds of story elements, he will accept them without question, and your transitions from scene to scene will go on unnoticed. That's your goal.

Mood Cues

Mood cues are more subtle and require more careful manipulation, but they are equally effective. The use of mood cues to make a transition effective is more often found in first-person narratives, told through a single character's point of view. The reader depends on everything the main character sees, feels, thinks, and ultimately decides.

> **TRADE TALK**
>
> **Mood cues** can take the form of a sudden idea, a revelation or an epiphany, an outburst, an attack, a retreat, an exit, or any other emotional or rational decision from within your character. They're all valid transition cues that move your reader to the next scene.

If your main character feels threatened, excited, tired, etc., the decision to react to those sensations creates a change in the narrative and a transition.

Word Cues

Believe it or not, you don't always need all that setting up and rationale. Sometimes your reader is simply ready for a shift, a relocation, a transition, and the only thing you need to do is add a little buzz phrase.

One of the oldest examples is, "Meanwhile, back at the ranch …." You may laugh, but it's perfectly valid once in a while, and with experience, you'll get a feel for when you can get away with dropping in an obvious phrase meant to make a quick move to a new scene. It's usually okay to employ when your narrative reaches a mini-resolution or climax and you and your readers are *expecting* something new to keep the story going.

> **TOM'S TIPS**
>
> Once we look at them so closely, transitions seem ridiculously obvious … and they are. They'll only present a problem for you when you don't include them in your narrative. On that note, the last thing I can say about transitions is: be certain your novel has them.

Point of View

Throughout the preceding chapters, I've been making direct as well as oblique references to this element, which basically answers the question: who's going to be telling your story? It sounds like an easy and obvious choice, but it's more complex than you might think. Many writers believe that deciding on the point of view (POV) affects everything that happens in your novel. I tend to agree.

You have three essential narrative viewpoints: first, second, and third person. You probably heard about these in your high school English classes, but they're going to take on extra meaning now. Two of them, as you'll see, are used far more often than the third one.

First Person

A first-person narration is when your character tells his or her own story. It's particularly popular in certain kinds of novels. Readers tend to like it when detectives and private investigators relate their experiences personally; the same goes for coming-of-age novels, historical romances, and heroic fantasies. But that may sound too restrictive—although those are some of the more widespread examples, any novel can be successfully written in first person.

In general, readers are very comfortable with first-person narration because it allows instant identification with the main character. Many writers claim first person is the easiest POV to master because it's the natural voice of all storytelling ("Hey, let me tell you what happened to me today ...."), and also because you can be confident you'll "come clean" with your readers by telling them everything you know about the story. If your main character doesn't know something that turns out to be crucial or important, then it's okay with your readers when he finds out later because they know he wasn't withholding information on purpose.

As easy as first-person narration may seem, you must be aware of the following issues that can cause problems in telling your story:

Because your narrator is telling the story, the reader can safely assume your main character survives whatever obstacles and conflicts your plot has in store for him. Therefore, you lose the element of doubt or possible suspense that something awful (like dying) could befall your narrator.

Yes, there are exceptions to every rule. We've all read stories in which the main character is the ghost or the dead guy, and we're told on page 1 this is the case. If you try to be overly clever by not telling the audience the narrator's dead, you run the risk of really angering your readers. (That's on the order of getting to the last page and finding out "it was all a dream," which as we all know is a real stink bomb of an ending.)

Your reader can only know what your narrator knows. In other words, your narrator can only experience what happens right in front of him. Anything else has to be relayed by another character, who has to run onstage saying the equivalent of "Hey, you shoulda seen what happened over there!" Or you need a device like TV, radio, or something else.

This is a limiting factor only in terms of scope, or what's going on in your story simultaneously on "other stages"—that is, other locations in your story. Once you're aware of this limitation, you can work within it. Good writers do it all the time.

Describing your main character is more challenging. What you don't want is a situation where your narrator has to describe himself ("I'm a big, strong guy at six-four, and I have to get my suits custom-made because my shoulders are so wide."). See how silly that reads? You'll want to include action and dialogue (mostly from other characters) to reveal him.

Second Person

Second-person POV is the one I won't need to cover in much depth. Narrating your novel using the word *you* (as opposed to *I* or *he/she*) is rarely, if ever, used at the novel level, unless the book is clearly "experimental" or "literary" (which, as you should know by now, are just other words for *pretentious* and *ostentatious*).

Many writers believe readers may not feel comfortable being referenced as already having personally done something their subconscious knows they didn't experience … and that's what second-person narration presumes—it says plainly *you* are doing things. So for our purposes, let's just forget about it, okay?

Third Person

Third-person POV is the most prevalent in the modern novel. Although it is not as easy to master as first-person POV, it gives writers the most latitude in their storytelling. The reason it is popular is obvious—the three innate first-person problems are gone. What makes things the most intriguing is that all bets are off on who survives to the final page. Even main characters can be killed off at any time.

Now as you might have figured, with a tool so powerful and popular as third-person POV, there are a number of ways you can execute it. Let's take that now-familiar closer look:

Omniscient point of view is basically telling the story as if you're the ruler of the universe. You know everything that's going on everywhere—at all the exotic locations and inside every character's head. Using this point of view, you can also make comments on the action or even make bold, unexpected warnings to the reader. But it can be tricky because there's the temptation to tell your audience too much of what's going on, and that undercuts some of the finest elements of storytelling, such as suspense and irony.

Another thing to avoid is being inconsistent in your use of the omniscient point of view—you can't slip in and out of it at your leisure. Readers will pick up on it, and they won't like it.

Cinematic point of view is the other side of the omniscient coin. As you might gather from its name, you write everything as if you were the lens of a movie camera, and you only tell the reader what happens directly in front of you. You don't include the internal thoughts or experiences of any of the characters, not even your main character or protagonist. This is obviously restrictive and serves little purpose in the novel-length story, which thrives on scope, range, and depth. Cinematic point of view is like the second person—both are best used sparingly and only work well in short stories. My advice? Don't use it.

Over-the-shoulder point of view is one of the most popular choices you'll see in modern novels. As the title suggests, the reader rides right alongside the head of the main character—seeing what that person sees, feels, and experiences and getting to know what's going on internally within your character's mind. The reader gets to share knowledge, experience, expectations, the full range of emotions, suppositions, plans, analysis … everything that could be going on inside the character's head.

This POV is very well suited to the modern novel and is especially effective when the focus of your story features one major character around whom everything else orbits. The key word here is *focus*, because over-the-shoulder point of view certainly does that. The reader's attention is narrowed down to one primary character, resulting in a narrative that's tight, engaging, and immediate.

Multiple points of view is my personal favorite, but that's not to say it should be yours, too. This POV is exactly like over-the-shoulder, but it's not for only one character. It's for as many characters as you want or need. With multiple points of view, you can get into the heads of as many characters as needed to tell your entire story. It tends to work best in novels that have a large scope or stage, like a family saga spanning many locations and generations, a global thriller that uses the entire planet as its stage, or any novel with a large cast of characters operating in separate locations.

However, free-wheeling freedom and expanded narrative power come with a price. It's harder to write in this mode because each character has to be sufficiently differentiated so when it changes from person to person, the point of view is obviously being channeled through a unique perspective. For example, if one character is a 50-year-old college professor and the other is a career Marine officer, each will have a completely different way of thinking, speaking, and perceiving the world, colored by a lifetime of different education and experience.

To use multiple POV effectively, you have to be skillful enough to control all the aspects of characters and make each POV stand on its own. The ultimate compliment will come when your readers won't need to be told which person is currently "onstage" because they'll be able to pick up on it by the character's style, language, and demeanor. This is a great POV to employ, if you're up for the challenge. And if you've hung around this long, I think you are.

A LIKELY STORY

An aging dictator in a third-world country decides to take the vice president of the United States hostage during a summit conference. Your hero is a Marine lieutenant who is a stowaway on the dictator's plane with the hostage VP. He must figure out a way to rescue the VP and escape the hostile country. This is a great framework on which to hang a multiple point of view. Are you up for it?

Pacing

When writers and editors talk about the pace of a novel, they're concerned with the flow of information and how it reaches the reader. The concept of pacing is what you use to maintain control of your narrative. Good storytelling is a series of natural ebbs and flows in the plot, with a single purpose of moving the story forward.

You can think of pacing as a kind of unconscious speedometer you consult periodically to see how things are moving along. If you feel you're getting too bogged down in details and dispensing necessary information, you'll need to hit the accelerator with a scene designed to pull the reader along at a crisp pace.

Conversely, if you have too many scenes in a row, all running at top speed, you'll need to insert something to slow things down like a very controlled conversation or leisurely observational narrative.

The Benefits of Good Pacing

Good pacing in your novel accomplishes several things:

Keeps the readers guessing. You always want to "be ahead" of your audience, and pacing allows you to keep your readers off-balance, unsure of what to expect next, while still keeping the narrative moving forward (one of your prime directives).

Allows all information to be processed. Some bits of the information your readers need to know require more attention, analysis, and reflection than others. Good pacing gives the audience a "breather" once in a while, where important details can be plugged in without fear they may be missed in a flurry of action.

Helps establish mood and atmosphere. The pace you choose for a particular scene contributes to its overall "feel." Different speeds of delivery, word choice, and content help you control your pacing.

Ensures rhythm and balance. These are actually your primary components of pacing. You can think of rhythm in a similar fashion to its musical counterpart, or even the way your English teachers tried to get you to notice "meter" in lines of poetry. Rhythm in sentences is more of an intuitive characteristic—you simply start to notice when some sentences seem to "flow" a lot better than others. There's nothing specific you need to watch for; it's just a sense you gradually develop the longer you write and the more you experiment with words (which is what writing really is).

Balance is a little trickier because it's not simply a question of alternating action and talking endlessly back and forth. Good balance in a narrative is unpredictable and should perhaps be called "off-balance." The idea is to shake up your pacing so it's always fresh.

Pacing Techniques

So how do you control the pace of your novel? To start, you need to have the idea of tempo in the back of your head all the time. The more you make yourself aware of it, the easier and more natural it becomes.

When you need an up-tempo scene, which usually will be descriptive action or confrontational dialogue (such as an argument), choose sentences that are generally shorter, punchier, and sometimes even clipped or abbreviated. Use punctuation such as periods and maybe a few em dashes. Short paragraphs also accelerate things unconsciously. Fights, chases, rescues, abductions, etc., are all well suited for up-tempo scenes.

When you need to slow things down, you can lengthen your sentences and choose words that are soft and languid and suggest calmness. Punctuation can help if you apply ellipses and use long paragraphs. Scenes that benefit from a slower pace are romantic scenes, exposition, nonconfrontational dialogue, setting scenes, and post-climax explanations.

The final important thing to remember about pacing is that it applies to the whole novel, from its largest segments like parts or chapters, to each scene within each chapter. It's not a good idea to have too many chapters in a row where the action is nonstop, just as it'd be a mistake to string together three or four chapters of dense exposition (like our brother writers in South America love to do).

Pacing, like all the other elements of writing, is simply one piece of the puzzle, and each piece is equally important and dependent upon the other pieces. Everything adds to or detracts from everything else. If one element is missing or deficient, it affects the remaining elements.

This many pages spent on the separate writing elements should do one thing, above all else: make you aware of them. Learning and mastering these elements are natural processes you'll make happen. But you can't make them happen if you don't know what they are and why you need them. Clueing you in was my job; yours is yet to come.

The Least You Need to Know

- Good transitions keep your story moving from scene to scene without feeling choppy or clumsy. If your novel has nice transitions, nobody will even notice them.

- Choosing point of view is one of the most important decisions you make when you begin telling your story. The primary thing to keep in mind regarding POV is to stay consistent—don't wander from one type to another.

- If your novel has good pacing, it has variety, unpredictability, and momentum, all of which drive it forward toward a satisfying resolution.

- Mastering transition, point of view, and pacing requires an awareness of their functions and careful attention to what's needed to keep them in effect. When they're done well, no one will ever notice them.

The Process of Writing a Novel

At this point, you should have a firm understanding of all the elements that comprise the body of a novel. Now it's time to have a close look at the *processes* you'll need to master so you can employ all the *elements* to your best ability.

If you look at the elements as being the big things, then the processes are more like the little things. But as you'll soon see, it's usually the little details that eventually make the difference between the mediocre and the sublime.

Research: Getting It Right

In This Chapter

- What you know and what you can find out
- The best places to find what you need
- What must be absolutely right
- Pitfalls and bad habits

Whenever I talk to students, young writers, or beginning novelists of any age, the topic of research eventually comes up. And before we even get into how to do it, or the kinds of research to do, or the sources, we usually talk about that old saw: *write what you know.*

This tends to bother young writers who don't think they've lived long enough to know much; and it also goes for older writers who've spent most of their lives within the confines of their occupation and don't feel they have much worldly experience. You'd be surprised how many women I've met who decide to be writers (after their kids are all out of the house and on their own) and then get depressed because they think the only novels they could ever write would be about taking care of a family in a familiar American home and neighborhood. Despite what the feminists would have us all believe, there are still plenty of women who feel that way—at least that's what they're telling me.

Experience Versus Research

What I'm getting at here is a kind of quiet controversy. Do you write what you know? Or do you research what you *don't* know?

You do *both*.

And you do both as much as you need to tell a good story. I think it's true a good writer can write just about *anything* and make it interesting. Part of making something good is making it believable. (And the opposite is also very true. A truly bad writer can take the most intriguing, fascinating material and make it as dull as the paint on a junkyard pickup.)

And that's what research is all about. Here's what I want you to learn from this chapter:

- Appreciate what effective research can do for your novel. If you have your facts straight, you'll be adding texture and detail to your settings and characters. Poe called it *verisimilitude*, which is the creation of a fictional world that feels "real." If you can do this, your readers will believe you and hang with you through just about anything.

- Recognize your research limits. Sometimes you'll start piling up too much data on a subject, and you'll need to know when to call it off. Other occasions may net you *too little* information, and you can get caught up in an obsessive search for a detail or a fact that's simply not available. Don't let research become a time waster.

- Locate some good, quick, accessible sources. You can do your research with less effort and more enjoyment when you have a good grasp on all the outlets available to you.

WORDS OF WISDOM

If you steal from one author, it's plagiarism; if you steal from many, it's research.

—Wilson Mizner

Sources

These days, with so many places where you can search and retrieve information, it's going to be hard to narrow down the most obvious and productive ones. So please realize I'm not going to be anywhere near as extensive or thorough as I could be. Entire books are devoted to the subject, so if you're that jazzed about research, get an entire tome on the subject or pursue a degree in library science.

Now let's take a closer look.

Unusual Occupations

This one is very important, especially if you have experience in a unique occupation, such as an astronaut, one of the ten guys around the world who knows how to extinguish an oil well fire, a biological nanotech engineer, or even something as mundane as a brain surgeon. You get the idea. I'm sure there are plenty of other jobs even *more* unusual—so much so, I can't even *think* of them at the moment. But why am I telling you? You'll know whether or not your occupation is all that unique. I'm just here to tell you: don't overlook it as a source.

In case you have such specialized knowledge, you need to research *yourself.* Not literally, but do take a hard look at yourself. Use your own expertise when you need a character like no other. And the nice part is, you don't need to be effusive and over the top in your details. If the occupation is esoteric enough, even a few odd facts will do the trick, and your audience will believe you.

Personal Experience

Personal experience is similar to the occupation source, but it applies more to one-time experiences that aren't duplicated very often. If you've wreck-dived the Bismarck or climbed K2, there's probably a story in it. If you survived a tornado that passed through your living room, you can most likely use it somewhere in your writing. Plane crashes, shipwrecks, car-jackings, and all the rest of those harrowing *I-faced-down-death* experiences are invaluable storehouses of research material not available to the average writer.

Now I'm not saying you have to limit your experiences to just near-death stuff, but that kind of thing is just so naturally intriguing, I used it as the prime example. You could also have been the person who polished the mirrors for the Hubble Telescope or discovered the potential force of a mega-tsunami in the Canary Islands.

Interviews

This is easily one of the best ways to do research. It not only gets you the information you're looking for, but you often discover so much additional information you could never have anticipated. When you conduct on-site interviews with your expert, you get a great chance to scope out your subject's working environment; see things up close; and maybe ask questions about equipment, procedures, or other details you may have otherwise missed.

The first time I employed the interview in my research was when I was writing a novel called *Night Train*, which used the New York City subway system as a major part of its setting. I set up meetings with a PR guy from the Transit Authority and went on tours of the entire subway infrastructure. I saw the way things worked and where and how they were controlled and organized. I met people who worked the same jobs some of my characters would be working. No question, the information I pulled from all the interviews and on-site tours made my book all the more credible and successful. (Even though it was just a paperback original, it stayed in print for more than 5 years, which is great for the average title.)

Travel

You would be surprised by how many people, when they take a scheduled vacation, do *the same thing* every year. If it's July, that means 2 weeks at a beach resort, or golf in the Berkshires, or skiing in Colorado. Year in and year out, they return to the same place, never even *thinking* of going anywhere else.

I don't know about you, but that strikes me as nutty. Life's too short, and even this little planetoid is too big to *not* try to see as much of it as possible. Not only are other cultures and locales inherently interesting just because they're different, but all the stuff you see is great grist for your writing mill. I've been all over the USA—every state and most of the bigger cities; at least half of South America; plus England, Scotland, Ireland, France, and Italy (including Sicily), and I don't feel like I've traveled much at all.

Still, I've used most of the locales I've visited in at least a short story or two and plenty of novels. I can't help it. Throwing in that kind of detail and little-known facts about places you've been to is irresistible, and your readers love it—especially if they've been there, too (because they'll know you're giving them the straight scoop).

Lastly, for the times when you can't get up and go there, you should have a good backup, which for me always was, and still is, that garish yellow monthly periodical capable of transporting you just about anywhere on the planet—the *National Geographic Society* magazine. In my pre-Internet days, it served as one of my primary sources of data on global settings as remote as Tunguska or as densely populated as Hong Kong.

There are two big pluses for *National Geographic:* it has great, in-depth articles full of texture, cultural referents, and style; and it has absolutely incredible photography, which gives a heads-up on your descriptive passages. The publishers also provide great indices, which can help you find an article on whatever you need.

Internet

In the last 15 years, if I had to point to the one thing that has literally *changed every-thing*, hands down, it has to be the Internet. I can't think of anything in my lifetime that has produced so many radical changes in the way we do business, communicate, amuse ourselves, or find information.

And television, which was a pretty big innovation in our lives, doesn't even come close to the Internet. I think the biggest difference between the two is a subtle but important one. TV is essentially a passive medium—you don't have to really do anything other than just *sit* there and keep your eyes open. The Internet is more active—you have to bring something to the table and read what's on the screen, ask questions, conduct searches, send notes, etc.

For writers, the Internet has opened up the entire world of information almost instantaneously available. I have no clue how something called a search engine works, but it is truly one of the most mind-bogglingly ingenious things I've ever seen. In terms of researching a topic, it's like having a genie sitting in the corner, just waiting for you to ask for something.

> **TOM'S TIPS**
>
> Here's a little trick to help you from getting bogged down. While writing your narrative, any time you get to a spot where you know you need more information to make the scene credible, just insert an extra line marked in the uppercase words MORE INFO. Then *keep writing!* The idea is not to stop in the middle of a productive writing session because you don't know the name of the street where the FBI Building is located. Mark each spot in the chapter that needs more research, and at the end of your writing session, search the MORE INFOs, do *all* the research you need to wrap up that chapter, and replace them with the real data.

I'm not going to go off on a long tangent regarding the variety of search engines and websites on the Internet because whole books are devoted to the subject, there are too many books about the Internet, and more are published every day. Just know that some are better than others, and none of them will give you *everything* you need. It's not magic; don't forget that.

The only problem with the Internet is that it's not up to date yet, and it may never be. All the stuff you can still find in great detail and thoroughness in a library is not yet digitized and available through a Google search. So if you're looking for really specialized information, or in-depth detail, the Net may not take you there. I'm sure this will eventually change, but the task of inputting all the knowledge of all the world's libraries seems pretty daunting to me, and unless I was sleeping, it isn't close to being done yet.

In addition, a lot of the search engines tend to find the *same* top-level sources, and if you don't dig down to the lower, more esoteric levels, you may miss out on some of the less-obvious data that may help you. I don't want to mention specific names like Wikipedia that may be suspiciously thin or even wrong in some of the information proffered there.

This means we still need our own magazines, books, and libraries.

Libraries

When I was in college, the only computers available were these tape-driven things that ate endless stacks of punch-cards and had to be kept at the same temperature as a head of fresh lettuce. They didn't do much, and the prospect for any of them taking over the world was downright laughable.

This meant I learned how to use the General Reference Room of my huge university's library. And even in these Google-guided days, you should learn how to conduct basic library research the old-fashioned way as well. You never know when you might need it.

Learn how to use the *Index to Periodicals*; book review indices; and countless archives of *monographs*, articles, and studies in every specialty discipline imaginable. Most universities also have extensive collections of newspapers on *microfilm* or microfiche, which date back at least 100 years and usually a lot farther. That's where you get the real authentic touches in the ads and the style of the articles and the politics of the era.

TRADE TALK

The *Index to Periodicals* is a huge, running set of thick books that lists every legitimate magazine published. The listing indicates what articles, topics, etc., appeared in the issue. Indices for various sources of book reviews can help you find all the places where a book by a particular author, or about a particular subject, may be located. **Monograph** is academese for a scholarly article usually written in the driest, stuffiest, and somnambulistic style imaginable. **Microfilm** was the only way to preserve crumbling documents such as newspapers before the advent of digital scanning and storage. It is a reel of photograph (positive) film you thread into a reader, a simple projector that displays the images on a screen.

I spent almost a month reading old New York and New Haven papers from the 1880s. I was researching a possible book (tentatively titled *The Bone Warriors*) about Othniel Marsh and Edward Drinker Cope, the two most famous paleontologists in history. I was going to do a big historical novel about their generation-long rivalry, but turned out to be about 6 months behind the curve. Just as my agent was getting ready to take out my proposal, he heard about a book just turned in at Crown Books called *The Gilded Dinosaur*, which was essentially the same book I had been planning to write.

If you've been paying attention, you'll note this is not the first time I've been snaked because I was late pulling the trigger on a marketable idea. Never say I didn't warn you. Snooze and possibly lose.

 A LIKELY STORY

How about this for a premise: a young computer wizard who works for the NSA as a cryptanalyst (breaking codes) is hired by an odd sect of monks living in upstate New York. They have discovered an ancient manuscript, which they believe may contain secrets of the earth's earliest history, and they ask our protagonist to use his skills to provide a key to translating this unknown language. He accepts but discovers that if he gives the key to his employers, they may unleash a terrible race of ancient beings upon the earth, which signals the end of our civilization as the old ones reinherit their world.

Great ideas tend to be contagious. And in case you think the research was wasted … nyah, I'm smarter because I did it, and that's always a good thing.

Things You Have to Get Right

The reason we do research in the first place is to ensure we get our facts down cold. The worst thing that can happen in your novel is to get caught dispensing information that's out of date, plain-headed wrong, or worst of all—something you lied about. Your readers who catch you may never forgive you.

And there are certain categories of facts and information more important than others, some in which there are lots of amateur experts who might be reading your books and *just waiting* in the hope of catching you. Let's at least have a look at some of the ones with the highest priorities.

History and Culture

I touched on this when we looked at genre fiction, such as Regency mysteries and historical novels in general. We're talking more than just dates and battles here. You need to know about the style of clothes, the popular books and plays, the politics, the favorite foods, the technology or lack of it, and even things like the music and the art of the periods. You may not use all of it, but you should know it. If you're going to make your characters move about in a historical era, you'd better know that era as well as the characters.

There are tons of ways to check your historical facts, and you should not be too lazy to confirm what you *think* is right. That means don't just rely on something you half-remember seeing on The History Channel or The Discovery Channel while surfing through on the way to HBO. That is *not* research.

Weaponry

Weaponry may sound like an odd topic at first, but believe me, misrepresenting it is one of the easiest ways to get caught with your facts down. Hundreds of thousands of serious gun enthusiasts and thousands of weapons "collectors" can tell you the difference between an ax and halberd, a dagger and a stiletto, etc. This means you'd better know at least as much and probably more than the collectors.

For modern weapons, you can get some pretty weird magazines that keep you up to date on names, models, ammo, range, accuracy, portability, and all the other details you need to know about guns and some really ugly knives. I can't remember any of the specific names, but you can find whole racks of them at any large newsstand or magazine section of a book and music "superstore." For historical stuff, you'd be amazed how well catalogued most of the devices are and how you can find illustrated books that cover everything we've ever used with which to kill each other.

Getting it right enriches you. For instance, you'll even be fascinated to discover that things like suits of armor we usually associated with medieval knights (because of dumb movies—so don't trust what you see on the screen!) did not really get much use until the late Renaissance. The stuff they wore in the Middle Ages was far more primitive.

Police Procedure and Forensics

If you're writing anything contemporary in the fields of mystery, suspense, horror, thrillers, espionage, and even some romance hybrids, you need to know how the cops and the coroners and the special-ops guys do their thing. Don't get lost in the details.

Be aware of certain mortal sins in these professions—things that are always done and things that are *never* done. Get caught violating these basics, and your novel's in the tank.

You can get up to speed with interviews and a couple guidebooks to crime-solving techniques and CSI/forensic stuff. Hey, I'm sure there are some *Complete Idiot's Guides* on those subjects that are great! (And no, I didn't write them.)

Geography

Geography can be as large in scope as the coastline of an entire continent or as small as the nearest drugstore next to the Banco Brasilia branch in downtown Lima. Geography is a lot more than knowing your state capitals and the boundaries between the states or countries. You need to know climates and topography; lakes and rivers; mountain ranges; state parks; national preserves; counties; and of course the highways, the landmarks, and things like that.

For instance, if you have your characters driving anywhere in the northern midsection of the country and you don't mention the endless signs for Wall Drug, people who've made that drive are going to get suspicious. Same goes for the South of the Border signs on I-95 along the East Coast.

What you know or don't know about the geography of the settings of your novels can very much influence what's going on in your story. If you haven't researched it any more than a cursory glance at your Rand-McNally Road Atlas, you might be in for a surprise … and not a nice one.

Professions

Certain professions, especially glamorous or nonordinary ones we like to reserve for our protagonists (such as fighter pilots, surgeons, actors, corporate CEOs, senators, etc.), require you to research more than others. The temptation is to rely on what we've learned through television and friends, but it's usually superficial at best, and dead wrong at worst.

The things that separate well-researched professions from ones done with less care and attention are the details you *won't* see on TV or even in a puff piece from *People* magazine. I'm talking about little observations or remembrances of people or incidents, or maybe even an anecdote that somehow captures or sums up some special aspect of the character's job.

Don't forget—many of us are defined by our jobs. What we do *is* who we are. Now I'm not saying that's necessarily a good thing, but it's a fact, and you need to keep it in mind when you create characters and give them professions. Be sure you've researched their job well enough to breathe some life and believability into it.

A Few Warnings

Doing research isn't a very dangerous or reckless pursuit, so putting out the caution flag might seem a bit supercilious. But not really. Research is one of those parts of the writing job that can become more of a curse and a problem than you could ever realize.

I'm going to wrap up this chapter by giving you several points to keep in mind. These should help you keep things in perspective.

How Much Is Enough?

This is a question I hear over and over when I teach a class or a workshop. How do you know when you've done enough research, when you have more than you'll ever need?

My standard answer is a hoary old sports axiom, which I turn into a fairly standard simile: research is like pitching in baseball—you can *never* have too much of it. The trick is learning what to keep in and what to *leave out* of your story.

The best tactic is to pile up more than you plan to use. What generally happens after that is kind of weird: all the facts and texture and anecdotes you can't possibly cram into your story kind of seep down into your mind and unconsciously saturate your settings and characters. The end result creates an unspoken familiarity with your material.

And *that's* the important part.

I'm not sure how it works, but that familiarity translates into a certain, palpable confidence in your writing. Readers can sense it, and they trust you because you really do sound like you know what you're talking about. With the material you've researched, it's not always the way you parrot it back to the reader that's going to be convincing. A lot of times, it's going to be more general and subtle.

This is a process that's harder to explain than to experience firsthand. Diligent research pays off in many ways. Writing with confidence is one of them.

WORDS OF WISDOM

Research is four things: brains with which to think, eyes with which to see, machines with which to measure and, fourth, time … sometimes also referred to as money.

—Albert Szent-Gyorgyi

Do You Want a Research Assistant?

Some writers have a whole staff to do all their research, fact-checking, and proofing. Must be nice. I wouldn't know anything about it.

I get asked about this one, too, and my answer is simple. It's expensive and counter-productive. Aside from the cost, why would a writer want to avoid doing the work, which helps immerse him more deeply into the entire world of the story?

I've always felt my research is a great warm-up to the material I'm going to be "making up." If I'd let somebody else do all that preliminary stuff, and I came to the story without steeping myself in the details, I can't imagine how I could write a good story or build anything convincing.

And yet, I've talked to writers who've done it this way their whole careers, and it seems to work for them. How, I have no idea. The thought of somebody retrofitting my facts to my novel, *after* I'd written it, sounds very dumb to me.

A Nice Place to Hide

This is a strange one. It's never happened to me, but I've heard other writers talk about it quite a bit, so it must be real, and bears mentioning.

It's actually related to writer's block (which is one of those phenomena I really don't believe exists) and is nothing more than a convenient and logical-sounding excuse for not writing.

Theoretically, it's a situation in which you become so wrapped up in your research you never really get around to writing your original project. People tell me they've let the research *become* the major project and almost forgot why they needed all the information in the first place. They start to hide in their research.

They do this to *avoid* writing. Or so they tell me. Seems to me you'd have to convince yourself that your readers are more interested in the details than the larger strokes of plot and the emotions and motivations of your characters. I think this "explanation" is just a fairly inventive, pseudo-intellectual excuse for not getting your pages written. For some writers, the act of writing is a torturous ordeal, so this kind of thing probably appeals to them. They hate writing and love having written.

My advice: don't be like them. Let yourself enjoy every aspect of the writing game. While you're sitting there, simply realize you're giving yourself and your readers a chance to see something no one ever does—your inner thoughts.

The Least You Need to Know

- Research balances your experience and fills in the cracks of your personal knowledge bank. Never shy away from it. Look on it as an enriching adventure.
- Sources of research come from within you as well as from all the people you can contact. The Internet has made research both easier and harder—because people tend to rely on it too much and expect more answers than are currently available. Old-fashioned library time is still time well spent.
- Remember: there are plenty of experts out there, and they're just waiting to catch you in a big mistake. So get your facts straight—especially in some of the most obvious categories of geography, occupations, history, weapons, and procedures.
- Don't let your research control your writing. Don't worry about having not enough or too much. Trust your instincts, and keep writing. Don't use research as a silly reason why you can't be writing.

Format, Presentation, Grammar, and Syntax

Chapter 12

In This Chapter

- Industry standards
- The extra touches
- Making good grammar decisions
- Understanding sentence structure

The process of writing a novel continues with four more topics, all of which contribute mightily to the success *or* failure of your novel—depending on how well you understand them. Because of that, I'm forced to include the following …

> *Warning:* The material contained within this chapter, if not thoroughly mastered, can be the cause of the following serious problems: sloppy presentation, unintelligible text, improper construction, and rejection slips.

It's Better to Look Good Than Feel Good

As you may recall, I used to read slush piles for a couple magazines, and my wife, Elizabeth, and I edit an anthology series of imaginative fiction. I've seen *countless* manuscripts submitted over the years, and some of them look good … and some of them don't.

It's a question of formatting your manuscript, and it might be the difference between your story or book getting read or returned to you with just a glance. You see, if a manuscript is formatted improperly, it screams the words *hopeless amateur!* at the editor, who probably sends it back with little or no attention.

Don't forget: first impressions are *everything* in this business. The way your submission *looks* is the first thing the editor sees—way before he or she might start reading it. If your manuscript looks like it's been prepared by a professional, you've cleared your first big hurdle.

It's best to think of formatting your manuscript as a standard way things are done throughout publishing. It's a series of little conventions that were adopted long ago and have just kind of concretized into the accepted *and* expected way to do it right.

Here are the basics (and I do mean *basic*):

Use regular white bond paper that measures 8.5×11 inches. This might sound silly, but don't use any of the other sizes available such as legal and something the Brits use called A4. Editors have shelves and niches designed to hold standard-size paper stacks, and you don't want to be the odd stack.

Use black ink. True, colored ink will make your manuscript stand out, but it will also make your submission very annoying. Also, only use the *front* of each page; nothing on the back side of each page.

Double-space your manuscript. There are a couple reasons for this—it's easier to read, and if, by chance, your novel is bought, the spaces between the lines make it easier to pencil in corrections, emendations, suggestions, or copyeditor queries.

Use margins that give the page an open, airy look. One inch all the way around should be fine. And you don't need to worry about justifying the type (making the right margin of type all line up as neatly as the left); a ragged-right margin is acceptable, and it's easier to read.

Add the important info at a glance. On the first page, in the upper-left corner, include your name, your agent (if you have one), the address (yours or your agent's, again, if you have one), phone numbers, and e-mails. In the upper-right corner, you can put the approximate wordage (if it's short fiction).

Also on the first page, centered and midway down, enter the novel's title in ALL CAPS. Below that, add your name (or your pen name).

Add a header. This is a line across the top of the page that includes at least a keyword from the title, followed by a slash, followed by your last name. Also include the page number. The header plus page number is *very* important because sometimes manuscripts come apart and pages get scattered. If your reader/editor can't figure out in what order the pages should be rearranged, guess who might be rejected?

It goes without saying (which means I have to say it anyway) that everything I just mentioned is for typed or machine-printed manuscripts—that is, *no* hand-printed or handwritten manuscripts—*ever.* If you're using a typewriter, it's better to have one that employs *pica*-size letters because they're bigger and easier to read than *elite.* If you're writing on a computer, your *font* size should be at least 12 points, and it can be as large as 14. You want to get between 23 and 27 lines per page. This is to approximate the size and word density of the *typed* manuscript page, which has become one of those industry standards.

> **TRADE TALK**
>
> Although they refer to typewriters, which few of us still use, the terms **elite** and **pica** persist. They are actually units of measurement. Elite is a fixed-width type that provides 12 characters per linear inch. Pica is larger, providing 10 characters per linear inch. Pica is easier to read. This is different from **font,** which is the style or "look" of the type.

I left the question of fonts until last because it's somewhat a matter of personal preference. The standard font is still Courier because it's so easy to read, and all the letters tend to be the same width, which helps editors and typesetters estimate the length of finished books. That being said, lots of writers, and even some editors, are tired of seeing Courier and are open to seeing manuscripts in other *readable* fonts such as Bookman, Times, Baskerville, Gatineau, and other serif (letters with little edges and "feet" like ... well, Courier). Just be sure you use a point size (12 to 14) that allows it to be read as easily as the old typewriter font—pica courier.

Now just to be sure you've got it right, I've included something to make it crystal clear—a sample cover page.

Tom Scrivo

Garrison Heath Smathers, agent

The Boutique Agency

000 Fifth Ave

NYC, NY 10000

1-212-555-5555

GHS@theboutiqueagency.com

Naked Came the Spy

by

Tom Scrivo

—————————————————————

—————————————————————

After the cover page, you begin your text, formatted as I previously indicated. Each page should also contain the book title, your last name, and the page number. This information is the header I told you about earlier, and here's how it should look:

Naked / Scrivo   page #

Okay? I can't make it any clearer than that.

Proper manuscript formatting may sound simple and not even necessary to go over in such detail, but you'd be surprised how many novel manuscripts come in on yellow paper or purple ink or even handwritten. All these standards might sound boring and uninteresting, but it's important that your submission stand out from the rest for the right reasons—not the *wrong* ones.

Making an Impressive Presentation

My wife, in addition to being a very beautiful and intelligent woman, is also a gourmet cook. She takes great pleasure in not only planning and preparing fantabulous epicurean extravaganzas, but also in creating just the right *presentation*.

If you've ever seen a table set for a dinner party with the silver flatware and charger plates under the service, you know how appealing that can be. When the courses are also presented in balanced, colorful, and appetizing ways, it's almost like an art form.

What's this have to do with writing your novel? Hang with me a second more, and you'll see.

Presentation is closely related to formatting, and equally important. To understand it, just think of it as the finishing touches to a properly formatted manuscript. You only need be aware of a few things to ensure a classy presentation.

The Cover Letter

This is what sits on top of your title page. This is the *true* first impression. Some writers and editors will tell you most covers get tossed unread into the Round File, but I don't believe them. If your cover letter is short, polite, and professional, it will probably get read; and that can't hurt.

Your cover letter should very briefly introduce your novel (without going into a long-winded synopsis of the plot—editors *hate* that) and a few brief words about yourself in terms of prior publishing credentials. If you don't have any, just move on to a simple last paragraph, in which you say thanks for the opportunity to submit your manuscript.

That's it. Your cover letter should be clear and succinct. Make your salient points, and close the letter. A cover letter thick with paragraphs of text is the mark of an amateur.

The Packaging

I always get a kick out of the scene you see in the movies when a character happens to be a writer and he's finishing his novel or the book is showing up on an agent or an editor's desk. In almost every case, the stack of pages looks *way* too thin (even the average length of a genre novel looks like the phone book of most medium-size cities), and the manuscript is *bound* in some fashion, usually with those big brass button-clips.

Friends, manuscripts are *never* submitted like that.

It's funny that movie people and even the screenwriters (who, for the most part, are *not* novelists and have no clue what goes into writing a novel) have apparently decided that a novel manuscript looks pretty much like a screenplay (which *is* around 110 pages and is usually bound with those brass things).

And with typical moviemaking arrogance, they assume that if, by chance, a novel manuscript doesn't *exactly* look like a screenplay … well, hey, nobody'll notice.

Well, *I* notice, and so does everybody else in publishing.

Now I know we're just talking about a movie prop, but it could give you the wrong idea. And that's why I'm here—to give you the *right* idea, which is this: do *not* bind your pages, and don't hole-punch them and put them in a loose-leaf booklet. Just pack the separate pages in a cardboard stationery box. And mail it. I know it doesn't sound very elegant or impressive, but believe me, that's what the editor *wants* and expects.

TOM'S TIPS

If you live in a small town that still has a mom 'n' pop "stationery store," you can ask them to save you some of the boxes their good papers come in. If you're stuck with a big-chain operation, go "make nice" with the clerk at the in-house "copy center," and see if they can save you some boxes. Also, whenever you get a package in the mail, ask yourself if the shipping box can be recycled to ship your manuscript. But the slickest trick is to go to your post office and "appropriate" a few of their priority mail boxes—the ones you have to fold into shape. The trick? Fold it inside out so all that red-white-and-blue is on the *inside*. Presto change-o! You have nice, sturdy packaging for whatever manner of shipping you choose.

The Bells and Whistles

With the advent of desktop publishing, writers can do all sorts of fancy prepress stuff that had previously been denied them. My advice here is, for the most part: don't do it.

Whatever great ideas you have to make your manuscript look cool or special are probably wrong-headed. Big, fancy, decorative title fonts, drop shadows, colors (aarrrgh!), and other neat stuff is not all that neat when you're submitting your manuscript.

Better to leave all that to the typesetters *after* they purchase your book, not before.

Back to Grammar School

Funny thing about the issue at hand: if you're not a writer, a discussion of English usage and composition would rank right up there with the care and storage of replacement erasers for your pencils. But if you really *are* a writer, then you most likely fell in love with the English language a long time ago. Learning about grammar and syntax is pretty much the same as learning how to write well.

I don't have the space to conduct an in-depth seminar on all the various exigencies of grammar that would possibly knock you silly. But I can give you a solid heads-up on the most important things to remember, avoid, and double-check in your revisions.

Grammar and syntax are really all about writing clear, structurally sound sentences that accurately *say what you mean*. It's about following an agreed-upon set of rules. Just like when we play a game or enact a procedure, we try to follow the rules. Put this way, it sounds so easy, so presumptuously facile, you might be wondering why we're even bothering with it.

WORDS OF WISDOM

Every writer should master the rules of grammar before he attempts to bend or break them.

—Robert Graves

Because, like everything else that goes into making your novel a reality, it's important. If you can write *clearly*, and your prose isn't cluttered up with lots of awkward, ungrammatical phrases, editors *will* notice your work. Really clear, tight writing rises above the pack. It's the single aspect of your manuscript that can determine very quickly whether or not the right people read it.

If I wanted to, I could spend the rest of the pages of this worthy tome on grammar and its various levels of complexity. But I don't want to. I believe you'll be writing clearly and mostly error-free if you pay attention to the basics to follow. I'm going to list and examine them in no particular order, but pretty much as they come to me.

Parts of Speech

To keep things moving, I'm going to do something very dangerous: I'm going to *assume* you already know what the parts of speech are (nouns, pronouns, verbs, adverbs, adjectives, prepositions, conjunctions, and interjections). Okay, so I listed them, just in case. The parts of speech are all the types of words we use to communicate. Each one has a different function; and if you want to be a writer, you need to be able to identify any of them in any sentence written in English in any book on any shelf.

If you can't do that, then maybe you should have bought the book on quilting instead of writing.

But I have faith in you. Point out the noun and the preposition in the previous sentence. Okay, you said *faith* is the noun and *in* is the preposition—underscoring my belief you bought the *right* book.

You know adverbs modify verbs, which means they tell you more information concerning the action; and adjectives modify nouns, telling us more about the persons, places, and things. Pronouns are the personal nouns that designate sex and number of characters. Conjunctions are used to join or connect words, phrases, and clauses, while prepositions are used to show relationships between nouns in the same sentence.

The only part of speech I'm not sure you need to know about is the stepchild of the family—the interjection. In fact, go to your standard grammar book (the one you *do* have, don't you?), and check on it yourself.

The most important thing to know about the parts of speech is what they are and the job they do in your sentences.

Agreement

Nothing irritates an editor more than reading sentence after sentence in which subjects don't "agree" with their verbs. Usually this is obvious stuff. Most of us do not confuse the differences between "he writes" and "they write." Very few writers would ever make the mistake of "he write" or "they writes."

That's the basic agreement between nouns (subjects) and verbs (predicates). But don't get too cocky; it can be a little trickier than that. And sometimes, a *lot* trickier.

When you have multiple subjects (such as Bill and Joe *work* on the Pentagon Project), you consider it as plural subject (as opposed to just Bill as the subject: Bill *works* on the Pentagon Project).

However, multiple subjects, when qualified by *each* and *every* or *neither/nor, not only/ but also,* and other similar connected qualifiers (such as *Each weapon and every bullet was used in the battle*), requires a *singular* verb agreement.

There are other agreement exceptions and rules, which are too numerous to mention here. The best I can do is mention the main points of grammar, and you must do your homework to ensure you get to be good at it.

Tense

One of the worst things writers can do is lose track of the tense they're writing in. If you're writing in the *present* tense, don't drift into the *past* tense.

This can happen in your first drafts, but watch for it and correct it in your revisions.

Punctuation

I can remember being at a big barbecue filled with people of all types. An older lady I was talking to remarked, when she learned I was a writer, that she could *never* do what I do because she'd "never been able to figure out where to put the commas, or any of that 'other punctuality.'"

Indeed.

Learning how to properly punctuate your sentences is a part of grammar both basic and essential to clear writing. A misplaced or omitted comma can truly change the meaning of a sentence.

Try to think of commas as natural pauses, just like taking a breath when we speak, and appearing in those places in the sentence where one meaning or point is completed and another is beginning. Commas are separators of ideas or concepts, or persons and places, and just about anything else. There is no real mystery to using them. I usually tell someone who asks how to use commas to read the sentence aloud paying attention to the *meaning* they intend to convey, and put the commas in the places where they just naturally paused while speaking the sentence aloud.

Semicolons are *not* like commas. Use them to divide complete sentences or clauses that share common elements. I use the semicolons when appropriate throughout this book; if you've been paying attention, you've already noticed.

Colons are used to designate some kind of list or catalogue is going to follow, or a specific point. Dashes can set off an item from the rest of the sentence—usually for emphasis. Ellipses tend to slow down and separate thoughts you want the reader to consider ... without haste or hurry. Because they often appear silly and excessive (even in dialogue), exclamation marks are to be used *very* sparingly!

As for the other points of punctuation, it'll be more or less your personal preference regarding how often you use them. They'll be part of your style without you really noticing it. The way you employ things like quotation marks, italics, and parentheses (among other grammatical devices) is important. It's also important to follow general rules of usage, which are somewhat intuitive if you read with care and genuine attention. Names of books and films are italicized. Titles of stories and articles are placed in quotation marks. Things like that.

> **TOM'S TIPS**
>
> Because I don't have the space to cover all the rules of grammar and usage in this chapter, I'm going to do what I've rarely done in this book—refer to some other guy's book. But in this case, I have no choice. One of the best books for writers is *The Elements of Style* by William I. Strunk and E. B. White. It's been in print for a long time, and it is a true classic. It's not a very big book, but it's crammed with all the things you need to make your writing clear and clean. Get it and read it. And reread it. Often. Also get a basic grammar book to answer niggling questions. Many are available, all of pretty much equal value.

Usage Rules

Usage covers a multitude of sins and questions—when to use that or which, lie or lay, should or would, was or the subjunctive were, adapt or adept, except or accept, allusion or illusion, assay or essay, etc.

Your knowledge of correct usage depends heavily on several factors: your elementary education on basic grammar and composition, the extent of your vocabulary, and how well you remember what you've read and seen employed by other writers.

There are also conventions to be followed regarding what gets capitalized and when, how you express numbers, the use of foreign expressions (*ad hoc*, *raison d'être*, *quid pro quo*, etc.), and how to hyphenate or divide long words.

In addition, you should know that synonyms are words with the same meaning (*carriage* and *wagon*), homonyms are words with the same sound but different meanings (*through* and *threw*), and antonyms are words with exact opposite meanings (*hot* and *cold*).

As I said before, I don't have the space to cover these topics in detail, but I at least want to point them out as areas of expertise you'll need to acquire.

Spelling

Orthography (need your dictionary for this one?) is one of those things at which some writers are naturally good, and some just totally suck. I'm not sure spelling can be taught or even encouraged. It's a brain thing. Spelling involves the same kind of biomechanism that allows (some) people to retain long series of digits and phone numbers and others to forget them instantly.

There used to be some great little books all typesetters (the guys who used to lock up real, lead type in wooden cases) kept in their hip pocket, and they were crammed full of all the words that could possibly be misspelled. Manual typesetting is disappearing and so are those books, but you don't need them as much either.

Word-processing programs and personal computers are usually equipped with spell-checkers that can do a pretty fair job of keeping your manuscript clean and accurate. But those programs usually don't catch the *form* instead of *from* and the optical character recognition (OCR) software that allows you to scan printed text directly into your word-processing program can make weird scanning errors such as reading *dean* instead of *clean*. Some grammar-checkers are getting good enough to at least *question* usage that looks odd, so things are looking up, but I would never depend on my software to ensure I'm writing well, and neither should you.

The bottom line when it comes to spelling is this: *don't trust your spell-checker.* You still need to proof your manuscript carefully and get someone else to provide backup. Inattention to spelling tells editors you're sloppy, and that's not going to help you sell your novel.

WORDS OF WISDOM

Would you convey my compliments to the purist who reads your proofs and tell him or her that I write in a sort of broken-down patois which is something like the way a Swiss waiter talks, and that when I split an infinitive, God damn it, I split it so it will stay split, and when I interrupt the velvety smoothness of my more or less literate syntax with a few sudden words of bar-room vernacular, that is done with the eyes wide open and the mind relaxed but attentive.

—Raymond Chandler

Syntax

In the strictest sense, syntax is a study of the structure of sentences. It's kind of like looking at the blueprint of a building to see how it was put together. The best thing about understanding syntax is the ability it gives you to vary the length, shape, and cadence of your sentences.

Writers can kind of narcotize themselves (and their readers) by falling into habits of expression. An example of this could be an endless progression of declarative sentences, which the subject, predicate, and object unroll over and over, like this:

> The soldier fired his weapon into the night. His ammo slammed into the tank. The explosion ripped open the sky. The shrapnel fell onto the earth. The …

See what I mean? It becomes deadening. A lively, engaging style keeps a reader *moving* through your text. This is what you want. You don't want to lull them into something that suggests repetition or predictability.

You can't avoid using declarative sentences—they're the backbone of narrative. But you need to substantially add to that basic structure. You do it by varying the length and, more importantly, the *syntax* of your sentences. It's easiest to accomplish this if you have an elementary grasp of dependent clauses and phrases.

You want to assemble a small arsenal of sentence-types, which you can juggle around and intersperse among your more direct, declarative sentences.

Use infinitive phrases. Consider starting off a sentence now and then with the verb form beginning with *to*:

> To become a better mother, Mary would need to become a better listener.

You should also use participles. Setting up the main thought in a sentence with an action clause is a great disguise for a declaration:

> Careening downhill with ever-increasing speed, the uncoupled boxcar was a rolling bomb.

Another good variant is opening with a nice, image-laden gerund construction, which we all know is a verb form being used as a noun:

> Swimming in the brackish current of the Rio Amazon, while exciting, is also dangerous.

A LIKELY STORY

Many zoologists and anthropologists are fascinated by the concept of communicating with animals. There have been attempts to create basic "languages" and simple rules of grammar for simians and dolphins. Write a story in which your protagonist is successful, but with unexpected consequences.

Finally, there are prepositions. And of course, all the old, reliable standbys—the phrases and clauses that begin with prepositions such as *when, where, what, how, if,* etc. The nice part of this usage is a choice of employing it at the beginning or the end of the sentence.

The end result is creating a narrative flow that's never predictable, never sing-song, and not marching to some rigid cadence. I can't really teach you how to do it, but I can make you aware of the *need* to do it. You'll get better at it the more you actually execute good syntax properly and with variety and imagination. You don't need to follow all the rules, but you need to at least know what they are.

In fact, the best writers *don't* follow all the rules.

The Least You Need to Know

- The mark of an amateur is a poorly formatted manuscript. Making your novel submission measure up to what editors expect is a big first step in getting their attention.

- The subtle touches of packaging and presentation, when done properly, are surefire ways to score points with first readers and editors. The idea is to get their attention for the *right* reasons.

- Make up your mind to have a firm grasp of good grammar. Do whatever it takes to learn it and employ it. Get *The Elements of Style* (by Strunk and White) and *The Elements of Grammar* (by Margaret Shertzer). And read them.

- If you have an intuitive feel for the syntax of your sentences, you can make your prose sing, sit up, or do just about any trick you want. The structure of your sentences is like the "delivery" an actor works on—in both cases, it's what makes words come to life.

Style and Voice: Finding Yours

Chapter

13

In This Chapter

- Style—it's who you are
- Interesting style developments
- Warning signs you're overdoing it
- Changing your voice

The last chapter stressed the need to understand the rules of writing and to be able to follow them with skill and confidence. Having said all that, now I'm forced to tell you something a little contradictory.

In order to develop your own individual style, you'll have to ignore a lot of the rules.

Or at least enough of them to make your prose *interesting* and unique.

You see, up until now, we've been talking more or less about all the aspects of writing that apply to *all* writers. But when we get into a discussion of style and voice, we're really talking more specifically about *you* and *your* writing. We're looking at your style, the way you express yourself with enough regularity for it to become codified and, therefore, capable of fitting a particular description.

I don't want it to sound more complicated than it is. But style is personal, and it comes from a lot of different places. In this chapter, we take a look at a few of them—to give you some insight—but not for the explicit purpose of "creating" a style for you. *Nurturing*, or *growing*, or *providing for* your style might all be better ways of looking at it.

The longer you write, the more comfortable you get with the mere act of sitting there and *doing* it, and the more automatic it becomes. The more you do it, month after month, year to year, the less you have to stop so often to actually *ponder* and *decide* how you will stage a particular scene, describe a character, or unfold a conversation. A magic thing begins to happen: you'll just *know* the right way to write the scene or line or paragraph because it's become a basic part of you. It becomes part of your style.

My Style

Over the years, people have occasionally asked me to describe my style, and I've always been a little hesitant to try. Why is that? I don't know, maybe equal parts wisdom and superstition.

I think it's tough for writers to recognize and label their style because they're so close to it all the time. It becomes so personal and habitual (in the best sense), it's close to invisible. Readers who have no psychological or emotional attachments to your personal means of expression are probably far better at describing how you write than you are.

> **WORDS OF WISDOM**
>
> There is such an animal as a nonstylist, only they're not writers—they're typists.
>
> —Truman Capote

My Influences

As far as my own self-assessment goes, I can now look back on my earliest stories (yes, I still have them) and see immediately how overwritten they were. Heavily freighted with extra adjectives and flowery description, my sentences, while grammatical, were overblown and kind of embarrassing.

In retrospect, I know exactly from where my excesses came. Early on, when I was 12 or so, I was reading a lot of Edgar Rice Burroughs's high-adventure stories (*Tarzan* and *John Carter of Mars*) as well as H. Rider Haggard (*King Solomon's Mines*, *She*, *Ayesha*). Both of these guys wrote in a full-blown "pulp" style with plenty of cumbersome, "purple" prose. I guess I figured this is what writing was supposed to be like. Then as I moved on in my reading, I got into Edgar Allan Poe and H. P. Lovecraft. I didn't realize it at the time, but I was being literally *firebombed* by their florid, Byzantine styles.

I liked the dense, heavy, and atmospheric writing (partly because it was pretty much all I knew), and when I started writing my own stories in my early teens, I tried to emulate the writers I loved to read. Some time afterward, I discovered a naturalist named Loren Eiseley who is known for his ornate, poetic style, and also the magical short stories of Ray Bradbury. Ray's style is deceptively clean and simple because he has perfect control of his images, his use of metaphor. But young writers invariably assume all his great imagery and emotion come from adjective and adverb overload—and that's just not the case.

Anyway, my style needed a lot of work, even by the time I was sending out story after story to all the fiction magazines. Gradually, I got things under control as I learned the difference between overwrought prose and good, clear writing.

A Matter of Trust

It was years before I arrived at a consistent, distinctive style I could depend on. I had finally stopped worrying about my style, stopped thinking consciously of how each sentence was going to come out. What happens, I think, as you mature as a writer, is that you learn to *trust* the way you express yourself. Once that takes place, your style goes on autopilot and it's just *there*, doing its job.

Lots of new writers tend to worry about their style. It ends up being wasted energy because your style *will* evolve on its own—no matter what you do.

WORDS OF WISDOM

Use plain, simple language, short words and brief sentences. That is the way to write English—it is the modern way and the best way. Stick to it; don't let fluff and flowers and verbosity creep in. When you catch an adjective, kill it. No, I don't mean utterly, but kill most of them—then the rest will be valuable. A wordy habit, once fastened upon a person, is as hard to get rid of as any other vice.

—Mark Twain

Your Style

Some of you aren't going to be satisfied with my assurances that your style will evolve into a comfortable means of expression with no self-conscious strings attached. You're sitting there fretting and wondering just what kind of style you have or have the potential for, and you want to know how to help it along, how to develop it.

And you know what? I'm going to throw out a few things for you to think about. Then after you've pondered the possibilities, I'm going to offer you a few techniques and pointers that may help you hone your style into the sharp, polished instrument you desire.

First, let's talk about what shapes your style.

Your Personality

This is probably the most overriding factor. To get this topic where it needs to go, you have to engage in a little self-analysis, some introspection. I'm not talking any deep psychological profiling, just a little surface-scan to see what defines you.

So what basic type are you? Do your friends and co-workers describe you as hyper, frenetic, active, restless? Are you always anxious to be doing something? Preferably something new and different? Are you always looking for things that need fixing? Are you driven to complete everything you do? Are you detail-oriented? If that describes you to any extent, then those traits may be reflected in the way you write. Your descriptions and dialogue may be very detailed. You may want to be sure to include *enough* to get the whole picture just right.

Or maybe people describe you as more of a free spirit. Details don't worry you. Maybe they even *bore* you? If you tend to have a more relaxed manner of task completion, and you trust others to understand what you mean with a minimum of instruction, that aspect of who you are will probably show up in your style. You may like *symbolism* and *surreal* styles. Or at least try your hand at them.

TRADE TALK

Symbolism in writing occurs when you use one object or idea to represent another (like the snake being a symbol for sexuality). **Surrealism** is a way of looking at the world in ways it never was. It is a juxtaposition of recognizable images in places that are not part of our reality. (Think of Salvador Dali's melting watches hanging from trees on an endless plain.)

If you're an abstract thinker or adept in math and the physical sciences, your prose may be very precise and measured.

Also, look at the way you do other things in your life, and you'll find some clues about what your true style might be. Have you ever tried your hand at painting;

drawing; music; or hobbies like needlepoint, knitting, or other crafts? What do you prefer—the loose look of charcoal, chalks, and watercolors, or the more precise, realistic lines of pen and ink, tempera, and oils?

In music, do you like the precision of Bach or the tempestuous spirit of Beethoven? Or do you like classic rock, country, or hip-hop? Your answers could be very reliable indicators of what might be reflected in your style.

Your Perceptivity

Another key to understanding your style is the way you perceive the world around you. Do you see it as a safe, comforting place? Or is it more foreboding and threatening? Or maybe it's a world full of wonder and adventure? The variety of filters you use to interpret your environment also color your style.

The same can be said for people. Some of us can "read" people better than others. Some of us trust everybody, while others trust *no one*. That brings more unexpected components to your style.

Remember, I'm not saying any of these personality traits or perceptions are any better or worse than any others. I just wanted to point out a few things that may be shaping the way you write other than the usual literary influences.

Developing Your Style

Here are a few brief suggestions and things to play around with that should help you get comfortable with the way you write. Because really, that's the secret of letting your style evolve and develop.

Try lots of techniques and strategies. And be patient and see what happens.

Always Build Your Vocabulary

Some writers I know like language so much, they "read" the dictionary. Others collect books of definitions of weird words. Others just make sure they look up the words they've never learned before when encountering them for the first time.

You should do this, too.

Pay Attention to Syntax

Noticing the syntax you use goes along with what I talked about in the last chapter—that is, what syntax is, and why it is necessary. Vary the length and structure of your sentences. See how it feels and what it does for your style.

> **TOM'S TIPS**
>
> It's okay to admire a favorite writer's style, but you should do your best not to imitate it slavishly. What happens is that you start making yourself crazy trying to re-create what somebody else is already doing. A better strategy is to take a little time to analyze what it is in your model's style that you like so much. Figure out what the writer is doing, and *incorporate* it into your own style. That way you're doing what all writers do; they arrive at their own style by cherry-picking from all the writers they like. And it doesn't happen overnight. It's a gradual process, but it works.

Figure Out What's Distinctive

This takes time because you need to amass a body of writing—journal entries, short stories, poems, novel chapters, whatever—so you have enough material to analyze. Do you like one-sentence paragraphs like Hemingway used? Or are you given over to the more heavily constructed and densely populated passages of Faulkner? Do you like to use em dashes—like this? What about ellipses …? Or are you like John Irving using italics *excessively?*

Again, there's no right or wrong answer here. There are just different modes of expression, and finding out what works for you.

Use Interesting Verbs

Using interesting verbs is more challenging and important than you think. Many young writers have a dependency on the verb *to be*, and it's so automatic, they never think about it. They describe people, places, and situations in terms of *is* and *was:* "The urban traffic was heavy and dangerous."

A more interesting way to do it would be to use verbs with more power: "The traffic brawled through the city streets, threatening to assault him."

It's impossible to entirely avoid using *is* and *was* (and the rest of their variations), and you actually need them in many cases. But when you don't, remind yourself to not be lazy and to use verbs that have power and description on their own.

A Lot of 'Splainin' to Do

Another point of style is how much you trust your powers of narrative. Some new writers worry that their readers are not "getting" everything, so they get into a mode where they explain everything *too* much. They *over*explain and *over*describe something in a scene.

This tends to make your style stuffy and inaccessible.

Watch Your Similes and Metaphors

An interesting style can be full of imagery and sense impression without overdoing it. A good way to do that is mastering the techniques of simile and metaphor—and using them with discretion. A really good comparative phrase can resonate with the reader and bring home a powerful set of images that will be memorable. The key is to not do it so much it becomes tired and familiar.

Check Your Clichés at the Door

Eliminating clichés is something you do in the second draft. When you're writing in the heat of the moment, it's more vital to just *get something down*. Later on, you can switch on your cliché radar and look for blips.

Trite phrases signal lazy writing. It's important to remove them from your final drafts.

Write in Your Journal

As I've said previously, some writers are very fastidious and habitual about making journal entries—daily or on some kind of schedule. Others (like me) just never get around to doing it.

If you like to keep a journal, it's a good place to work on style because you can write with the unspoken assumption no one is going to be reading it but you. So you can be as free or as anal-retentive as you want. You can experiment.

Hunt Down Your Adverbs and Adjectives

Make a conscious effort to take note of how often you feel the need to drop modifiers into your sentences. Again, I'm not saying adverbs and adjectives don't have a place in your prose—they do. But I want to foster an *awareness* in you of how much or how little you're relying on these parts of speech.

I've seen story submissions in which *every* last noun in *every* sentence has at least one, sometimes more, adjectives in front of it. The writers of these manuscripts clearly don't realize what they're doing, and I don't want you to be one of them.

Understand Usage and Diction

Every so often, remind yourself to look at your sentences for things like the outright *misuse* of a word, or using a word that is *close* to what you really mean, but not as precise as it should be. Also, be careful not to let the *same* word show up in several sentences in a row … and definitely never in the *same* sentence.

For example, if you're describing a car chase, you'd better have an ample supply of words to carry the action other than *car, car,* and *car.* I may have used this example before, but that's okay—it's a good one. And it bears repeating.

Style Warnings

It's very common for writers to become obsessed about style, or more specifically *their* style. I've been to more than a few symposia and seminars (always within the halls of universities) where some guy who calls himself an "author," rather than a writer (which is *always* a bad sign), makes this proclamation to the masses: "If I can carefully craft at least one good sentence a day, I feel as if I've done a good day's work."

One good sentence.

Yeah, I've heard more than a few pompous people say nonsense like that. I don't know what they're thinking or trying to put over on their audiences. That writing is so hard, you should be *lucky* to write even one intelligible sentence a *day?* That style is so important and so hard to achieve it can actually take that long to write a sentence?

You can see where I'm going with this. You can become so self-conscious about what your style actually is that it becomes the primary *reason* you write. You sit down every day to evolve your style instead of telling a good story.

Friends, down that path lay madness. *And* pomposity, pretentiousness, and laughable turgidity. Don't go there.

And while I'm at it, here's a little heads-up when you're reading reviews of new books—especially the "contemporary" or "literary" novels. If you notice the reviewer throwing around phrases that extol the writer's "bold, stylistic explorations" or "exquisite narrative voice" or any other such flattery, which conveniently skirts the pesky issues of *plot* and *storytelling*, it's a great bet the novel is close to unreadable. Writers and critics who adhere to the idea that good writing is all style and little story don't get read much.

> **WORDS OF WISDOM**
>
> Every fine story must leave in the mind of the reader a quality of voice that is exclusively the writer's own.
>
> —Willa Cather

My advice is not to think so much about your style. Try to employ some of the exercises and techniques I talked about in this chapter, and things will automatically happen. Just be patient, keep writing, and your style will evolve on its own.

Finding Your Voice

Voice is sometimes confused with style. Although the two are definitely related, they enjoy subtle differences. Your style—once it develops and stabilizes—remains fairly constant, but your voice can vary from book to book or character to character. And that's okay. Sometimes it's necessary.

Reaching for the Tone Control

Voice is the way you speak on paper. It's all about the *tone* you employ. Are you being irreverent? Chastising? Inspirational? Atmospheric? Paranoid?

Do you see what I'm getting at here? Think of your writing voice as the one you would employ if you were *telling* the story aloud. If you were reading a children's book, you wouldn't use the same voice as when you were reading a ghost story. The books of Mickey Spillane convey his tough-guy voice; while the deceptively quiet voices of the narrators in the stories of M. R. James seem to make things more unsettling than reassuring.

Nothing Automatic

Also unlike style (which becomes more automatic and unconscious the longer you write), your voice becomes increasingly *more* under your control. You can alter your narrative voice at any time. There's no autopilot for your voice, and there shouldn't be.

Just as you select the right voice for the kind of story you're telling at the moment, you also want to apply the same decisions to the kind of characters you're bringing to life.

If you're writing a story in the first person, the voice you create can be very close to protagonist's dialogue—a little less colloquial, but essentially the same voice. When you write in the third person, you can choose a voice that fits the third-person narrator—whether it's over a character's shoulder or an omniscient voice of authority, it will be dictated by your story and characters.

The other major consideration for the best use of voice is the novel of multiple viewpoints. This kind of narration gives you a chance to experiment with voice and your range of control over it. The narrative voice of a child or a teenager should be different from that of a cop waiting to retire. If you have that kind of range in your characters, you'll be challenged (in a fun, interesting way) to make everybody sound as realistic and believable as possible.

WORDS OF WISDOM

In the long run, however you talk or even think about it, the most durable thing in writing is style, and style is the most valuable investment a writer can make with his time.

—Raymond Chandler

Finding Your Own Comfort Level

The most important thing to retain from this chapter about style is to *not* worry about yours. Every writer has a unique style, and you're no different. Whether or not yours is any good, or distinctive, or compelling is not for us to decide at this point.

Learning to get familiar with your own style takes time. The longer you write, the easier it will get. It's like that old saying about not being comfortable in your own skin—getting used to the way you express yourself is a gradual process that involves an increasing level of comfort and confidence.

Trust yourself and your abilities. They're not as good as they'll be tomorrow or next year, but that's the fun part about writing. The coolest part is that you just keep getting better; and your style is one of the best indicators of that process.

The Least You Need to Know

- Style is a reflection of who you are and how you interact with the world.
- Achieving an effective narrative voice is a constantly changing challenge that presents itself with every new character and story premise.
- Don't ever let style trump your need to tell a good story. Good novels have substance because they entertain us with memorable characters and engaging plots, rarely because they have only style.
- Be patient. A good, serviceable style requires mostly time to develop and mature.
- Your voice can vary from book to book, depending on the tone and the sense of character and mood you want to convey.

Time Management and Discipline

In This Chapter

- Time equals pages
- Analyzing your time and you
- Making a schedule that works
- Making the best of the worst

If you ask writers to name the most important writing skills to master, most of them will include *discipline* and *time management* way up there on the list. Thinking about writing is nice, but actually making the time to sit down and *do* it is a lot more crucial. You can have all the skills and tricks and sheer talent of any of us, but if you don't make time in your life to write, your novel is *not* going to happen.

The Secret of the Universe

Whenever I talk about writing at a school, a college, or even a convention of readers and fans, I ask the audience if they think they could write just *3* pages a day. I usually get a lot of cautious affirmatives, and even some indignant responses of "Of course I can!"

I smile, and I tell them I've just given them the Secret of the Universe. If you want to write novels, just *write those 3 pages a day*. Figure it out: 3 pages a day (and let's take off weekends for whatever else needs attention in your life) works out to 15 pages a week, and around 60 pages a month. In 6 months, you will have a 360-page manuscript. That's not a large novel, but it's not a small one, either.

When people hear this, they are amazed because they've probably never bothered to do the math. It inspires new writers and aspiring novelists because it reduces the task of creating all those pages into something that at least *seems* doable.

And I gotta tell ya: every time I finish a book, and finally print out all the pages at once and take a look at that *huge* stack of pages bigger than the phone books of most cities, I'm still amazed that anybody can write that much about anything. And hey, *I* did it!

But then, after I sit there for a few minutes, I get this great feeling of satisfaction and accomplishment. *Yeah*, I think, *I did that, and it feels good.* You can get that feeling, too, and believe me, there's nothing like it.

 WORDS OF WISDOM

When I start a book, I always think it's patently absurd that I can write one. No one, certainly not me, can write a book 500 pages long. But I know I can write 15 pages, and if I write 15 pages every day, eventually I will have 500 of them.

—John Saul

But there's an important corollary to that Secret of the Universe: you *have* to write those 3 pages every day. Or you have to write enough over a 5-day period to average 3 pages a day. That requires something all real writers have—discipline. It's the ability to *make yourself* do the writing. It's being so dedicated to a goal, you don't let anything get in your way of achieving it.

News flash: the only way you're going to make discipline a part of your life is by learning how to manage your time. But don't worry about it; in this chapter, I show you some ways to do it. No time like now, so let's get started.

Analyze Your Time and Yourself

Before you can get serious about discipline, you have to take a good, hard, honest look at the hours in your day and your week. If you're into charts and that kind of thing, then by all means, make one that gives you a picture of your life in terms of the hours and days and *who* wants a piece of you and *when*.

If you're like most people, you have some kind of job that takes up a considerable chunk of your time. That is obviously time you need to … ah, work around, as they say.

Answers please:

> Who are you and what do you do?

This is a question only you can answer, but I can speculate a bit, and maybe anticipate some of the scenarios that may apply to you and your situation.

Right up front, I'm going to tell you finding time to write is not just possible; it's easy. My experience, and from what I hear from other successful writers, tells me a major source of discipline comes from the desire to write. If you *want* to write, you *will*.

If you want to make excuses for not writing, you'll do that, too. But we don't need to dwell on that one. You probably know about that all too well.

Time is what it's all about. Your job is to *find the time* to do what you want in your life. It's there, but you might have to work hard to uncover it.

WORDS OF WISDOM

Don't say you don't have enough time. You have exactly the same number of hours as were given to Helen Keller, Pasteur, Michelangelo, Mother Teresa, Leonardo da Vinci, Thomas Jefferson, and Albert Einstein.

—H. Jackson Brown

Getting Jobbed

If you have a full-time job, no matter what you do, you have anywhere from 7 to 10 hours of your day already spoken for. I have a friend who drives in and out of Boston each week and spends *3 hours* every day doing that. It is essentially wasted time (if we can discount the vigilance and skill required to keep him from auto accidents and related mayhem).

If that describes you, you might want to think about using that time to dictate stories, journal entries, story plots, character profiles, scenes of dialogue, or even whole chapters. This may be awkward at first, but if you get a voice-activated digital dictation recorder, you can give it a shot and see how it feels.

I'm not sure it was true, but I can remember somebody telling me Ellery Queen (actually two people—Fredric Dannay and Manfred B. Lee) never wrote a word. He (they) dictated everything, gave it to a secretary, then went over it with a red pencil, before giving it back to her for another run through the typewriter. So it might work for you, too. It sure beats just sitting there staring at the license plate of that car in front of you.

Writing for Your Supper

If your job requires you to do a lot of writing each day, that could have a definite effect on the amount of writing you get done when you're *not* at work. If you write for a newspaper, advertising or government agency, a law firm, or even an insurance company, you might be burned out by the time you get home. The *last* thing you feel like doing is *more* writing … and that's lethal.

The worst situation is having a job in which the writing you do at work is *competing* with the writing you want to do on your own. That can be discouraging and depressing and may eventually force you to make a very serious decision. And I'm talking about a life-changing one, like quit the job or quit writing.

I think I said in an earlier chapter how important it is to have a job that *keeps* you from writing. I repeat this point because it also relates to time management and discipline. If you're doing something all day that has *nothing* to do with writing, all the better. Psychologically, you're pumped to get home and get a few words down.

Being a Creature of Habit

How are you on deadlines? Repetitive tasks? Routines?

Do you keep your lawn maintained on a regular basis? Change the oil in your car when you're supposed to? Call your mother, your kids, your friends timely enough for them not to wonder if you stumbled into some fissure in the earth?

What does your basement look like? Your garage, or your workbench? Do you like to hang things on pegboard? How do you feel about filing cabinets? A lot of writers I know feel very comfortable walking around in office supply stores; do you?

Your answers to these questions will give you some insight on the kind of personality you have and just how easy or tough it is for you to stay organized enough to create a writing schedule and stick to it. And I don't mean you have to be some obsessive-compulsive automaton or a loony neat-nik, either. My desk and office get progressively cluttered and full of paper the deeper I get into a project. Anyone who walks in will think a tornado takes a regular spin through the place—and it does, the tornado of mutant thoughts in my head all day long.

But don't think I'm not organized, because I am. I know what each flung paper is and why I'm keeping it around. When I finish the story, article, column, book, script, or whatever, I pick up everything, file it or toss it, neaten up the office, and move on to the next project.

Okay, enough about me. The previous points should get you thinking about the way you work and the work habits you'll need to cultivate or change to fit the writing regimen you need to create. We all have good habits and bad ones. You need to make *writing something* (good or bad) a part of your day. You need to make it a necessary habit (like brushing your teeth) you'll feel bad about shirking.

WORDS OF WISDOM

There is no perfect time to write. There is only now.

—Barbara Kingsolver

Schedules

Everybody is different, and everybody has a load of different parameters running through their lives. So it's not that important *what* your schedule actually is ... only that you have one.

I can't spend a lot of time on this because a schedule is a personal thing. For instance, unless I have a very pressing deadline, I practically never write on weekends, which are reserved for family stuff, but some writers (who have so little time during the week) use their weekends to do all their writing each week.

The other thing about making and keeping to a schedule is that you shouldn't carve it into a stone tablet. Take it for a given that some days things just aren't going to work out and you're going to miss the hours and pages you planned.

Don't let it bug you. Forget it, and move on to the next day. And don't try to make up the page tomorrow. You'll make yourself nuts if you try to crank out *double* the amount you decided was feasible in the first place. Never look back, only ahead.

Some writers keep one of those erasable plastic schedule-makers on their wall next to the desk. They write in what they need to do for a week or two in advance, look at it each day, and check off how well or poorly they're doing. If it works for you, keep doing it. But watch it. Some of the wall-chart people I know get carried away with it and start figuring out ways to run statistical analysis on their productivity with time-motion studies and percentage pie-charts and a bunch of other stuff that becomes the reason for its own existence and ends up stealing away writing time—or worse, becomes an excuse *not* to write.

My best advice is to keep experimenting with your schedule until you find one that …

- Is realistic in terms of pages per day. Three pages is doable for most people. Fifteen is not.

- Doesn't conflict with the needs and schedules of others in your life—such as bosses, spouses, kids, friends, etc.

- Is flexible enough to absorb the unexpected changes it will endure.

The important thing about your writing schedule is it *feels right* to you. It should work well enough for you to feel good about sticking to it, and the results you get. A bad schedule is one you look at like a jail sentence of any required repetitive task you don't like doing (one of mine is mowing a lawn—man, I *hate* that!).

WORDS OF WISDOM

A good plan today is better than a perfect plan tomorrow.

—George S. Patton

Just remember: the longer you do something, the more likely it will become ingrained and easier to do the next time. Kind of like the muscle-memory thing with a golf swing. It takes a while to kick in, but when it does, you stop thinking about it so much, and just do it.

The Rules of the Game

Now to make your schedule easier to maintain, I'm going to lay out a few tips, which are actually rules. Not titanium-clad, but still, you better pay attention.

Avoid Distractions

This is very crucial. Don't set yourself up to be interrupted. So tell yourself—and mean it—you're not going to answer the door or the phone. If you don't have an answering machine, get one. At the least, get caller ID so you can answer the phone if it's urgent or an emergency.

If you are a computer person, don't schedule your time on the Internet and e-mail as the same time for your writing. The Internet is great and so is e-mail, but they can be huge time sinks for writers. Peter Straub once told me he added the amount of e-mail he wrote over an average 6-month period, and he said the wordage equaled a small novel(!), which made him think twice about responding so dutifully to all his correspondents.

Make a general announcement to the rest of the family or roommates that you *cannot* be interrupted when you're writing. At first, nobody will take you seriously, but if you establish up front that repeated distractions will make you very cranky, you will get the respect you need. Be insistent. Nobody will take it seriously unless you do.

Lastly, if something is distracting you on a consistent basis and messing with your output, you need to isolate it and *remove* it from your writing environment. Don't ignore the problem. It's only going to make things worse.

Hide the Remote

One of the worst time-eaters in our lives is the television. True, it has been a fantastic invention, but I don't think I'm being hyperbolic when I say that even with 200+ channels of all-digital cable TV, there are many occasions when there isn't a thing worth watching.

In other words, stop watching so much TV. If you add the number of hours you watch in a week, you'll get depressed because it's time you can't get back—time you could have spent writing.

Tell yourself you're not one of the watchers; you're one of the creators. You are one of the people who *create* the stories the herd of "sheeple" want to watch.

Write Fast

Years ago, when I was still in graduate school, the only time I had to write was late at night—between 10 P.M. and midnight. The lateness didn't really bother me. I was younger, and it wasn't that big a deal to subsist on 4 or 5 hours' sleep just about every night. What *did* present a problem was the lack of continuous hours in which to write.

I remember one evening I had gone over to the University of Maryland campus to listen to a friend of mine, the late Roger Zelazny, who was scheduled to do a reading to the college science fiction society. He was an established writer, and he did this sort of thing a lot. Afterward, we went out for coffee and talked writing. I guess I'd been complaining because I recall Roger telling me his solution to short windows of opportunity: faster writing.

At first, I figured he was kidding around, but he shook his head. He meant it. He said it was all in the way you looked at it, and the best way was to pretend you were giving yourself an "essay exam" like the ones in college. You remember them—you had 45 minutes to fill as many "bluebooks" as possible and, therefore, convince your professor you were brimming over with information and knowledge. And that's the point. I know it sounds silly, but write *faster*. (And yeah, I can hear some of you yelling and screaming, but I already told you how I feel about the "one good sentence" phonies, right?)

If you can teach yourself to write as fast as possible, the results will be obvious— you'll have more material to work with. And with computers playing so heavily in writer's lives these days, the idea of typing so fast your manuscript gets full of mistakes is not so terrible. (But don't forget: Roger was telling me this *before* the computer age. So he wasn't being glib about not worrying about how easy it would be to fix typos.)

TOM'S TIPS

The value in writing fast is you end up getting *something* on paper. I'm tempted to say get *anything* on paper because the biggest stack of bad writing is infinitely better than *no* writing.

Okay, bear with me for a second here, while I wax metaphorical—by using sculpture as an example. If you're trying to create a statue, and you have to mix your materials from scratch, the idea would be to get the clay, or mud, or plaster (or whatever your *glop* might be ...) into some kind of recognizable shape as quickly as you can. Then you can take a more leisurely time shaping and sculpting your basic form. The idea is to achieve an elementary shape that can be tweaked and fine-tuned later.

Space Versus Time

Finding a *space* where you can do your writing is a major factor of time management. Ideally, you can sequester yourself in a spare bedroom, a "sewing" room, a den, or even a little cubicle in the basement. If you have to invent a new space in the attic or over the garage, well, maybe you better grab your toolbox and your measuring tape.

Having a special writing space set aside can have a great impact on the amount of real writing you get done. If you have a desk where you can spread out your papers, your reference materials, notebooks, files, etc., and leave them there all the time, you have just gained many writing hours over the course of a year. Think about it. If you're forced to write in a space where you must *set up* each time you want to write, you waste time doing that.

Keep Out!

One of the other things you want in your writing space is a door to keep yourself in and everybody else out. There's nothing worse than getting interrupted repeatedly when you only have limited amounts of time at your disposal. And if the door has a lock on it, even better.

WORDS OF WISDOM

People on the outside think there's something magical about writing, that you go up into the attic at midnight and cast the bones and come down in the morning with a story, but it isn't like that. You sit in front of the typewriter and you work, that's all there is to it.

—Harlan Ellison

If your space has a phone in it, unplug it. Leave it out in the hall. The worst habit to get into, when you're locked away, is to let the world in *with* you when you're supposed to be letting *out* the world inside you. Same goes for a window—you don't need one. But if you have one, be sure you have curtains, or that it looks out on something essentially bland and not very distracting. A brick wall would be great.

And lastly, if you don't have a spare room, a basement, or garage loft, set up and start typing in the bedroom or at the kitchen table. Plenty of great books have been written in both locations. Remember when I told you I used to write on the dining room table in my graduate school apartment? I wrote maybe 20 short stories with that setup. Then I moved to this really tiny townhouse and my desk was in the living room—a space that held my big, ugly IBM Selectric on a desk ... but no television. I wrote a couple novels in that wide-open, high-traffic area.

If you have a laptop computer, you can write no matter where you go. In the car on long trips (when you're not the driver), in planes and airports, and even doctors' and dentists' offices. In fact, I'm sitting at my Mercedes dealership as I write this sentence, waiting for my 120,000-mile check-up to be finished. (Everybody else in here with me is sitting around with kind of slack expressions on their faces. But me, hey, I'm being my usual creative self.)

The point is clear: you find whatever space you can, and you put it to the best use you can.

Final Considerations

Okay, everything I've been talking about is all well and good, but what do you do if none of it's working?

In other words, your job and your commitments to family friends, organizations, etc., are so great (at least for the present) that there's no way you can write 3 pages a day. No way you can even write anything *every* day. You've looked at things realistically, and you don't see a regular schedule—the schedule needed to produce a novel— available until some wholesale changes can be made or planned that will take some time into the future (like a new baby gets older, you or your spouse find a different job, you get a new roommate, a change occurs in your relationship with spouse or otherwise special person, etc.).

So what do you do? A couple things.

Start writing other kinds of things. If all you have time for is a journal entry, do it. Even if you hate poetry, try your hand at it. Or write a quick essay in which you express an opinion about something that really upsets you (they're the easiest ones to do). Try your hand at short stories. The idea is to take on projects that you know you can complete within the parameters of your daily routine.

Keep the novel as your primary project. Write scenes, character sketches and biographies, plot outlines, and other parts of the process that are short enough to be adapted to your fractured, or nonexistent, schedule.

 WORDS OF WISDOM

Being a writer is like having homework for the rest of your life.

—Lawrence Kasdan

Don't give up. No matter how hard it is for you to find time and maintain discipline, tell yourself you're not giving up—*ever.* That's why selecting projects with finite, close-at-hand end-points is so important. If you can create a psychological atmosphere in which the time you do spend results in some *finished* projects, you'll be in better shape to persevere.

The Least You Need to Know

- Time management and discipline are two of the most important skills a writer can develop. If you don't spend the time writing, nothing gets done.
- You will be able to create a realistic, workable writing schedule only after making a realistic assessment of your habits, personality traits, obligations, and daily routine.
- Train yourself to be disciplined and follow your schedule. Many other parts of your life will want to intrude on your writing. Do whatever it takes to shut them down.
- Don't be discouraged. Writing takes time. Your time. Whatever time you can invest will be rewarded.

Another Name for Writing Is *Rewriting*

Chapter 15

In This Chapter

- When your first draft is done
- General revision tactics
- More specific revisions
- Proofing the galleys and beyond

Okay, you've just typed the final page of your novel. Just for good measure, you type "The End" after the last line. You know you've accomplished something only an infinitesimal percentage of the country's population could even *think about*, much less do.

It feels great, so take a few minutes to radiate some of that home-cooked self-satisfaction before you have to get ready for the next stage of the writing process: revising your first draft. In this chapter, I show you the most efficient and painless way to do it.

Creating the Second Draft

A lot of writers and most editors will tell you that *rewriting* your novel is way more important than getting it down in the first place. I'm not so sure about that. Getting the vision and the energy and the discipline all working together to create a first draft of 300 or 400 pages is pretty important to me. Most people dream about it but never make it happen. But getting through a second draft is still essential.

Rewriting may not be fun, but I think it's easier than the initial creation of your book, especially after you read this chapter and learn what to look for and how to do it with skill and confidence.

This is probably no news flash, but revisions and rewriting are a *whole lot* easier since we all started writing on computers. I bought my first computer in 1982, and even though the earliest word-processing programs were crude and clumsy, I knew my writing life had become a lot less burdensome thanks to that machine. I can remember critics of personal computers claiming the computers would make writers lazy and "too plentiful" (because it was "supposedly" easier, more clowns would start writing). And to this day, I have a couple writer friends who claim to hate computers and, despite being called Luddites, *continue* to write on typewriters.

I think all those early fears and suspicions proved to be exaggerated. There's no doubt the computer made me a far better writer. How? Because it changed the way I did revisions.

A Little History Lesson

I wrote my first *eight* novels on electric typewriters—a cheesy Smith-Corona, and later, a big IBM Selectric dreadnaught. As I look back, through the distorted lens of the Computer Age, I have no idea how I did it. Mainly because I'm not, and never was, a touch-typist. I taught myself how to type when I was 12, and evolved a fairly efficient three-fingers/two-fingers system I still employ today for a decent 60 words per minute. Sure, I have to look at the keys, with an occasional look at the screen to ensure I'm not making too many mistakes. But this is a perfectly fine method for a writer like me who writes by the seat of his pants—right out of my head, first draft on-the-fly.

The problem, especially back in the Typewriter Era, arose when I had to revise my first draft, rewrite it, and of necessity *retype* it.

I was in very deep brown matter because I had to read the revised page, read it *again* as I re-created it on the keyboard, and read it a *third* time on the paper. Friends, the word *painful* doesn't begin to describe the process. It was absurdly slow and only a little more enjoyable than working a chain gang.

 A LIKELY STORY

A man is unjustly arrested and convicted of a capital crime in a state where chain gangs have been reinstated as a form of punishment. He is serving his sentence on the road and escapes. Write a story about his time on the run in which he attempts to prove his innocence.

You see where this is going—I didn't despise editing, revising, and rewriting my stories and novel, but I hated all the retyping.

But the distinction didn't matter. Because the whole process was so hard and so time-consuming, I did as little as I could get away with. My stories and novels suffered because I simply didn't have an extra 6 months every year to spend retyping everything.

After a couple mediocre paperback novels, I realized I was going to have to change the way I worked. When I finished the first draft of my next novel, I went through it with a heavy editing pen—cutting, slashing, re-structuring everything that fell beneath my baleful gaze. *Ruthless* is a good word to describe the way I worked on that first draft. It felt good to be really doing an exhaustive set of revisions (especially because I *knew* I'd never done it before).

The reason I'd become so effusive in my revisions was simple: I'd hired a lady in the neighborhood to *retype* my manuscript with all my changes scrawled all over it. Back then, cut-and-paste had a far more literal meaning, and I gave the poor woman tons of pages that looked like they'd been part of a Ginsu knife commercial. Hey, what'd I care? *I* didn't have to retype it.

Okay, so what's the point of all this ancient history? Two things:

- When I knew I didn't have to waste time retyping my entire manuscript, I was much more willing to be a merciless rewriter of my material.

- I was very much aware of the need and value of revising and rewriting my work.

TOM'S TIPS

Don't forget—revising and rewriting has its own learning curve, and you're going to be teaching yourself a process of *how* to do it. You will be figuring out what works for you and what doesn't. It's subjective and full of ego. Even though ego is one of the things you don't need at this point, it's part of the process. Roll with it.

Which brings us back to *now*, and your obligation to revise and rewrite your novel. My little anecdote is nothing but a preamble to embarrass you into realizing how absurdly *easy* it is to perform major surgery on your manuscript in these "modern times." If you wrote your novel on a computer, you have no excuse for not going through it like a Panzer division through France. You save your original draft and then start hacking and chopping and re-arranging things.

What we're going to do next is look at some general techniques to get you into a good revision mode. Then we'll move into more specific things you should be looking for, and maybe even a few tricks along the way.

Finally, accept that there will be stuff in your manuscript you'll be totally *blind* to. Stuff so wrong, yet so invisible to you, you're going to feel stupid when somebody else points it out to you. Again, this is all part of a great universal process all writers endure. If you're in this for the long haul, get used to it.

Getting Started

Keeping in mind there's much to this whole process dependent on personal taste, I think if we start off with a few universal points of revisions and rewriting, you'll be off on the right track no matter what.

WORDS OF WISDOM

Books aren't written, they're rewritten. Including your own. It is one of the hardest things to accept, especially after the seventh rewrite hasn't quite done it.

—Michael Crichton

Take a Break

After you finish the novel, don't even *think* about starting to revise it right away. I don't care how great you think it is, or how fast you want to get it into a slush pile reader's grubby hands.

The first thing to do after typing "The End" is print it out in double- or triple-space, pack it neatly in one of those boxes I told you about, then *put it away*. For at *least* a couple weeks. You need to put some distance between you and the book, mainly because you've been so close to it, you can't possibly have much objectivity working for you.

Time away from your novel will give you some perspective you just don't have when you're hip-deep in the actual writing. Use the time to try something new. Write a short story or two, or a few outlines for a *new* novel, or maybe some journal entries.

It doesn't matter what you write as long as you write something. You don't want to treat your novel and your writing as something from which you need a "vacation," like grown-up people's jobs. If writing is really a vital part of your life, be sure you cultivate that reality.

Sit Down and Read

Okay, it's a few weeks later, and it's time to get out your novel and start the process of making it better. The best way to get reacquainted with your work is to sit back in a comfortable chair and do something you couldn't do while you were writing it—read it straight through the way you would any other book.

You shouldn't plan on much editing on this first read-through. I don't recommend you do *any* (unless you find something so egregiously bad you can't bear the thought of ever reading it again, and you just have to strike it out of existence). What you're looking for at this early stage is a general feeling of how the narrative flows.

Shopping Lists and Red Pens

Write down a list of the things that jumped out at you during the initial read-through— the good stuff and the bad stuff. Remind yourself that you've just skimmed across the surface; there's plenty you missed for one reason or another, and there's no sense worrying about it. Just believe all the missteps will be caught sooner or later. Trust me. You'll sleep better that way.

Write down whatever leaps out during this first run through the narrative, and mark the page number. Mark missing transitions, thin characterization, wooden dialogue, too much description (or not enough), and anything else apparent at this stage. A good test for whether a questionable passage works or is smoothly written is to use the old reading-it-aloud trick. Do this as often as necessary.

After this, you're ready for the next step, which is to reach for the red pen or, as they used to call it, the "blue pencil." (I have no idea why …) Oh, and did I tell you? Put the manuscript away again. But just for a few days this time, while you build up enough steam for the next big push through the manuscript.

It's Clobberin' Time!

If you were a comic book reader, you may recall the member of *The Fantastic Four* known simply as "The Thing" saying this when the time for action arrived. And so it is with your manuscript—time to whack it around a bit and then flense all the blubber from its sorry carcass.

On this second read-through, keep your pen in hand and use it *frequently* to make margin notes, write questions, circle questionable passages, make x-outs, enter line and word replacements, fix strange spellings, and all the rest of the things you'll need to signal yourself to adjust, revise, or remove.

Exactly what you'll be looking for and how you'll suggest changes will be examined in closer detail in the next section. But before we get into that, it's time to discuss the possibility of another reader, besides yourself, sharing in the revision process.

WORDS OF WISDOM

It's perfectly okay to write garbage—as long as you edit brilliantly.

—C. J. Cherryh

A Second Opinion

This is one of those things every writer needs, and some are actually fortunate enough to have. After you've read your book all the way through for the first time, you'll have a better idea of what it would be like for a reader coming to it cold. But not the *best* idea. There's no substitute for getting someone, especially someone who's never encountered a whisper of it previously, to read it.

So who is this person? Well, for me, it's my wife, Elizabeth, who works as an editor and is my harshest critic. She doesn't worry about hurting my feelings and goes after my writing with steel-eyed objectivity. I love it, and I trust her judgment because she has been a reader all her life, has edited anthologies, loves books in general, and is just about the most perceptive person I've ever known.

You can't use Elizabeth, so you need to find a reader who can do the job. Ideally, this person should be a voracious reader (preferably of the type of novels you write, to have a valid point of reference and comparison), and he or she should also be as bright and perceptive as possible. But the most important qualification this reader must possess is *honesty*. Your reader must be willing to be brutal in telling you what is wrong with your novel and what needs fixing. You don't want to hear "It's nice." You want to hear the *truth*.

Now only you will be able to tell if you have a potential second reader. But if you do, don't hesitate to use that person. You're looking for a valid appraisal of your novel; as if someone walked into a bookstore, pulled it off the shelf, and started reading it.

The Devil's in the Details

Detail is just another word for getting specific. This is where I talk about just exactly *what* you're going to be looking for when you pick up your red pen. Revising your novel is actually a conglomerate process that involves close reading, editing, critiquing, and rewriting. It's a process you need to learn, and you have to teach it to yourself. It's not hard, but it can be tedious if your heart's not in it.

A good point to remember is that revision is closely related to style and syntax, which I covered earlier. When you write a first draft, and you have so many balls juggling in the air, the things you notice the least can often be spelling, usage, grammar, and punctuation. The time to focus on those issues (and some other important stuff) is now.

So grab that list you made during the initial read-through, and get going.

The Good Ol' Spellchecker

If you wrote your novel on a computer, you've got software to check your spelling and grammar. I usually run mine when I finish the first draft of a chapter, but if you haven't done it yet, do it now.

But don't trust it!

I mentioned this before, and I meant it: spellcheckers are not fool-proof. My experience with the grammar checkers has also been hit-or-miss, and I'm not sure they've become sophisticated enough to catch enough to make me believe in them. I still think you should run both the spelling and grammar checkers, but with the understanding they *need* to be followed up by good ol' human intervention.

Especially watch for the homonyms—those words that sound alike but are spelled differently (for example, *here/hear, they're/there, your/you're, its/it's*). Sometimes, when I'm typing really fast, I go into brainlock and key in the wrong one. Maybe you do, too.

Sentence Structure

Teach yourself to study the "picture" of your pages, which is just looking at the whole page as a collection of arranged words. Are there lots of long, convoluted ones? Hmmm, might be a warning flag for run-on sentences. Are there too many short, declarative ones? That should tell you to watch out for that sing-song cadence you want to avoid. Also check for variety, not just in length, but in construction and use of dependent clauses. A nonuniformity is what you want here. It keeps your narrative fresh and interesting on an unconscious level.

Be hard on yourself. If a sentence isn't saying exactly what you mean, circle it, and put a note or a question mark in the margin.

And this is important, so I'll mention it right at the beginning of this section: *don't try to rewrite every error or mistake as you find them.* Just identify them with the red pen and *move on.* The actual rewriting happens later, and I'll talk about it soon enough. Be patient.

Intros and Outros

Pay close attention to the way each chapter opens and closes. Especially the first chapter. Make believe you're browsing in a bookstore and you read the very first paragraph of your novel. Did you get yanked in? Was there something there to compel you to keep reading without pausing to decide if you *should?* If the opening didn't work, mark it for big changes or maybe even a total excision.

It's crucial that you pull your reader into each chapter and, when you wrap it up, leave them in suspense, wanting more, wanting answers. In talking with many writers over the years, I've probably heard it said more often than anything else—during the revisions of their own books, many writers were surprised how often the openings and closings needed revision. Do yours?

Diction

Another thing to watch out for is your diction—your choice of a word to pin down exactly what you mean. Don't write *dais* when you mean *lectern*, or *boycott* when you mean *embargo*. Employing good diction is the difference between writing that's as clear as a mountain lake and writing that's … let's say a bit murky. Your reader will put up with a few instances of a loss of clarity, but an entire book of what is essentially sloppy writing is just not going to make you a lot of new friends.

WORDS OF WISDOM

The difference between the right word and the almost right word is the difference between lightning and a lightning *bug.*

—Mark Twain

Also, watch out for too many "big" words. It's a common misconception that having a good vocabulary means throwing around as many multi-syllabic words as possible. Not true. It means knowing lots of words and knowing when to use them. Once in a while, an unusual and striking word can be powerful. Used too often, they become ponderous and ostentatious. Like I said in a previous chapter: eschew obfuscation.

Colloquialisms

This one is a bit tricky. Slang and *colloquial* expressions are fine in your dialogue, and even in a first-person narration, if they fit the personality of your protagonist. But you have to watch it in your general, third-person narrative voice. It's more a question of tone and familiarity than anything else.

> **TRADE TALK**
>
> **Colloquial** means being conversational. It suggests an informal way of communicating—the way people really talk to one another, rather than in some formal or idealized way. This book, in case you hadn't noticed, is colloquial because I intended it to be an easy read and, therefore, accessible.

If you want to establish that kind of informal relationship with your readers, that's acceptable, but you have to maintain it throughout your novel. I'm not saying you can never use a colloquial style; just be consistent. You're either going to employ it throughout the book, or not at all.

Repeating Words

Another common error ripe for revision is the overuse of the same words. The most obvious errors occur within the same sentences. For example, when you're describing a car chase, you use the word *car* over and over instead of dropping in an occasional *auto*, *vehicle*, or even a specific name or model.

Variety is what keeps narrative fresh. Over-reliance on the same basic set of words will show up big time in a novel-length manuscript. Be on the lookout.

Transitions and Agreements

Transitions and agreement problems can be subtle and more easily overlooked.

But *you* can't miss them. You must look for them. Basically you need to do a quick check to see that singular nouns are hooking up with singular verbs ("Johnny sings well" not "Johnny sing well"); plurals with plurals, and other things like that. Be sure phrases and clauses refer to proper nouns or pronouns ("The cop, who fired his weapon, shot him" not "The cop shot him who fired his weapon"), and other issues of tense consistency. Readers may not catch errors like this, but they will unconsciously know *something's* not right, and that will distract them from your story. Not good.

Transitions are even more subjective. You have to check the ways you move from scene to scene and character to character. Look for instances where transitions are abrupt, clumsy, or even *absent*. The best transitions are the ones you don't even notice, so that should make your task a little easier. Only the bad ones are going to be evident.

Punctuation

Although very basic, you should make certain all your dialogue is punctuated properly, with everything in and out of the quotation marks where they should be. Another thing to watch is how you use commas and indicate possession with apostrophes.

If you need a refresher, turn back to Chapter 12, where I get more specific about this.

Other Stuff

Here are some additional things to look for:

- Character disagreement, which happens when a writer types in the wrong character's name (no big deal, just a little more of that brainlock that happens to everybody)

- Mistaken geographic data (such as directions, north/south/east/west stuff, landmarks, highways, etc.)

- The spelling of foreign words and places, plus the proper placement and direction of accent marks

Is It Getting Drafty in Here?

Okay, so now you've gone through the manuscript twice, and if your second reader marked up his or her copy, you'll have a fairly extensive catalog of things that may need alteration or removal.

The easiest way to do it from here is to sit down at a desk with plenty of clear space, with both manuscripts side by side. Designate one of them as the master copy, and incorporate all emendations from the other one into it. That way, you have one set of suggested revisions.

Now it's time to put on the work gloves and do some heavy lifting.

Rewriting for Real

This is where you'll be glad the computer was invented.

The first thing to do is create a new subdirectory or folder called "Revised Novel" and date it. This is where you're going to save each chapter after you've rewritten it. That way, you'll still have your original first draft, and a new, revised, second draft. You may need them later.

It's also a good idea to make backup copies of your novel. Store them on flash drives, upload them to a remote server or your website, or burn them to a CD. Then put the copies in a very safe place like a friend's house or a safe-deposit box at your bank. If anything happens to your house or your computer, you still have copies of something that cannot be replaced by an insurance policy.

I always carry a flash drive in my pocket that holds all my works in progress. If my house catches fire, I'm safe. The only problem with this plan is if *I* catch on fire ….

Next, take all your notes and your master revision copy, and go through each page on paper and your screen simultaneously. Be thorough, and don't try to rush the process. Consider this stage where you input your changes as a kind of third draft because you get to reevaluate the changes you red-penciled before you type them in.

WORDS OF WISDOM

The beautiful part of writing is that you don't have to get it right the first time, unlike, say, a brain surgeon. You can always do it better, find the exact word, the apt phrase, the leaping simile.

—Robert Cormier

What ...? *Again?*

By this time, you should feel very familiar with your novel and all its components, and that will naturally make you feel better about any editorial changes you plug in. The nice thing about doing all this revising and rewriting is that you're not carving this all into granite. You can always go back and restore a prior version or revise it even more. You don't have to get it right the first time as long as you do eventually.

Also, don't worry about the time required to get the revisions completed. Whatever it takes is fine. It's far more important that you feel *good* about whatever you revised.

One more thing: if, by chance, you wrote your novel in longhand, or on a typewriter, you have the same choice I used to have: hope you have lots of spare time on your hands as you retype hundreds of pages (and keep a bottle of Wite-Out handy for all the mistakes), or hire someone to type your final draft (with the favored odds being on your typist to save your manuscript on a computer).

Copyediting and Proofing Galleys

Okay, we're just about finished with this topic, but I want to leave you with a few words about reading a copyedited manuscript and galley proofs.

Let's assume you sent in the final draft of your novel and an editor buys it. Your editor may have suggestions for additional changes. If that happens, you will most likely make any and *all* of them (because, if you're like most of us, you would trade your mother for a first novel sale). That means more revising and rewriting. So what? This is not the time to complain.

Then after the editor's revisions are accepted, your manuscript is going to get *another* heavy-duty working over by the publisher's copyeditor. Eventually, you'll get your manuscript back with the copyeditor's remarks, questions, and suggested changes all over it.

The copyeditor will most likely use a panoply of odd little marks and squiggles called proofreaders' marks—a kind of shorthand for editors and typesetters. It will be a good idea for you to familiarize yourself with them. To take a look at some proofreading marks, visit www.utexas.edu/visualguidelines/proofreaders.html.

However, this time-honored practice is also changing. Lots of editors now send back your pages in a digital file with their edits/changes/suggestions plugged in through a "track changes" or "edit" mode. It's the future, and it's already here.

Bottom line: regardless of *how* you get your novel copyedited, it means you're going to have to go through the revision/rewriting process *one final time*. Bear in mind you aren't as duty-bound to accept all your copyeditor's suggested changes, but they do deserve your careful consideration.

The next time you see your manuscript, it will be in the form of publisher's *galleys* or *galley proofs*. A galley is a storage tray of wood or sheet of steel printers use. These hold typeset pages that will be put on the presses for final printing.

> **TRADE TALK**
>
> A **galley proof** is a copy of the page as it will look in your book. The copy was traditionally on cheesy paper (such as newsprint), and was not designed to last longer than it took for you to check it out for any errors that happened during typesetting. Now that photocopying and laser printing are more economical, the paper is usually better. Typical errors are missing pages, broken lines and paragraphs, nonitalicized words, and things like that.

There's only one problem with getting galleys. By this time, you've been over your novel so many times, you may very well be *sick* of it, even if its deathless prose matches up nicely with Shakespeare and Dostoyevsky. From my own experience, it is very tough to catch errors in galleys because you are so darned familiar with what the copy is *supposed* to say.

My advice: get your second reader or some other trusted person like an English teacher or professor to proof the galleys. Odds are very high they'll do a better job than you at this point.

And that's the last of the revisions. The only thing left for you to do now is wait for your copy of the first edition.

The Least You Need to Know

- Don't be afraid of the revision process. It's easier now with computers, and it invariably makes your novel better.
- Get a second reader if at all possible. The additional objective perspective is invaluable in the revision stage.
- Back up everything you do. Then be as thorough and ruthless as you want. Read questionable passages aloud—you'll be amazed what a different "take" on the material you get.
- Consider the revision and rewriting process as a learning experience. This is when you teach yourself to be critical of your own work, to edit your writing, and to become a better writer. Be confident that you can always revise and rewrite as many times as necessary.

Revisions and Beyond

We're making the final turn, friends. Now that you have a good understanding of everything that comprises the actual writing of your novel, we need to look at what happens after you type "The End."

First, we make a brief examination into some New! Different! Innovative! publishing alternatives. Then we review what you've learned by pointing out common mistakes you *won't* be making. Then we take a brief survey of other sources that may improve your skills. After that, we investigate ways in which you can assume some control over how your book is presented to the public and how it's sold. As we head into the final turn, you get a quick course in the business side of what you want to do, as well as a summary of introductions to the kind of people you're going to meet as you blaze your trail across the landscape of publishing.

Alternative Publishing

In This Chapter

- The history of alternative publishing
- New publishing pathways
- The power to be *you*
- Publishing on the fringe

As we shamble forward ever farther into the twenty-first century, we have taken big bites from the digital (no pun intended) and woven the computer, in all its various shapes and sizes, into the deepest fabrics of our lives—desktop, laptop, PDA, cell phone, MP3, CD, DVD, and whatever I've either forgotten to mention or has already become obsolete.

As far as writers and publishers are concerned, things started to get really interesting in the early 1980s with the sudden (and outrageously expensive) availability of personal computers on which we could write our novels. It was a strange and magical time, and it literally changed the way writers write. But back then, few of us ever imagined that it would also be changing the way we *read* and the way we *publish*.

Although the concept is older than the last decade, the idea and practice of electronic publishing, or e-publishing, didn't get much traction until around the start of the new millennium. As I look back at its earliest mentions and appearances, I guess I should have recognized it for the potential world-changer it may actually be.

But I didn't. I kinda smiled patronizingly and regarded e-publishing as the red-headed stepchild of the computer age. I thought the idea was new and quirky but ultimately about as useful as an 8-track tape.

And for a while there, I was pretty much correct.

But as we enter the second decade of this new century, I'm beginning to realize I was probably being a dope and an old fart when it came to e-publishing. And so, in this chapter, I want to do a quick and dirty overview of some of the nontraditional pathways new writers can travel in their quest to get published. I'm tempted to hang a sign over the off-ramp to these new territories with that old reminder that "Here There Be Dragons," but I'm going to resist the urge. I have a feeling I might be wrong.

Defining the Moment

E-publishing is, in essence, the publication of material without physically *printing* it—that is, without putting little black squigglies of ink on paper. No pamphlets, magazines, or books of any kind need apply.

> **TRADE TALK**
>
> **E-publishing** is basically an umbrella term used to cover any type of nonpaper publication such as CD-ROM, DVD, PDF files, or any other digital format.

In place of these time-honored vessels of The Word, what we write can be placed online at a website, digitized on a CD or a flash drive, or displayed on a computer screen or a smaller electronic e-book reader.

Although I had been aware of e-publishing more than 10 years ago, I hadn't paid much attention to it until I began reading submissions for *Borderlands*, an anthology series of imaginative fiction I edit with my wife, Elizabeth. We received lots of unsolicited stories from newer writers, and a lot of them were listing publication credits in magazines we'd never heard of nor seen on any newsstands. And quite a few of these new writers were listing credentials that seemed hard to believe—such as *150 short stories* published in a seemingly endless venue of publications.

Frankly, I found this hard to believe. I mean, I've published around a 100 short stories, but it has taken me 3 decades to do it—partially because they're hard to write, and also because there just aren't that many markets for them. So how were these (presumably) new, young writers doing it? So many stories ... so many publishers?

The answer was simple—their stories weren't in print; they were appearing in that weird, other-worldly dimension called cyberspace. These people were getting "published" online, and their words were showing up on websites calling themselves "online magazines."

Once I discovered this, I began exploring some of the venues listed among the credits of many would-be contributors to our anthology series. A lot of what I expected turned out to be true.

That is, many of the "magazines" were simply web pages thrown up by amateurs who lacked finely honed editorial skills or experience and tended to "publish" whatever stories were e-mailed to them. I discovered that very few of these online publications paid anything, and a lot of the fiction was very short and most of it very poorly written. I could imagine vast hoards of fledgling writers sending off endless files of 1,000-word fictions and an equally endless number of people with computers, domain names, and time on their hands slinging it across the ether.

This, we thought, is not publishing. It's something far closer to a hobby or something most of us do by ourselves when we're feeling lonely.

But we were wrong. It *was* publishing—just not very good publishing. Yet. What we were witnessing were the birth cries of a new way to reach an audience. And like most new ideas, it tended to get better with age and experience.

I think everybody realized the innate power of e-publishing when Stephen King published a novella called *Riding the Bullet* exclusively online. I don't have the exact numbers available, but I remember that more than 400,000 readers downloaded the story within the first week or so.

Amazing? Yes, it was. And even though the outrageous volume is almost totally attributable to the King's popularity, the incident served as a pretty loud warning shot across the bow of conventional, traditional publishing. And the message beneath all the noise and smoke was simple—if you already have an audience, or if you can find an audience, you can sell an impressive number of copies.

And that was kind of the pre–Cambrian era of e-publishing. It's gotten far more sophisticated and pervasive since King showed us all how it could work when all the stars and planets are in alignment. Today, there are thousands and thousands of online publications ranging from columns to blogs to magazines and newspapers as well as academic journals, trade newsletters, and just about anything else that ever found its way to a printing press. Readers buy subscriptions and download their content to computers or portable devices.

And then, for some weird reason, many newspapers have even started putting their daily edition online for *free*, and now the circulation of most major urban papers are on a downward spiral with a revenue engine in flame-out. Books and magazines didn't make the same mistake, and it seems to be working just fine.

If you've been thinking about e-publishing, and whether or not it's right for you, a brief look at what it's all about is probably a good idea. So let's examine the major benefits and drawbacks to e-publishing before we make any rash judgments or decisions.

WORDS OF WISDOM

My writing career isn't about printing my words on paper. It's about reaching readers with my words. If readers want to read my words electronically, I'd be stupid not to give them what they want.

—J. A. Konrath

E-Publishing Advantages and Disadvantages

I'm going to break out the pros and cons of e-publishing into three sections:

- The good
- The bad
- The ugly

Or something like that. Let's take a look.

The (Pretty) Good

First up, there's the cost. Other than the minimal fees to maintain a website, publishing online is almost free—especially if the writer is not getting paid for the "exposure" or is getting a per-piece pay rate based on the number of downloads.

And then there's speed. Back when I used to sell my short fiction to genre magazines, the *lead time* probably averaged 8 or 9 months. And for a novel, usually a year or so. With e-publishing, the lead time shrinks from almost zero to maybe a couple weeks, max.

TRADE TALK

Lead time is how much time elapses between the moment the story is accepted and paid for and when it actually appears in print. Depending on the magazine or book publisher's schedule, this can vary from 3 or 4 months to a *year* or two. In addition to the possibility of your material losing its freshness or relevancy, the publisher could go out of business in the interim. Lead time is also very crucial if you agreed to be paid on publication date rather than upon acceptance. Yeah, that happens.

Talk about a Final Frontier …. E-books don't take up all that much space. You can store hundreds or maybe even thousands of books on a device that fits in your pocket. No library can compete with that.

And when your story appears in a magazine or even in a book, it has a shelf life, after which it is pulled from the rack or the shelf to make room for the next offering by a writer who is *not* you. This is not an issue for e-publications. Your work can reside in the essentially infinite space of servers and file directories for a limitless period—and with no need for maintenance or any additional cost. No matter when someone discovers you and wants to find more fiction by you, you will never be *out of print* (three very dirty words for writers).

And what about your retention of rights? If you put your work online, historically, your publisher does not attempt to obtain any additional rights (such as print, film, video game, etc.). This is because there's usually no advance, and you're compensated on a per-order basis. Print publishers almost demand additional rights or at least a percentage of them from newer writers and use it as leverage to threaten the initial purchase without them.

In the paper world, writers can receive royalty rates anywhere from 4 to 15 percent, depending on a large number of factors not worth listing here. However, all that changes in the electronic world. Because of many of the aforementioned factors, you can expect to get anywhere from 50 to 75 percent of the proceeds of each transaction. This is a huge departure from "the way we've always done it."

Finally, your work is not immutable (as when it appears in cold print) and can be updated for errata or any other reason. It's a simple, painless series of mouse-clicks and file replacement.

The (Not-So) Bad

I talked about credibility earlier. If your only publishing credentials are in the electronic realm, you're still not as highly regarded as your brothers and sisters of the printed page. If you've already established yourself as a "paper pro," this isn't as much of a problem. And it is slowly changing. With the proliferation of blogs and columns and the availability of best-selling novels in e-book formats, this stigma is gradually washing away.

Because writers generally get a much higher percentage of the sales of each book (your royalties), most e-book publishers don't offer an advance against those earnings. This isn't really all that troublesome because you can set up a payment schedule that's a lot more writer-friendly than twiddling your thumbs through the traditional 6-month royalty statement period that makes writers crazy waiting for checks. Getting paid monthly or even quarterly is an obvious improvement over the old method, which is apparently supervised by guys sitting on tall stools wearing black armbands and green eyeshades and wielding quill pens.

And because your book doesn't exist as a physical entity, people cannot readily *see* it—either in a library or on a bookstore display table, paperback rack, or even in spines-out bookcases. That makes marketing and advertising even more important than ever for writers trying to reach and find an audience. The responsibility to publicize and sell your e-books is on you, but this isn't really all that different from what happens for most in-print novels.

If you're not a best-selling author, most publishers don't spend much time or money on promoting you anyway. As I reiterate elsewhere in this book, the smart writer recognizes not only the value but also the *necessity* of marketing and publicizing his own books. If you don't do it, it ain't gonna happen.

I've heard this a lot when readers talk about e-books: "I like the feel of a book in my hand, and I like to see a room with books on the shelves." Generations of people who've grown up with the traditional reading experience of holding an actual book in their hands and turning the pages feel very comfortable with that model. The idea of reading off a screen and never seeing the vast library suddenly available to you is not appealing to book-lovers. In addition, many dedicated readers collect books and could never imagine living their lives *not* surrounded by walls and shelves of their paper and cloth-bound friends.

I think this resistance will gradually fade away and either printed books and their electronic counterparts will learn to co-exist or bibliophiles and their libraries will become quaint reminders of how silly we all were to want those dusty volumes cluttering up our lives.

And the (Man-This-Is-Gonna-Get) Ugly

Let's talk money. Unless you're already a best-selling writer, you're not going to make a lot of money e-publishing your novels—especially if that's the only place your books appear. Now this is probably going to be a temporary state of affairs because as we all know technology has a way of changing rapidly and with lots of unanticipated domino-effect results.

But let's face it. You are writing for two reasons: you love to/have to do it or you like the idea of getting paid for it. So I'm thinking you should be prepared to let this concept evolve and grow and gain acceptance—much like people now get their music as downloadable MP3 files instead of on CD.

Although the techno-crowd has been playing around with ways to protect your e-books and copyright, there still appears to be plenty of opportunity for abject piracy. I've heard the story (maybe apocryphal, maybe not) that when Stephen King offered his online novella for sale, hackers learned how to overcome its "protection" within 24 hours. Not long after that, so the rumor goes, *Riding the Bullet* was riding the cyber-freeway to millions of people all over the planetoid. For free.

This yanks us into the *digital rights management* (*DRM*) arena, and a proper discussion of the various ramifications is beyond the scope and word space I have in this chapter. But I do have a few thoughts on the issue.

TRADE TALK

Digital rights management (DRM) is an issue being debated by everyone in the information and entertainment industries. It centers on how creative material (also called "intellectual properties") can be protected from piracy. It's a difficult problem to solve because the technology is ever-evolving, and DRM is subject to the Law of Unintended Consequences, just like everything else.

Similar fears surfaced about lost sales and lost copyrights when photocopiers became part of the office techno-culture. However, it turned out that standing in front of a copier for 3 hours to make a copy of an entire book was not exactly the definition of a fun day for most people. Sure, students copied short passages for their footnotes and secondary sources, but the wholesale freebooting of entire books was negligible.

But nobody has to wait more than a few seconds to make a digital copy of your e-book and then broadcast it to the world. The same situation occurs in the music and film industries, and there's no consensus yet on how much or how little potential piracy will hurt sales. Some e-book enthusiasts believe the proliferation of your work—even through bootlegging—makes you a brand name and creates a larger fan base than you could ever hope for through traditional means. This increased popularity, they argue, will encourage readers to seek out your "real world" books as well.

We'll see about that, won't we?

Finally, let's talk money. It's no fun sitting at your desk or balancing your laptop on your knees, mouse-scrolling down an endless toilet paper–like roll of text, reading a book on a low-res screen. Add to that the nonergonomic posture that makes you feel like Readasaurus Rex. Something had to be done to make reading e-books more pleasant, and a variety of electronic solutions have hit the scene in the form of portable e-book readers like Amazon.com's Kindle and Barnes & Noble's Nook. Other devices are debuting with regularity. But the problem for now is that they cost a lot. At this writing, most of them are around $250, and that's prohibitive for people who are balking at buying a paperback for $7.99.

I have a feeling this is a fleeting issue, though. The more a technology sells, the more affordable it becomes. VCRs once cost over a grand; DVD players that now sell for $29.95 used to soak you for $500 or more. So I think it's a pretty safe bet to count on the prices of e-book reading devices to drive themselves off a cliff when proliferation and good old American free market competition kicks in.

WORDS OF WISDOM

There are as many advantages to eBooks as there are disadvantages—all depending on the reader. However, having been addicted to books for decades now, I have found digital words to be the same as ink and paper words. They carry the same message. They produce the same images. They satisfy the same need.

—Michael Knost

Final Thoughts

Whether or not you get involved in e-book publishing is a personal option at this point, but I wanted to give you a bit of a heads-up as to what it may become in the near future. If nothing else, it provides you with a few new and potentially exciting new methods to reach your audience.

It also affords you the choice of hooking up with an established e-book publisher or starting your own electronic "house" and selling your books yourself. Plenty of websites are doing this already, and there's always room for one more with your name on it.

Invasion of the POD People

Another way the computer changed writing and publishing was the ability to create typeset press-ready pages on any mook's desktop. Software from companies like Adobe and Microsoft has allowed all of us to become book designers, layout experts, and publishers. It has made the whole idea of self-publishing far easier and more affordable.

How It Works

One of the most high-profile results of the new technology is the concept of *print-on-demand (POD) publishing*. It changes the basic ways the printing of books and getting them to market are accomplished.

> **TRADE TALK**
>
> **Print-on-demand (POD) publishing** is the ability of a publisher to print very small numbers of a book at a time. It can be very useful when introducing a new writer to the marketplace because books can be printed as they're ordered and purchased. Digital printing technology has made POD a viable and not prohibitively expensive alternative.

Traditionally, a publisher (whether that's you or somebody in New York like Random House) always employed the same strategy—select a novel to print, run off the number of copies ideally hoped to sell, and get them into the hands of distributors and booksellers.

POD allows publishers, especially small presses or individuals, to only print as many copies as needed to fill existing orders. As new orders come in, another batch of already-sold books can be printed.

This method of getting out books by newer authors has been a godsend to small presses who are now willing to take a chance on an unknown writer because the specter of having 987 of 1,000 copies unsold has been eliminated.

What's more, the quality of POD books is not all that different from paperbacks and hard covers printed in the more familiar ways.

Printers Versus Publishers

If POD interests you, you can make it happen in several ways. You can enlist the services of companies set up as POD specialists. Some of them are just printers, while others are full-scale publishers. What's the difference? Only everything.

A POD printer has no editorial input or after-press services. They don't care how good or bad your novel is. All they want to know is how many copies you want, will it be cash or charge, and if you want fries with it.

When you're dealing with a printer, you're bankrolling the entire project. Not only are you writing your novel, you are typesetting it, designing the layout, arranging for any cover art and lettering, as well as doing the advertising, order-taking, shipping, and accounting.

If you go to a POD publisher, you might encounter several variations, depending on the entity you select. Some are just like any other publisher who uses editors to select material they think is sellable—they'll provide you with all the editorial and production services, print as many copies as they can get orders for, and divvy up the profits with you along the lines of whatever contract the both of you sign. This is just like any other book sale to any traditional publisher—except your print run is tied directly to the amount of demand created for your novel.

The second type of POD publisher is more like a glorified printer in that they offer you a whole slate of editorial and production services, but it all comes at a price. These companies either enter into a joint venture with you to get your book published and sold, or they let you fund the entire effort while taking advantage of their large roster of services.

Some Good, Some Not-So-Good

Especially in the genres that support the small press fairly well (horror, dark fantasy, and mystery), I've seen many new writers get their first novels published via the POD model. And as with anything else in the universe, the bell curve pretty much applies to their efforts. Some writers have made a nice splash and succeeded in introducing their work to an audience that gradually grew and continued to buy their book. Others only managed to sell copies to a few friends, neighbors, and relatives.

Regardless of what appeals to you the most, there is one upside to the whole POD method: you can get your book published and get it done fast. You can also find out how well your book is selling almost instantly.

> **TOM'S TIPS**
>
> Before you decide to get involved in any of these alternative publishing ventures, you must do your homework. What I've been telling you in these pages is not much more than keys that open the doors. You need to step inside, walk around, and see what's in the closets and basements. Don't expend time, energy, and money on anything until you understand the process as completely as possible.

Thy Name Is *Subsidy* ... or Is It *Vanity?*

These alternative publishing concepts are similar to some of the POD models I just talked about. They differ in the amount of time it takes to get a finished product and in the number of copies printed. But there are a few other things to consider as well.

We Want to Publish Your Book!

Back when I was first getting started, each month my subscription copy of *Writer's Digest* would show up in my apartment mailbox, and each month there would be ads in the back pages announcing the fervent desire of "publishers" who were clamoring to see my novel so they could rush it into print. They called themselves "subsidy publishers," and they always had very stodgy names that suggested they'd been around forever like the "The Stableford Press" or "Montaigne House Publishers." (I made those up, but you get the idea.)

The ads were always written with great energy and optimism, and for the first few months, when I was really a babe in the woods, I fell for their natural allurements. I sent in samples of my work, and I got back expensive brochures full of color photos and testimonials of previous writers who'd published with them.

However, as I read their promotional stuff closely, I discovered they were not *real* publishers. Real publishers paid writers money for their book and then published it. These subsidy fellows wanted *me* to pay *them* the money to get published. Funny thing, but none of this sounded exactly right to me. And while I never had the funds nor the inclination to get published in this fashion, thousands of other writers had done so, and continue to this day. And most of the books published were done in "hard" print runs—thousands of copies to make the press time even minimally economical.

Many subsidy publishers give you the impression they *might* want to share in the expenses to get you into print, but I have a feeling that happens about as often as we pass through the tail of a comet.

What's in a Name?

As I began to interact with other writers, editors, and agents, I learned that the preferred industry name for subsidy publishers was the *vanity press*. The name is fairly self-explanatory, and if you sense a pejorative fog settling over the term, you are correct.

TRADE TALK

Vanity presses publish books at the total expense of the author—either through an independent "publisher" who is actually just a glorified printer, or by the author himself and the aid of a printer.

Despite vanity publishers' claims of generating reviews, publicity, distribution, and sales, *very* few of them are even a little bit successful at any of those endeavors.

Vanity press books—especially the ones produced by the biggest companies who afford the splashiest ads in the writers' magazines, and were, therefore, the most recognizable—were the pariahs of the industry. They were *never* reviewed by any of the trade journals or newspapers or magazines, libraries never bought copies, distributors by and large ignored them, and most bookstores—either chains or mom 'n' pops—refused to carry them.

Wow, that sounds like a *lot* of copies piling up in attics, basements, and garden sheds around the country.

Fringe Is Not a Dirty Word

A couple other alternative publishing venues merit mention. I guess you could say they are something like cousins of e-publishing because they've both grown out of the new technologies and everyman's ability to use them in the comfort of their own homes.

I'm talking about audiobooks and podcasts; but again, as you might expect, there are distinctions to be made among the various types of these publishing venues.

Listen to Me

"Reading" your novel or story by listening to it is not new. In the past, the terms *talking books* or *books on tape* described the basic idea of getting someone to record your novel so others might hear it. Many New York publishers offered the audio rights to third-party companies who would produce the recording, but now, many of the larger publishers have begun to create their *own* audio divisions.

As we have become a very mobile society and the ease of carrying our entertainment along for the ride has also increased, *audiobooks* have become much more popular. Although they are still fairly expensive bookstore items, they are also available on CD, as well as in a downloadable form, from libraries all over the country. They can be played in car stereos or piped through iPods and other MP3 players.

> **TRADE TALK**
>
> **Audiobooks** are digital versions of books, often read by the author or an actor and recorded on CD or saved as an audio file. They're not considered another "edition" of most mass-market books. Digital technology has allowed publishers to create accessible and very portable versions of books.

Ideally, audiobooks are read by professional actors or speakers who have a great facility for reading aloud and also for dramatizing the material.

As Read by the Author …

And all this new technology enables writers to take the audiobook to new levels. By using shareware recording software and computers, writers have begun to record themselves reading their novels and stories and burning them to CD or preserving them as MP3 files.

What happens next is a matter of choice or strategy on the writer's part. Some writers use their self-created audio presentations as promotional items, giving them away at conventions, conferences, book signings, or speaking engagements. Others package them smartly and sell them at the same gatherings or on their websites.

Such recordings can be a valuable addition to your arsenal of ways to find an audience. But you have to do it right. Most writers I've heard reading their own work have little idea how to do it with any style or sense of drama. Actually, I'm being kind. Most writers read their own work with all the panache of a funeral director announcing his price list.

Get a microphone, plug it into your computer, and record yourself reading your work. What comes next is the hard part—honestly assess your performance. And I stress the word *performance* because that's what your reading should be. Listen to yourself, and if you aren't very good at it, you need to do one of two things: practice a lot, or forget about it.

Becoming a really good reader requires a lot of time and talent. Please believe me on this one—if your potential audience is turned off by an amateur reading and recording, they will be much less willing to *read* you, and for a very simple reason—it's easy to listen, but picking up a book and reading it is a much more committed effort. Think about it.

Is This Thing On ...?

Closely related to audio versions of your stories and novels is the *podcast*. This is another innovative by-product of the digital age—a "show" produced like a segment for radio or TV that you can package as a digital file and listen to on your laptop or a portable MP3 player like an iPod or one of its competitors.

TRADE TALK

Podcasts are recorded segments of "shows" packaged and stored for playback on digital equipment. They can be produced just like a radio program or an audiobook, and plenty of software out there enables you to do your own podcast about you and your work. Many venues list and serve podcasts, and your listeners can "subscribe" to your show and download you. Amazing stuff.

The general format of the podcast is simple: it's part of a series of presentations all dealing with the same thematic material, with possible syndication, and distributed via the Internet.

Thousands and thousands of people are doing podcasts, which are available through services like iTunes or Podcast Alley, and more source platforms are coming online all the time. Podcasters either give away their podcasts for free or set up a subscription and charge a fee. They offer them as downloads from their own websites as well as through larger platforms that offer entire menus of podcast categories. Podcasts have become increasingly popular and can be a source of revenue if you can find your audience.

The idea is for you to do a podcast about your writing. If you have noticed how many best-selling books have achieved that status because their authors are regular commentators on talk radio or television, perhaps I don't need to tell you how a successful podcast could substantially increase your audience.

I have been writing an award-winning column about writing and publishing for 30 years, and I have toyed with the idea of doing it as a podcast because I have a fairly large audience who would support it. But one thing is keeping me from jumping in with both feet—time. To do a really professional job of it will require time I have up until now been devoting to writing or thinking, which leads to writing.

And that's the final barometer on these fringe publishing alternatives—does the amount of *time* they will take away from your writing balance out the increases you may enjoy in terms of audience and income?

As with most of what I've been telling you in this book, it's something for you to think about.

The Least You Need to Know

- E-publishing is here to stay. There's no way to predict the impact it will have on your sales or success of your writing career, so you need to decide how to use this new form of publishing to your advantage.
- Print-on-demand is not for everyone. Evaluate its good and bad points before making your decision.
- No matter what name you put on it—subsidy or vanity publishing—by self-publishing, you're making a fairly large investment in yourself. Only you can determine if you're worth it.
- Audiobooks, podcasts, online columns, and related programming about your craft are excellent ways to advertise and market your talent. Just because they're new avenues is no reason to discount them.

Common Mistakes

In This Chapter

- Appearance, talking, and academia
- Characters, dialogue, and plot
- Watching your language
- Structural problems

Everybody makes mistakes.

And that's what this chapter's all about. We're going to talk about the myriad ways writers can screw up their novels. Once we isolate the major problems, you will know enough to avoid them.

Sounds easy, right? Well, yes and no. The funny thing about writing is that you can know what makes a novel great, what makes a writer popular, what makes a style effective … but putting that knowledge into practice is another story.

The most important general advice I can give you about making mistakes in your writing is this: don't worry about it. It's not a sign of incompetence or ineptitude; it's merely an indicator of your unrelenting humanity. The key is to learn from your mistakes and resolve to not repeat them.

One more thing: it's no accident many of these common errors are reiterations of points I've already made in previous chapters. Writers make these mistakes because they've not learned properly the things I've been telling you.

In that sense, this chapter is a review of all that's come before and a checklist of things you *should* know not to do.

General Appearance

Never send an agent or editor a manuscript that looks sloppy, shabby, or beat up. If you do, the message you've sent to your recipient is: this novel has been making the rounds. If it *looks* like it's been previously read and handled by others, you're telling the latest editor you don't care enough to clean it up, reprint it, or repackage it.

WORDS OF WISDOM

The greatest mistake a writer can make in life is to be continually fearing you will make one.

—Elbert Hubbard

That's right, even the box you ship it in is important. It doesn't do much good to put a pristine copy of your novel in a box that's warped, crushed, and covered with the remnants of torn-off labels and postage from earlier trips around the country. Use a nice, clean package. Treat your prospective agent or editor with respect, and save the beat-up, recycled packaging for your cousin Frankie.

In case you're skeptical about appearance being important, here's an anecdote. I told you before that my wife and I read unsolicited manuscripts for an anthology series we edit. Every once in a while, we get a manuscript that looks like it has spent its earlier existence lining a bird cage or keeping coffee rings off the furniture. Do you think we read it?

Enough said.

Don't Talk It … Write It

Early on in my writing career, I discovered an interesting dynamic—if I came up with a great idea for a story or novel, and I told somebody about it … I *never* got around to actually writing the story.

After several years of this, I noticed a pattern, and I started to wonder what was going on. Why was it happening? It's pretty simple if you think about it. A significant part of the writing process is walking around all the time with this burning *need* to tell a story, to let something out of your inner thoughts and give it shape and life.

If you think of a fascinating premise or plot for a story and you talk about it with others, you've essentially "let it out of you," and because it's no longer heating up like a banked coal in your unconscious, you no longer feel the driving need to write it down. Once the idea or the actual storyline has been told—*in any form*—it has been released from its state of "not-yet-there," and you've lost your need to make it real because you already did.

Okay, I know this sounds dangerously close to the psycho-babble I *loathe*, but in this instance, it makes a lot of sense to me. Trust me—don't talk about what you want to write until *after* you've written it in some form.

The Groves of Academe

In case you've spent lots of time studying writing and literature at your favorite university, I have a small caveat—don't fall prey to the position that style and dazzling prose are acceptable substitutes for *story*.

We both know they're not.

WORDS OF WISDOM

Everywhere I go, I'm asked if I think the university stifles writers. My opinion is that they don't stifle *enough* of them.

—Flannery O'Connor

Don't get me wrong; I'm not smearing the study of literature at the university level. I have a Master's degree in English, and went ABD (all but dissertation) before quitting to write fiction full time. I think it's a great benefit to a writer to have gained a deep, scholarly appreciation of literature. But there's a prevailing attitude in many English departments around the country that proclaims if you write "commercial" fiction, two things immediately obtain: you can't possibly be a good writer, and earning a living wage from your writing somehow "cheapens" the art of writing.

This is, of course, a load of ordure.

Most of the best examples of enduring English and American fiction were done by the crassest commercial writers of their time—Twain, Poe, Dickens, Melville, Hawthorne, Dreiser, London, and too many others to list here.

Never try to alter what you write to fit the expectations of a flimsy academic template. Tell a good story well, and people will want to read you. And most of them *won't* be wearing tweed jackets with leather buttons and those annoying suede ellipsoids on the elbows.

The Missing Hook

Many new writers, especially novelists, believe the sheer size of the book gives them the space and the time to *develop* reader interest as they slowly build their story. Not true. Big mistake.

They compound this error by starting the story at the beginning, a point that may *not* be a moment of high drama and interest. That comes from an attachment to a strict chronological unraveling of your story ... and it can have drastic results.

Look in your story for a moment of tension and drama that can naturally evoke a reader's interest and attention. Use that moment to hook the reader, reel them in, and capture them for the rest of your narrative. That is the true beginning of your tale.

Who's In Charge?

Going right along with the error of the missing hook is the very common error of not getting your protagonist or antagonist onstage quickly enough. Readers want to be cheering (or jeering) for someone as soon as possible. When they start a new novel and the pages drag on without a clear-cut "hero" or major "bad guy" emerging, many readers start losing interest fast.

It's a big mistake to load in too much introductory description or setup without getting any of the main players on the field. Your major objective, when you open your novel, is to captivate your audience. Interesting major characters—whether good guys or bad guys—are what your readers are looking for. Don't withhold them for more than a few pages in Chapter 1.

> **TOM'S TIPS**
>
> Make a little billboard you can tape to your computer monitor, or from the bottom of the shelf above your desk (if you have one), or any conveniently prominent place. On it, neatly list the most heinous common errors you can make while writing your novel. That way, they're constantly in your face.

You Need a Motive

Another common character development mistake is forcing characters to do something you *need* them to do rather than having them act out of any logical motivation within your narrative. Be certain the decisions your characters make flow organically—obeying the simplest laws of cause and effect or stimulus/response.

It is essential that you avoid acting out of authorial convenience. Seasoned readers and even the newest editors will call you on it every time.

Who Said That?

One of the most obvious signs of an unpublishable novel is bad dialogue. In Chapter 9, when I stressed the importance of reading your dialogue aloud, I was *not* kidding. You simply *have* to do this—for years if necessary, or until you're certain you've developed a great ear for the way people really talk.

Even if you hate them, go to a few stage plays. The dialogue in an effective play carries the plot, creates the characters, and controls the pacing. You could do a lot worse.

Dumb Luck and Coincidence

Be sure everything in your narrative makes *logical* sense. I'm talking plot here. Remember, plot is a series of plausible, dramatic moments, caused by complication, that must be resolved or allowed to grow into a *worse* complication.

Things must happen in your story out of a natural progression of events and situations. Veteran editors will groan out loud if you rely on shaky or totally absent cause-and-effect.

Here are the biggest offenders:

- *Luck.* Never use this as an explanation why anything happened.

- *Coincidence.* This is very similar to luck and is only worse when you have a character actually exclaim "What a coincidence!"

- *Author's convenience.* This is the worst plot offense. You've given no reason for why something has just happened, other than the unspoken one that you desperately *needed* it to. (Reread the "You Need a Motive" section earlier in this chapter if you tend to make this mistake.)

Here's the end note on this: be sure your plot flows organically from one event to the other. You're not writing a Greek epic, so please, no lightning bolts from Zeus. (Which we all know is called *Deus ex machina*.)

What would happen if an archaeologist found irrefutable proof that a super civilization existed on Earth more than a million years ago, more advanced than our own? He also discovers that a catastrophic climatic event wiped out almost every trace of it … and the event is about to repeat itself. Would he reveal his knowledge to the public? If he did, what would happen?

Can You Describe It for Me?

Common errors of description occupy both sides of the coin—either too much or too little. Description is a necessary part of narrative, but there's a knack to doing it right.

New writers have a tendency to describe a new character in one large, expository clump, never giving the reader another cue about the character's appearance, mannerisms, etc. Ditto for places and other objects. The best way to describe people and places is in small packets inserted throughout your story. That way, the reader acquires a gradual familiarity with the people and places that feels more natural to the reader.

Too much description all at once can be overwhelming. It can also be an inducement for the reader to start skimming—something you don't ever want.

Too little description makes your story too vague and unanchored in the imagination of your audience. This stretches their patience, and you risk losing them because they don't feel connected with the people and places you're talking about.

So pay attention to the way you describe things. The watchword is *balance*. Your goal is to give your readers a good visual feel for everything over the course of the novel.

WORDS OF WISDOM

It's only those who do nothing that make no mistakes.

—Joseph Conrad

Where Are We Now?

Very much related to how you describe things is how well you establish a *sense of place*. It's a common mistake for writers to assume the reader is as familiar and comfortable with the setting of a scene as they are. As you read over your first draft, check each scene to ensure it's properly identified for the reader.

Sometimes it's not enough to merely establish the sense of place; you need to maintain it by reminding the reader now and again with a word, phrase, or something that anchors or establishes the location—a smell, a sound, a texture, or even an evocation.

Did You Wear a Watch?

Along the same lines, be sure your reader doesn't get lost in any passages of time you've previously *assumed* were obvious. Keeping your audience plugged in to changes in time is crucial to good pacing. Good descriptive power includes the ability to portray and handle the ever-changing dimension of time.

Trite Expressions

These are things you want to look for when you're revising your first draft. All writers get lazy once in a while and drop in a cliché or a shopworn phrase just to keep the narrative going. If you do it, don't worry about it—as long as you catch them in revisions and excise them for the verbal tumors they are.

Trite, overfamiliar writing is a signal of two things: lazy writing or inept ability. You don't want to wave either of those flags at a potential editor.

If you spot a cliché, and you can't think of an original way to phrase it, you're in big trouble. There is *always* a fresh way to say something, but if you can't think of it, it's better to say nothing at all.

Stereotypes

A close relative of the cliché is the stereotyped character. I talked about these folks in Chapter 7, but a little reminder can't hurt.

Be ever mindful of employing preestablished "labels" for your characters instead of stepping up and creating truly original ones. No tough Irish cops or Brooklyn mobsters or American Indians talking about powwows, okay?

You Talkin' to Me?!

The tone and the amount of exposition you employ in your book say a lot about the audience you're writing for. If you're doing a definite genre novel such as mystery or science fiction or romance, be sure your narrative speaks to a readership already familiar with the trappings and conventions of the particular genre you've chosen.

If you overexplain everything, your reader will wonder why you're doing it. If they read a lot of Regency romances, they probably know the history of the period better than you. A polite nod or mention is more than enough to cue all the necessary resonances. The same goes for science fiction. For example, it would be superfluous and a little insulting to bog down your narrative with a discussion of FTL (faster than light) travel when it has become an accepted staple of the genre.

So keep a firm vision of whom you're writing for. Don't do anything that will insult them or tell them you're not as familiar with the material as they might be.

Imagery and Language

It's very easy to lapse into what I call a "workmanlike" style, although it's not so much a style as a set of convenient, workable writing methods that get you through your daily word count. Other writers have called this "the plain style."

Although there's nothing wrong with evolving a plain style, I find it to be too universal, too nondescript. Even though it contains no grammatical errors or narrative miscues, to me, it still lacks something, something that makes it lively and intrinsically interesting.

What I'm getting at is a general *dullness*. It's hard to describe, but I know it when I encounter it. Sometimes it can be a lack of fresh images or challenging imagery or a dependency on the plainest words, as if the writer was consciously avoiding *any* esoteric vocabulary. Other symptoms can be a paucity of metaphors and similes, or anything that smacks of the lyrical or the poetic.

I'm not saying your prose has to sing like that of the great romantic poets Keats or Shelley, but you should pay attention to its overall feel. Granted, this is more subjective than anything else, but you should develop some basic radar to detect dull, albeit syntactically correct, writing.

WORDS OF WISDOM

An expert is someone who knows the worst mistakes that can be made in his field ... because he's probably already made them.

—John DeChancie

Structure

This is probably the most difficult one to detect and correct until your novel is complete. Don't confuse it with plot—it's more about the overall effect your story has on the reader. Structure is all about traditional storytelling—beginning, middle, and end.

Beware the most common errors associated with structure:

Slow beginnings. I've already addressed this in several places, but I cannot emphasize enough how important it is. If you lose your audience at the start of your book, you will *never* get them back.

Sagging middles. This is not just a problem for aging athletes. Your story cannot lose direction in the center of your book. When plots don't have enough complication, they tend to start meandering and trying to double back on themselves, flirting with repetitive scenes. This is the kind of mistake that causes readers to put down a book and "forget" to pick it back up again.

Unsatisfying endings. Coming up with a good ending is one of the biggest challenges in modern storytelling because readers are getting very sophisticated. "They lived happily ever after" usually won't cut it.

An ending might not work for lots of reasons. A very common error is when the writer wraps up things too fast and too neatly. Another occurs when the ending just kind of fizzles out with people dying or disappearing and no real resolution is at hand. Look closely at the way you end your story. Even if it begs for a sequel (or you intended to write one as part of a series), your ending must resolve enough questions and problems to satisfy your audience's need for order in the universe.

Loose ends. These are issues, problems, and questions you wrote into your story and just plain *forgot* about resolving. Take the time to check for things like a letter that somebody mailed and you never mentioned anyone receiving it; a character getting locked in a closet and no one ever letting them out; or … hey, you've got the idea.

Okay, we're about to put the lid on common mistakes you can make. Now that we've reminded ourselves, and even made a little warning board, they should be less of a problem to all but the most obtuse among you.

The most encouraging message I can leave you with in a chapter about making a mistake is this: don't be afraid to make them. Rather, be afraid of not catching them.

The Least You Need to Know

- Every writer makes mistakes, so stop feeling bad if you do, too.
- Mistakes are no problem—as long as you catch them and fix them.
- The time to look for common errors is in the reading and revision stage of your first draft. You don't want to be still making them during your final rewrite.

Other Sources of Help

Chapter

18

In This Chapter

- Magazines, books, newsletters, and more
- Immersing yourself in instruction
- Joining organizations
- Helpful software

When I was first getting started as a writer, there was no Internet, which, as we all know, is an unbelievably easy way to be connected to *any* kind of information you might need. And so, as I sat quietly in front of my typewriter, even though I *sensed* a whole world of writers and stuff about writing out there, I couldn't help feeling very much apart and adrift from it.

Being cut off like that was not a serious obstacle to my writing, but I knew I would be better off if I could eventually connect to things related to writing and publishing. And that's what this chapter is all about—the peripheral aspects of the profession that keep you informed, focused, and writing at the top of your game.

Publications

Books and periodicals about writing have been around a long time, especially in America. They're a tradition born of the widespread literacy that set us apart from many countries in Europe during the eighteenth century. Let's take a closer look.

A Few Good Mags

One of the (many) great things about America is that no matter what kind of hobby, pastime, or profession you may be into, there's a magazine for you. Bottle collecting, hamster breeding, home beer brewing, rice-grain engraving … I'm sure they've all been covered in *somebody's* publication. And writing's no different.

Early in my career, there were basically two magazines for people who wanted to write. One was a rather staid-looking pamphlet-size mag called *The Writer,* which looked very serious, very professional, and not terribly friendly. The other, loud and splashy and the same size as *Time* or *Newsweek,* was called *Writer's Digest.* The latter looked like a lot more fun, and it usually had an article or two by a writer I knew.

I started buying *Writer's Digest* on the newsstand and then later subscribed. I read the articles and columns, learned what I could, and felt connected, even if in a rudimentary way, to the world of writing at large. This is where I learned the basics of the profession, and if you don't regularly read a magazine about writing, you should for just that reason. You'll get some current information on the publishing scene, and you'll get refresher material on the things you need to know to write well. There's also an inspirational side. Every time the periodical arrives in the mail, it's a reminder that you *are* a writer, regardless of what the rejection slips are telling you.

 WORDS OF WISDOM

I don't think it's very useful to open wide the door for young artists; the ones who break down the door are more interesting.

—Paul Schrader

Lots of Books

If there's one thing writers love to write about, it's writing. There are plenty of novels about writers, but there are hundreds, probably thousands of nonfiction books about writing.

The best ones I've seen tend to be about writing in general. Some have been reprinted endlessly and have become minor classics, such as *On Becoming a Novelist* by John Gardner and the one I told you about in a previous chapter, *The Elements of Style* by Strunk and White. A relative newcomer, *On Writing* by Stephen King, fits in this category, too.

But most of the others narrow their focus, concentrating on particular kinds of writing—poetry, nonfiction, or various kinds of fiction—especially the genres. These can be very useful because they're usually written by writers who've earned their stripes writing mysteries, romances, and science fiction, and they can give you some valuable information they've gathered from working on the inside.

I found a book called *Writing Science Fiction* by L. Sprague De-Camp in a used bookshop. It was probably 20 years old when I bought it, but it contained some universal wisdom that never goes out of style. I read the book over and over, as well as one by Kingsley Amis called *New Maps of Hell*, which is an analysis of modern genre fiction—especially SF. At the time, I wanted to write science fiction, and discovering these books was like finding buried treasure. If you want to work in a specific genre, an easy search on Amazon.com should yield you plenty of material.

There's another subclass of writing books, one that gets even *more* specific in what they try to teach you. I'm talking whole books about creating believable characters, building plots that work, writing great dialogue, etc. And you know what? I think books with such a narrow focus are highly suspect—there just isn't all that much you need to know to fill 300 pages, even in EZ-Eye type. Seems to me you're getting lots of padding and repetition. My advice? Fuggghedddaboudit.

If you want my honest opinion, you don't really need *any* books about writing other than the one in your hands right now. Hey, don't laugh; you had to know I was gonna tell you that.

And if you've stuck with me this far, then you know I'm giving you the real thing.

How-To Manuals

I just told you all you need to know about *other* books.

Market Newsletters

Market newsletter publications vary widely in their scope and usefulness. They are basically a list of magazines, anthologies, and book publishers who are looking for material. A good market newsletter tells you circulation, payment rates, frequency of publication, examples of previously published material, plus all the usual contact information.

> **TOM'S TIPS**
>
> You can find lots of market reports by looking in the classified section of writers' magazines and also through web search engines. Lots of them offer sample issues for a reasonable fee, and it's usually worth trying a few to see if one is right for you.

Newsletters of this type used to be exclusively distributed by third-class mail, making the freshness of the markets a little dated. Now many are sold through e-mail subscription, which tends to make this more current and useful.

Instruction

Okay, so other than the bookstores and libraries, where else do you go to get an edge or a leg-up on your writing? Some of you will look to the classroom, and naturally, I've got a few thoughts about that, too.

Writing Classes

After I finished my Master's degree, I took an evening class in creative writing. I didn't do it so much to learn how to write as I did to get objective feedback. I'm not so sure you can be taught how to write "creatively." I think most of us just sit down and do it. Whether or not we do it *well* is another story. And I think we basically teach ourselves how to write by the sheer repetition of doing it. You can get a line on what good writing should be, but the act of writing, and writing, and writing is the way it finally happens.

So what's with the writing classes? Are they any good? They *can* be, if you approach them with the right attitude and expectations. If you're like most new writers, you sit and you write, and you're basically the only person reading your stuff. But what you need is feedback—how others receive your work. This is where the writing classes can give you exactly what you want.

But a few warnings are in order.

Choose your writing class carefully. You want it to be large enough to have a wide range of readers besides you and the instructor—at least 10 others, but even more people would be better. If you have a local college or university, you can probably enroll in a good-size class. If it's offered by a local library or ladies' auxiliary or maybe a church group, well, be prepared to not find much more than a mutual admiration society.

TOM'S TIPS

There's only one way to make a writing class work—take it seriously, do the assignments (whether you like them or not), spend the time learning how to provide honest feedback to others, and *require* the same from everybody else in the class.

I remember a writing class I once joined. It had about 18 people in it, all fitting into one of three categories: college kids taking an elective, middle-age housewives who liked writing stories about their pets, and a few of us who were very serious about our writing.

Workshops

An interesting variant of the formal writing class is a writers' workshop. There's no single, correct way to run a workshop, nor is there a set length on them. Some workshops run for 4 to 6 weeks, with guest lecturers (like me); while others are set up to operate within the confines of a single weekend.

Back when I had yet to sell my first story, I wrangled an invitation to a weekend workshop run by Ted White, who was the senior editor at a venerable science fiction magazine called *Amazing Stories*. Seven other writers were there—all guys in their 20s—and I was the only one who had not sold anything professionally. We all arrived early on a Friday afternoon and got started almost immediately.

Each one of us brought two stories, and we had to read everyone else's stories. So I read seven stories on Friday night, and compiled heavy-duty notes on all of them, even though I wasn't sure what I was doing.

WORDS OF WISDOM

Your manuscript is both good and original; but the part that is good is not original, the part that is original is not good.

—Samuel Johnson

On Saturday morning, we got up, grabbed the obligatory coffees and donuts, and arranged ourselves in a big circle. All eight stories had been tossed into a box, and the moderator pulled out the first one, handed it to the first guy, and we were off. Each story got a thorough working-over by each of us, taking anywhere from an hour to an hour and a half to get all the way around the circle.

When we broke for dinner, we were all exhausted from being so "on" for so long. But that evening, we still had three more stories to critique and then we had to read seven *additional* ones for Sunday's session. By the time I fell asleep that night, I felt like I'd been interrogated by a guy using a rubber hose.

The next day we did it all over again, and I held my own against the other guys. My critiques were fairly well reasoned and as astute as anybody else's, other than Ted White's, who was just marvelous at figuring why a story worked or failed. The level of criticism in general was as impressive as it was blunt. Nobody made any efforts to soften blows.

My two submissions had batted .500—they hated the one on Saturday, and they liked the one on Sunday. Ted White told me I had some ability and he would be happy to read new stories I might submit to his magazine. I ended up revising my workshop story and eventually selling it to him—my first professional sale.

Overall, my initial workshop experience was very positive, and not just because it produced my first check. I learned a lot about how to critique a story and even more about how to improve my own work. It was very tough physically and psychologically, and I wouldn't recommend it for everybody. I'd always been an adventurous kind of guy, so it worked out great for me, but if you're a more fragile type … it could be a very long weekend.

Only you can decide whether a workshop is going to work for you. The ones that run for a 3-day weekend are the most intense. The longer ones that are held over a week or longer tend to be more relaxed. Some people prefer a less pressure-packed environment.

I have been an instructor at the Borderlands Press Writers Boot Camp for many years, and its success is pretty impressive. More than 20 attendees have gone on to publish their first novels and at least twice that number have sold their short fiction.

The Boot Camp is open to all genres and features instructors who have been professional writers for decades, as well as at least one senior editor from a New York publishing house. We've had instructors such as David Morrell, F. Paul Wilson, Thomas Tessier, Jack Ketchum, Gary Braunbeck, Elizabeth Massie, Mort Castle, and Douglas E. Winter and editors Richard Chizmar, Ginjer Buchanan, and Jaime Levine. And of course, me.

If you're interested in meeting me or the others and working almost one-on-one, click on the Boot Camp banner at borderlandspress.com.

You can find other workshops advertised in the classified sections of writers' magazines, genre writers' organization newsletters, and of course, Internet search engines.

Conferences, Seminars, and Symposia

The third type of "class" we should look at is of the day-long variety—sometimes called a seminar or a symposium. To be honest, I think this type of instruction is the least valuable of any you may be seeking.

Most of the ones I've either attended or in which I've appeared as a guest speaker have been rather formal and structured, which doesn't leave much room for the spontaneity that can evolve in a regular class. Usually, there's a panel of speakers and a moderator who asks everybody a series of the same questions, and everybody answers them.

Big whoop.

The better ones also give the audience a chance to ask questions, but in general, they can be kind of stultifying. They normally don't have much of a hands-on, instructional feel to them. They are more abstract and theoretical, and if you have too many academics in attendance, things can get downright stuffy, and (dare I say it?) *boring*.

If you think I'm a little harsh on the professors and their ilk, it's because I've had a *lot* of experience with them. They don't often get out in the trenches where the action is, so they often end up saying things that, to my trained ear, sound several standard deviations this side of uninformed.

Okay, I've said enough. If you see a symposium on writing in your area, check it out and decide for yourself if you found it valuable or if you would want to go to another one. So much about writing is subjective, as we all know. My job is to just make sure you know about this stuff. What you do with it is up to you.

Clan Gatherings

Besides formal gatherings in the classroom or the auditorium, there are other ways to surround yourself with people interested in writing. Writers go to book fairs and conventions, they join organizations, and (with the emergence of the Internet) they network among themselves. You should have a passing acquaintance with these gatherings of the writing clan.

Just know: as with everything else, some of these will be good for you and others not so good. So experiment. Pick and choose. The main thing to remember is this stuff has got to be fun—that's the first requirement. If you don't enjoy it, stop doing it.

Conventions

There are so many book and writing conventions, I couldn't possibly list them all here. A few annual gatherings are created by the pooled funds of all the publishing houses and appear under names like Book Expo, Publishing Expo, and Book Fair. These are huge events that fill big city exhibit halls, and they tend to emphasize the commercial side of writing and publishing rather than the esthetic or how-to side of the industry.

If you attend one of these mega-events, you may be able to find panels of writers or publishers who talk about current trends in their field, but then again, you may not. I think you'll have far more success learning about the field by attending regional and specialized conventions.

These are held on just about every weekend of the year in one city or another. They're specialized because they tend to focus on a particular kind of writing—the genres in particular. Science fiction, crime, mystery, and romance are the subject of so many "cons" (short for *conventions*), so there's no question you can find one in your area. Lots of writers attend these gatherings because they like to meet other writers, and lots of devoted readers come to meet their favorite writers.

Conventions can be a great source of information about writing because they typically feature an entire program of panels hosted by writers, editors, and agents, as well as readings by authors and even Q&A sessions with fans and aspiring writers. The atmosphere at these cons is amiable, and many writers are more than willing to share their experience and wisdom with new writers.

But they're an acquired taste, especially the ones dedicated to media such as role-playing and video games, television, or the movies. You're going to run into a certain percentage of people in strange costumes and others with psycho-social profiles that fall outside the boundaries of the norm.

I tend to regard conventions as a place to meet writers and editors who are exchanging information and ideas on what's currently hot in the industry. For instance, I can remember going to one in the early 1990s and sitting at the hotel bar with a bunch of the usual suspects of editors and agents. The general buzz was that the "train to catch" was going to be something they called "legal thrillers."

And you know what? They were right. (For a while, anyway ….)

Writers' Organizations

Writers' organizations are as numerous as they are diverse in their purposes and usefulness. Many national writers' organizations, regional branches, clubs, and even a few real unions all bring writers together for any number of reasons.

As with the conventions, many of the organizations have formed out of the genres. The Mystery Writers of America, the Science Fiction and Fantasy Writers of America, the Romance Writers, the Horror Writers Association, and many others have large memberships. Almost all of them are professional organizations, which means they require their members to have sold a specific number of stories or books to legitimate professional publishers.

These are not "clubs." They are a collection of working pros who share similar goals and who try to represent their interests and needs to publishers through a united front. But it's not all business and no fun. Most of these groups confer awards for superior achievement, and they throw banquets in New York hotels, where everybody comes for a weekend of panels and publishers' parties. These can be a great place to meet other writers and stay on top of what's going on in your own area of interest.

Oh, and remember when I mentioned market newsletters in an earlier section of this chapter? Well, almost every one of these organizations publishes its own newsletter, which focuses on the needs of the particular genre they serve. These can be very helpful when you're trying to learn who's buying what and in what quantities.

As with much of what I've been talking about in this chapter, you can find information on most of these organizations by a quick Google search. Every large professional writers' organization has its own website, full of everything you could possibly want to know.

WORDS OF WISDOM

What a heartbreaking job it is trying to combine writers for their own protection! I had ten years of it on the Committee of Management of the Society of Authors; and the first lesson I learned was that if you take the field for the authors, you will be safer without a breastplate than a backplate.

—George Bernard Shaw

I can't tell you whether or not you should join a specific organization. I have friends who love them and others who have no use for them. It depends on why you might want to join in the first place and what you expect it to do for you. My experience with the few writers' organizations in which I've been a member is that they're long on camaraderie and short on any kind of unionlike activities. Writers are solitary and individualistic, and it's tough to get them all focused on *any* single goal.

My job, as you will recall, is to simply steer you in the right direction on matters such as this one. You'll know if you're a "joiner" or not.

Networking

The whole idea of contacting other writers like yourself is a good idea because you spend so much time alone and around people who have no idea what you're going through. That's why writers' conventions and organizations can be so helpful in keeping you informed and focused.

The Internet has made this exchange of ideas, experience, and friendship unbelievably easier, and so many websites, chatrooms, and e-mail address books have been established for writers, I couldn't begin to list them all, much less discuss them. If you surf the Internet, spend a little time looking through the websites that bring writers closer together.

The feeling of working in a vacuum, of not being understood by the rest of the people in your life isn't fun, and I know many writers feel that way. But it doesn't have to be like that.

Software

I've already discussed the advantages of using a computer when writing, and I glossed over the word-processing software that helps you in both the writing and the revision phases of your novel. But other programs you might not know about can help you in other ways.

A LIKELY STORY

Suppose you invented a software program that could write brilliant prose and riveting, original plots. Would you sell it to the masses? Or keep it for yourself? Write a story that explores these questions.

Many software manufacturers have add-on packages that hook you into a whole shelf of reference books writers may need at any time. Dictionaries for meaning and synonyms, encyclopedias, biographical indices, and concordances are available for every taste and budget. I like the ones that can operate in the background while you're writing. You can pull up anything you need with a few extra keystrokes instead of getting up from your desk to grab a big book off a shelf.

Another family of programs purports to help you with the more subjective aspects of writing, such as plotting and the actual construction of your story. I've never taken the time to learn any of these types of software, and I have heard conflicting reviews from other writers who have tried to use them.

To be honest, I'm skeptical of software doing a writer's job of storytelling. If there's value in this kind of interface between a writer and the cold lines of computer code, I think it can be found in teaching writers how to "see" the way a plot works or how a story is constructed from more basic components. If the software can explain things like complication, motivation, and transcendence, well, that's a big bonus.

If you feel that plotting or understanding story-concept are personal weaknesses for you, you might want to investigate this kind of software. I don't feel comfortable pumping any particular program over any other, but as with almost anything these days, a quick Internet search will get you up to speed on what's currently available.

The last type of software that *may* be of help to you is one that enables you to sit back and talk to your computer and its word-processing program. There are at least two fairly well-known ones on the market, and I keep telling myself I want to try them.

But the biggest problem I've found is that you have to "train" the program to get comfortable with the way you pronounce your words. Depending on the speed of the CPU (central processing unit—think of this as the brains of your computer) in your computer and the severity of any regional accent you may have, this training *could be* extensive, which means time-consuming. Most writers I know who've tried to teach their PCs to take dictation lose patience with the training process. I'm going to predict that as the programs get more sophisticated, these type of programs will become more popular.

For me, I think I still need to see the words on the page as I'm writing them. I've tried dictating my column I do for a bimonthly magazine, and it feels very awkward, even though I know exactly what I want to say. I suspect it's a question of learning a new way of expressing yourself, and the more I do it, the more comfortable it will become. I'll let you know.

The Least You Need to Know

- A variety of sources can provide inspiration, support, and valuable information for writers. It's not a good idea to work in a vacuum, and you should sample these sources to see what's best for you.

- Magazines and newsletters can arm you with great reference material and keep you up to date on the state of the publishing industry. Books can also be helpful in polishing specific skills. Of course, the book you're reading right now is priceless and will be the sole cause of your success.

- Attending a writers' workshop, conference, or even a "boot camp" can be a life-changing experience. You can learn more in a weekend than a whole year of knocking your head against the keyboard might produce.

- There's some truth to the old saw about birds of a feather. You might enjoy joining a writers' organization and hanging out with others who share your dreams. Some people are joiners; some are not.

- Even though plenty of software is out there, claiming to make you a better writer, I would approach with a "show me" attitude rather than a blind faith that buying a particular program is going to transform you into a great novelist. I don't know … I just have this feeling it's not that easy.

Marketing and Publicity

In This Chapter

- Understanding the marketplace
- Creating interest in your novel
- Pushing your novel yourself
- Playing the publicity game

Okay, it's time to talk about getting your book sold to as many readers as possible. Your publisher considers your book a *product* that must be distributed to the marketplace. To do that, marketing and publicity come into play.

It's hard to believe, but plenty of writers tell me they have little or no interest in how their book is marketed or publicized. They claim they're "too busy being creative to worry with such things …" or some such nonsense. Any writer who expresses that sentiment is a dunderhead of the first mark. A writer talented enough to sell his book to a legitimate publisher *must* be concerned with how it will be advertised and sold to the public.

There's a lot to know about selling and publicizing a novel—more than I can fit into a small chapter like this one. I touch on the main points in this chapter and trust I've inspired you to probe deeper into the subject. Some very good books, websites, and professional services can get you up to speed. The absolute best is John Kremer's bookmarket.com. His book *1001 Ways to Market Your Books* is a classic. You can do the usual research to find secondary material.

Your mission is to stay focused on what happens to your novel *after* you've proofed and turned in the typeset galleys. So let's get started.

The Major Goals

Marketing and publicity are basically aimed at getting three things accomplished:

- *Finding your "target audience."* This is mainly common sense. If you've written a mystery novel, you want the large pool of mystery readers to receive the majority of information about your book. Your publisher should have a handle on this.

- *Giving them the hype.* This includes publication date, plot summary, advance reviews, endorsements from other writers, and anything else to get them interested in what you've written.

- *Make them read it.* You can nudge this one along in lots of ways. I get into them in greater detail when we talk about publicity.

WORDS OF WISDOM

If a writer proclaims himself to be isolated, uninfluenced, and responsible to no one, he should not be surprised if he is ignored, uninfluential, and perceived as irresponsible.

—Charles Newman

The Marketplace

The book business has undergone many changes in the last 25 years—some good, some not so good. The small, mom 'n' pop bookstores have been crowded out by national chain bookstores; giga-superstores like Borders and Barnes & Noble; and even the lower-rent outlets like BJ's, Sam's Club, and Walmart. More recently, online booksellers like Amazon.com have entered the arena, selling books without the overhead of maintaining and staffing brick-and-mortar stores.

All those outlets can sell their books at immediate discounts off the cover price because they are buying in huge volumes to get better discounts from distributors and publishers. The small, independently owned bookshops can't do this, so they're forced to buy fewer books at higher prices. The math doesn't look good for little stores.

The end result has been a big decline in the number of bookstores … other than the really huge ones. That means fewer places to display all the new books published each year. The industry types call this *shelf space* or *rack space*, and it's getting smaller and more concentrated each year.

A LIKELY STORY

An amateur inventor spends 20 years of his life on a device that will revolutionize his industry. When he shares his prototype and plans with his employer, he loses *all* rights to his life's work because he signed a contract when he was first hired that grants the company ownership of *anything* he creates while working for them. He attempts to reason with the owner of the company but gets nowhere. Driven to despair, the inventor resorts to violence, killing the owner's wife and kidnapping his son.

I've heard lots of publishers, editors, and agents say the same thing: too many books are being published. I don't know if that's true or just the usual insider carping. But they did publish around 300,000 titles in the United States during 2009, which means lots of books to be squeezed into a limited number of slots on a limited number of shelves.

This begs the question: how long does a book stay on sale and in print before a new one crowds it out of the marketplace? There's no definitive answer, but ... let me tell you a little story about O'Hare International Airport in Chicago.

Adventures in Time and Space

O'Hare is a very big airport, with many, many newsstands and shops scattered throughout all the levels, terminals, and buildings. All these venues offer magazines and books for sale, and they sell a *lot* of them every day. They sell so much reading material that O'Hare is considered a kind of gold mine for book publishers and distributors—everybody is going crazy to get their titles in the airport shops because the buying is brisk.

Every day, new shipments of books arrive at the airport. There are so many books, in fact, that they have a guy who does nothing but drive all over the mammoth airport in a little electric truck full of magazines and books, going from shop to shop, endlessly restocking the reading material. I've heard it takes him about 36 hours to make a complete circuit of all the shops and newsstands in the airport—before starting the process all over again.

Now here's where it gets interesting for us writer types.

When he gets back to a store last visited 36 hours ago, he looks to see which books have sold and which have not. If the five copies of, say, book A he put out on the last trip have sold out, he restocks *five more* copies of book A. That's great. No problem.

But let's say book B on the next slot over only sold one copy, or maybe even *no* copies … well, then we have a different situation. He takes down book B and *replaces* it with a new book we'll call C. As he goes along through the rest of the circuit of shops, he replaces sold book B copies with copies he's pulled from previous stores … unless he continues to find book B *unsold* on too many shelves. If that appears to be the pattern over his entire circuit, he yanks book B from *all* the shelves, and it will never be sold in the airport again.

So let's recap. Your book (or anyone else's book) is basically getting *3 days* of shelf life to get peoples' attention and sell, or it is effectively *gone*. This is how it goes in the busiest, hottest book-selling airport in the world.

Other Venues

The O'Hare tale is an extreme case, mind you, but I mention it to show you the level of competition for space and sales and how much time you may have to get people reading your novel.

In the super-bookstores, your novel may make the "new release" table or shelf, or it may get placed in the shelves with just the spine facing outward, which means nobody's going to find it unless they go on an expedition to specifically do so. It will, however, have a decent shelf life, and it won't be yanked in terms of hours or weeks. Months is more like it.

The big consideration is the competition with all the other titles. There's no way to avoid it because most publishers are pumping out new books on a *monthly* basis.

Marketing in General

If you've generated a good working relationship with your editor, tell him or her you want to be as involved in the marketing and publicity as you can. Tell them you'll do signings and tours, stand in booths at book fairs, hand out flyers, spin plates on sticks, or whatever they want.

Now especially with new writers and first novels, publishers don't have excess time and money to develop a big-time marketing plan. Unless you've been talented enough to land a very big advance, your publisher won't be highly motivated to do much to get back their investment. Most publishers of first novels are content to let such books "seek their own level," which is a polite way of saying "sink or swim."

That's where you come in. Your job is to ensure a variety of marketing strategies take place, even if your publisher doesn't have the resources to assist you. It may sound like a tough assignment, but it's worth the effort. Believe me.

Let's consider some marketing strategies.

Timing

If you listen to editors and agents, you might get the impression that there's practically *no* good time of the year to publish a book. The summer is when people travel and stay outside a lot—no time to read (unless it's that elusive "beach book"). Autumn competes with the "back to school" rush. There are so many books released for Christmas, yours may get lost in the crush. And of course, nobody buys anything for *months* after Christmas, which gives you a very small window in the springtime to sell books.

This is an exaggeration, of course, but different seasons do bring out different marketing strategies. So when your publisher gives you a pub date, you should at least consider how it will fit into the season that will greet it.

I can remember one Christmas season when a paperback edition of an anthology series I'd edited was published. I scheduled myriad signings in mall bookstores throughout the mid-Atlantic and sold a *ton* of books to people looking for inexpensive, original gifts. You never know what's going to work, but you try to be adventurous and optimistic. Every sale is important because that's one more person who may like your work and recommend it to *another* person.

Timing can work for or against you. If your book centers upon the dramatic events of, say, a nuclear power plant meltdown, and a *real* one happens a few days after your novel is published, you can "catch the wave" and ride it all the way to the money-shore. But just as easily, a book's appearance and possible attention can be dwarfed or overwhelmed by events taking place on the world or national stage. But that's beyond anyone's control.

Signings and Tours

Normally, with a first novel, a publisher isn't going to invest the time and money to advertise a new writer and send him out on the promotion trail to hawk sales. They don't see it as an economically viable proposition. They have let their cost accountants tell them how many books they can print and expect to sell *without* any additional expenses. This is perfectly reasonable. Publishers roll the dice with new novelists—sometimes winning, and more often than not, losing.

This does not, however, mean you shouldn't consider doing a series of book signings that may be of a ... oh, let's say, less than national scope.

Bookstores—large and small—absolutely *love* to have authors on the premises signing their books. It's good for business and it costs the stores *nothing.*

If your book takes place in a singular and high-profile region of the country (such as Gettysburg, the Everglades, New Orleans, or any of a hundred other recognizable locales), you might want to explore some publicity in the region and schedule appearances to sign books and drum up some sales. If your book centers on a particular occupation or event, you may want to try to arrange for appearances that tie in with them. For example, if your story is about firefighters, you could do promotions with regional fire departments and do events at firehouses.

You have to be creative and prescient and willing to take chances. Book signings are weird. Sometimes they are very successful, and sometimes they are complete flops. Some of the big superstores schedule a group of writers and trump it up as an "event" and even have the writers read selections and answer questions. This can be great if you have an electric and engaging personality like me. It can be less than great if you have the personal charm of, say, a newel post.

The bottom line is to be willing to get out and befriend your potential readers. Bookstores are great places to meet readers. Funny thing about that.

Your Book's Cover

The tired old axiom says, "You can't tell a book by its cover," but I'm here to tell you millions of people do just that.

And here's some more bad news: most writers have absolutely no control over what their book cover is going to look like. A lot of people are surprised when they hear this; they wrongly assume the writer gets to somehow choose the appearance of his or her book.

No way.

If this is *ever* going to happen, it will be only after a writer's been with a publishing house for an extended number of books and years. And even then it's not guaranteed.

Before we go too far here, let me explain a few things. A book's *cover* can mean different things, depending on the type of edition we're talking about. In general, the cover is the very front of the book, the "face" the public sees first. Hardcover books usually have their cover depicted on the *dust jacket,* or the paper wrapper that folds over the boards. Also called DJs, they can be foiled and embossed, and they're usually gloss-laminated. Trade paperbacks and the smaller mass-market paperbacks (which used to be called pocket books) don't have dust jackets; they just have a cover, which is a thicker, often laminated paper that encloses the inner pages. All references to covers in this discussion refer to whatever is on the front of the book.

Now some covers proclaim a book to be classy and upscale and all that stuff—these tend to have more type and less illustration. If there is a graphic image, it tends to be more symbolic or abstract. Editors and publishers call the pictures on books either *cover art* or *cover illustration,* depending on how the book is being marketed.

> **TRADE TALK**
>
> **Cover art** is usually what art directors call the graphic image on a dust jacket. The same thing on a paperback is called **cover illustration.** There's a kind of unarticulated snobbery going on here. Art is, as we all know, better than mere illustration; hardcovers are, of course, more prestigious than paperbacks. *Of course.*

The cover of your book is out of your control; and the only reason I'm even mentioning it is to give you a clue about how your publisher intends to market your novel. Go into any bookstore, and compare the covers of other books on various shelves and categories, and it won't take you long to figure out where your own cover is going to show up—depending on the genre or category.

And from that assessment, adjust and focus your *own* marketing program to best suit the "look" of your book. As an example, if you've written a fine historical romance and your publisher dressed it up in a lavishly illustrated, colorful painting of a bare-chested man holding a swooning heroine, well, that's probably not going to market well to a speaking gig at the Elks Lodge or a literary symposium at Princeton. See what I mean?

Website and Samples

The cyberspace arena has opened up a variety of new marketing channels to writers who are motivated and forward-thinking. Months before your book is published you should set up a website. I don't have the space here to go into detail about how to make it happen, but plenty of people and agencies out there can help you.

Surf around and check out other writers' websites. Get ideas. Steal what looks good; blow off what looks silly. Think of it as a freewheeling idea database. Go out there and see what people are doing to sell books.

The main point is to get it done. Have a series of web pages devoted to you and your book. Pictures, advance quotes, reviews, and some biographical stuff on you are all good, standard inclusions. But you will also want to think about setting up links with either your publisher or other booksellers so people who hit your site and want to buy the book can just click right through and make the purchase.

Another intriguing way to get people to try your work is to offer a *free sample* of your writing. This is usually done in either a file prospective buyers can download, or a page on your site where they can read it on-screen. Be sure you get permission from your publisher to do this and then *do* it. I know several writers who have established a substantial readership by doing things like this.

WORDS OF WISDOM

If being an egomaniac means believing in what I do, and in my art and my music, then in that respect, you can call me that ... I believe in what I do and I'll say it to whomever will listen.

—John Lennon

You will also want to find large, generic websites that post links to other writers and readers. The idea of linking into web-rings (lists and links of sites that share common themes) is also helpful. Your website guru/consultant will help you with this stuff.

The basic effect should be friendly, accessible, and modern. Do *not* make your website all stuffy and authorlike. That bit is beat, not to mention boring.

Word of Mouth

Another powerful tool to sell copies of your book is by the old jungle telegraph—I tell somebody how good your novel is and that person reads it and tells somebody else.

It's a slow process that gradually builds from an arithmetic increase of one at a time into a geometric expansion in which 10 people each eventually tell 10 each and up the line until your book has been mentioned to hundreds of thousands of people.

Word of mouth does work. But it requires time and patience.

You can nudge it along by telling everyone you know about your book and outright *telling them* to mention it to everybody they know.

The best way to make this happen is to have enough contributor's copies of your book to give away to people you meet who you believe have the influence to spread the word to a lot of other people. You can usually buy extra copies of your book from your publisher at a very reasonable rate due to the deep author's discount.

Do yourself a favor and buy a hundred copies. They beat the living tar out of a business card. You can go to sleep on *that* one.

Publicity

Publicity is all about you getting into the spotlight and telling everybody how cool you are and how great your book is. It's the blood relative of marketing, and you need to learn how to make the most of whatever publicity you can generate. And never forget the etiology of the word—which is from the root, *public*. That means getting out in the public and making people notice you and your novel.

It's supposed to be an unquestioned wisdom that writing is a solitary and lonely business. There are some who'd like you to believe it's a profession you do by yourself and is best suited for introverts and social cripples.

> **TOM'S TIPS**
>
> Don't think you're too good to talk about your work; also don't feel embarrassed if you want to talk about your book. Don't be shy. In this business, humility is for chumps.

Friends, after spending all this time with me, you should have already put the lie to that kind of talk. I have lots of friends and a majority of them are writers, and I'm not exactly what you would call shy or socially inept. I believe the most successful writers working today are those who are as facile and adept in public as they are in front of their keyboards.

And if you're not, you can certainly train yourself to be. In case you haven't noticed, you can be as unproductive or successful as *you* want to be. Your internal choices about yourself control everything else.

Okay, we need to talk about getting the word out on your novel. We start with one of the oldest chestnuts in the barrel.

The Press Release

You've probably heard of these things, even if you've never seen or written one. They're basically a notice—always only *one* page—sent to the media to announce something they don't know about.

Every publisher has a publicity department, but you cannot count on it to work as hard for your book as *you* would. Such departments are usually small, understaffed, and under orders to pump up the "lead titles" each month—for which the publisher paid the most money. That's another way of saying you're going to be bugging them for help, not the other way around.

Anyway, if you ask your publicity department for copies of press releases they have sent out on previous titles, you can get a great idea of how you're going to do your own. Essentially, the press release addresses the standard questions of classic journalism—*who, what, where, when,* and *how?*

A good press release has a banner or headline running in bold type across the top of the page. This single line should be catchy and sharp and, ideally, it should summarize the theme and unique points of your novel. This is not easy—in fact, there's an art to doing it with most novels because fiction is generally more complex and layered than nonfiction. Media-types get hundreds of press releases every day. You need to make yours stand out from the rest by making it as intriguing and irresistible as possible.

You need to ask yourself some questions. *What is the one most intriguing aspect of my novel? Does it posit a new idea? Does it answer an old, familiar mystery? Does it create a new way of seeing the familiar?* These and other questions you must ask will steer you toward the perfect banner for your press release. I prefer banners that ask a question—a question so original and curious the media-types can't resist reading on to get the answer (which may or may *not* be there …).

Here's an example of a catchy banner:

> What Happened to a President Who Faked His Own Assassination?

Okay, so let's assume you have the banner that will grab everyone's attention. What else do you need? You want a short line or two that gives the basics of the book: title, author, publisher, publication date, price, and ISBN number (a universal identifying code assigned to each book published anywhere in the world, making it unique and retrievable).

Then you post a few trenchant *blurbs* that make your book (and you) sound like it's headed for instant best-seller status. Next, a few paragraphs summarize the plot and explain why this novel is relevant to today at this very moment and why everybody *must* read it. Optionally, you can answer the question you may have posed in the banner-hook and then wrap things up with the usual numbers and e-mails for you and your publisher who may be contacted for more information, interviews, and *free* copies of your novel.

> **TRADE TALK**
>
> A **blurb** is essentially a one-sentence endorsement of your novel by a famous, best-selling writer (if possible), or at least by a recognizable name. This is done to give credibility to your ability to tell a good story. It's difficult to assess the value of blurbs, but because publishers continue to ask for and use them, they must help.

It is very important that your press release be *one page only*, and that there's plenty of "air" in it—open space between lines and short paragraphs that make it easy to read. You only have a few seconds to grab your target's attention, so make it as easy as possible.

Radio

You may be wondering, *Okay, I have this great press release … now, what do I do with it?*

Good question. You're going to make a lot of copies, and you're going to send them out to an enormous number of places. One of the best places to send your release is the world of radio—especially the burgeoning arena of talk radio. They will be quite receptive to it. Thousands of radio stations all over the country are *constantly* looking for interesting program material. If the program directors of these outlets like your press release, you will be invited to do a "book spot" on one of their daily shows.

It works like this: you'll get a call from a station producer, who will want to talk to you and see what your voice, pronunciation, and general delivery sound like. The producer will tell you he's calling to schedule you for a spot, but believe me, he is also making sure you speak well enough to be on the air. If you talk like you have mud and marbles in your mouth or you have a very heavy regional accent, the producer may suddenly have trouble finding a good time slot and promise to call you back. Right, sure … right after that geologic era sometime after *never.*

TOM'S TIPS

When the radio producers start calling, be sure to speak clearly and with lots of energy. You simply cannot sound low-key or boring. You have to be totally excited about your book, and you have to be engaging and entertaining. There's nothing worse than hearing a writer talk about his work if he is thunderingly boring.

And by the way, the best way to reach hundreds of radio stations in a short amount of time is to buy a current listing of their *fax* numbers, the names of the talk show hosts, and the addresses. The best place I can recommend is a company called Bradley Communications (1-800-989-1400). You can either spend first-class postage to mail each station the press release, or the cost of the fax call; it's your choice.

I have done this myself many times and have easily scheduled between 50 and 100 stations for each new book I write. The best schedule features a lot of "drive time" spots, which hook you into a maximum number of listeners per station. And I can personally vouch for this strategy. I have noticed dramatic increases in the sales of my books that received the radio coverage over ones that did not.

I didn't even mention your local radio stations, but you should be on the phone and in your car personally pitching all the local producers to put you on the air. It should be an easy sell because local authors have lots of regional interest.

Television

Getting your pretty face on TV is another story. Your chances are probably better if you live in what's called a small market rather than one of the big cities. But even then, television broadcast facilities are not as plentiful as radio stations, and they cover larger geographic areas.

It's the usual percentage game—with fewer television venues in which you might appear, you will have a higher number of people vying for the same number of slots. Unless you get some gigs on that dying dinosaur, public television, you won't have airtime to sit and discuss your novel and how you came to write it. Commercial TV rarely interviews novelists unless they are quasi-famous best-sellers. When they do talk to a regular writer about his novel, they normally do it with a slant that links it to a topic that's currently "hot" in the newsroom studios.

That ties into what I was saying earlier about timing. I did a novel that examined some rather original applications of cloning (*way* before *Jurassic Park*, thank you), and I did a fair number of appearances talking about the whole concept. That book (*The Blood of the Lamb*) sold out of its entire print run in hardcover and stayed in print in paperback for 12 years … which is excellent shelf life.

Getting on national television to talk about your novel is one of those things I would rank down there with your odds of getting hit by a meteor while sitting in the upper deck of Yankee Stadium. Unless you rocket to the top of the best-seller list, there isn't a whole lot you can do to make it happen. All the faxes, phone calls, e-mails, postcards, and letters won't make a dent in the juggernaut of network broadcasting.

Now you could get very blessed and have the president of the United States tell a meeting of the National Press Club how great your first novel is (which is exactly what happened to my high school classmate, Tom Clancy), which would most likely propel you onto the charts.

But don't count on it.

Book Reviews

A lot of new writers don't realize the value of book reviews and the importance of having them appear in the right places. The one thing you can count on from your publisher's publicity folks is getting out review copies. They do it for every book and hope it gets the reviewers' attention.

If you've written a genre book, you have a better chance of getting reviewed because more magazines, newsletters, and websites are devoted to the various categories of fiction than those written for a mainstream audience.

National publications receive thousands of books per month for possible review and can only give attention to a very small percentage of them. To get reviewed in the Sunday *New York Times* is tantamount to winning the lottery or getting knighted. National news and entertainment periodicals review even fewer titles.

Your initial efforts to get reviewed should be with your local and regional newspapers and other publications. Most are very well disposed to local authors and will be happy to help you get some coverage. Collect all those appearances in print, and attach them to review copies for other media. Every little bit helps.

Oh, one last thing. If your novel is a paperback original (no prior hardcover edition), your chances of getting national reviews are practically nil. Traditionally, only hardcovers receive consideration. You can still get genre paperbacks reviewed in magazines and websites devoted to particular fiction categories.

With the recent trend toward new novels published as trade paperbacks, which are paperbacks with trim sizes comparable to hardcovers, book reviewers tend to give them more attention than the old mass-market (standard size) paperbacks.

Postcards

If you're willing to spend a little money, you can get your book some decent attention. With a full-color reproduction of your book's cover on the front and a half-panel for reviews, hype, and order information, you can reach targeted audiences and get people to *notice* you, even if they don't buy your book.

Send the postcards to local newspapers, radio stations, book reviewers, special events directors at big bookstore chains, and anyone else who can help you sell your book. A color repro of your book cover gets noticed.

And don't forget, getting noticed is what this chapter is all about.

A caveat: postcards and postage are costly and definitely low-tech. However, that may be just what you need to get your book publicity to stand out from the rest. Very few people do it anymore and, therefore, you can achieve a more distinctive profile if you go *against* the trend.

E-Mail

The potential to reach millions and millions of potential readers makes the allure of e-mail so enticing, but most e-mail advertising is considered spam, the lowest of the low. I've talked to other writers and publishers about e-mail's place in book publicity, and I get a variety of opinions that cover the spectrum from useless to invaluable.

I'm still not sure how it's going to shake out. The idea of opt-in e-mail lists sounds like the only way to reach a potential audience without alienating yourself from it. In theory, the only people who will receive your book are those who have *asked* to get notices about cool books and writers. They have exercised the *opt*ion to be *in*cluded in your mailing, hence the abbreviation.

It's still too early in the game to see how opt-in e-mail will work, but it bears watching. As the industry becomes more sophisticated, we will all learn more about how well it succeeds or fails. In the meantime, you can find opt-in e-mail suppliers on the web who will send your message for a price.

I know writers who don't care if a thousand people hit the Delete key for each one who reads about their book. When you're dealing in the millions, those one-in-a-thousands add up. And maybe that's the best attitude to take on this one—play the sheer numbers game, and don't worry about the people who don't care.

Internet Communities

Recently, the Internet has become the home for blogs, message boards, forums, and community kiosks like Facebook, Twitter, and MySpace. These are all ways to reach lots of people instantly, and if you have an important message to deliver—like the publication of your new book—it can be a generator of interest and sales. However, these communities tend to be trendy and may fall out of favor as newer venues present themselves. So I wouldn't be surprised to discover that all these examples could become very old news in a hurry.

I know several writers who have cultivated the message boards and kiosks to specifically create ever-expanding communities of people who like and buy their books.

This is an avenue for exploration, and you shouldn't ignore it just because you may not understand it or use it on a regular basis. You owe it to the success of your book to examine and tinker with the power of the Internet as a marketing and publicity tool.

Publicists

The best way to get out the word on your new novel is to get a professional involved. It's also the most expensive. But big-time publicists, if based in New York or Los Angeles, are well connected to most of the media outlets. If they are good at what they do, publicists will know the "right" people on a first-name basis and can get your book seen by influential reviewers and other decision-makers.

WORDS OF WISDOM

There's no such thing as bad publicity except your own obituary.

—Brendan Behan

Every industry is based partly upon the who-you-know factor. A successful publicist gets results by getting clients' books *past* the gatekeepers and screeners whose job is to filter out 95 percent of the books thrown at them each month. And you simply can't do that unless you know people. I hired a publicist for a novel I knew had a unique premise, and it was selected as a *New York Times* Notable Book of the Year, as well as winning a major writing award. Coincidence? Maybe not.

That's why a really good publicist will charge anywhere from $10,000 to $20,000 to promote your book. It's clearly not an option for everyone, but if you can swing that kind of cash, it's a consideration. There's a story in publishing that a very famous best-selling novelist had a very wealthy husband who spent close to a million promoting her first novel and literally *forced* it onto The List. When that happened, and she became a brand name, her success was assured.

The Least You Need to Know

- Figuring out the best audience for your book is important. *Selling* it to them is essential.
- Novels don't have a long life span if no one notices them. The time to begin marketing your book is several months *before* it's published.
- There are many ways to publicize your novel. Don't overlook any of them, and make generating publicity a vital part of your writing process.
- You cannot, under any circumstances, be shy or retiring or (*gasp!*) humble regarding your novel. You must be in love with what you have written and be driven to make others feel the same way.

The Business of Writing

Chapter 20

In This Chapter

- Working around other jobs
- How you get paid
- What you are selling
- An inside look at publishing

One of the big problems you might have when you decide to write your novel is how to budget your time—because your time is your money.

Now that previous sentence purposely contained a couple slightly radioactive "keywords"—*budget* and *money*. This chapter examines what they really mean and looks at the side of writing that most writers never want to think about: the business side.

If you want to write a novel or spend the rest of your life writing novels, you can pretty much count on it being a full-time job. Even when you're not writing your novel, you should be spending time *thinking* about writing your novel. That's not exactly thinking like a businessperson, but you will need to be aware that you *are* in a business.

Two Things You Need Lots of: Time and Money

You're going to need a lot of time to complete your novel. You will also need money on which to live. If you are working another full-time job (to get the money, you see), the time to finish your novel will stretch out to a much longer completion date.

So what's the solution? You might want to work a part-time job and set up things so your support group (remember we discussed this way back in Chapter 1?) can take up some of the slack. There are a lot of ways to make this happen, including having a spouse who enjoys a great job with plenty of income and benefits to take care of both of you; or having recently inherited enough money to pay your expenses while you write; or sharing housing and food expenses with others in a similar situation as yourself (like the old college dorm days, but extended into adulthood); or maybe even joining a Communist artist colony. (Just kidding about that last one. Everybody should know by now that communism was a bust.)

WORDS OF WISDOM

Money to a writer is time to write.

—Frank Herbert

Finding the Time

When I was first getting started, I didn't actually plan my finances and business arrangements; instead I chose to let them "happen" in a free-form kind of way. After graduating from college, I took a part-time job working in a bookstore, attended a few graduate school courses, and wrote my stories and books late at night. I remember that the apartment I shared with my old college roommates was a second-floor unit above a guy who was a supermarket manager and had to wake up at 5 A.M. every day.

You can see where this is headed. He was getting ready to hit the sack at just about the exact time I was sitting down to write. It doesn't sound like a problem until you remember this was taking place in the Permian era, back before anyone had ever heard of Apple Computer or Microsoft, and you were a modern, well-to-do writer if you were using an electric typewriter. Not being able to afford one, I was still using a big, old, clunky manual typewriter, which squatted on a chrome-legged dining room table. It was decently noisy, and the pounding on the keys must have reverberated at a pretty good decibel level down the metal table legs and through the floor.

I say this with a lot of certainty because my downstairs neighbor would start banging on his ceiling with a broom handle as soon as I started writing. I tried to damp down the machine by putting a layer of foam rubber and a bath towel under it, but it never really approached the total silence my neighbor wanted.

He couldn't understand why anyone would want to start typing at such a late hour … and even if someone did, he couldn't imagine what would require *all that* typing.

I'm not even going to bother telling you about the battles that raged between us until he finally moved out.

Cutting to the chase, I ended up writing three novels—over the next two years— between the hours of 10 P.M. and 2 A.M., but I don't recommend a schedule like that to anyone. The only reason I was able to keep writing like that was my youth, energy, and an unstoppable mission to become a professional writer. You may not have all, or any, of the three.

> **TOM'S TIPS**
>
> You have to convince yourself that writing your novel is your real job, and that anything else you do in your week-to-week existence to earn money is merely a necessary obstacle to that real job.

Working for Yourself

How does this apply to you? Well, I guess this is just a long-winded way of telling you writing is a business and can be a demanding one. If you sell the novel you're going to write, you will be a professional writer, a freelance writer (which means that you'll be an independent contractor), or self-employed.

For some of you, that concept will sound very unsettling and worrisome. If you've spent all your adult life working for a company or for someone else, the idea of working for yourself can sound very alien and not very feasible. Well, I'm here to tell you: don't let it bother you. Being self-employed is just like anything else—it has its advantages and its downsides, its pluses and minuses, its X's and O's. The bottom line is that you should understand the business side of writing.

The following section explains the real world of the publishing business and how it will directly affect you.

How It Works

If you sell your novel to a publishing house, the financial side can play out in several ways. If you've turned in a complete manuscript and your editor wants to buy it, he or she will offer you what is called an *advance*, which is an amount of Federal Reserve Notes based on the amount your editor and publisher think they can recoup in sales of your book.

The reason the industry calls the first money they pay you an *advance* is because it's up-front money that's charged against whatever royalties your book earns. Royalties are the dollars you earn for each book you sell.

TOM'S TIPS

Learn very early in the game how to read your contracts. Don't trust your agent or lawyer to understand the language and terms and always get it right. If you fully comprehend your contract, you have an equal understanding of how much your work is worth. You also need to know how to read your royalty statements.

Let's consider an example; I'll use round, simple numbers to keep the math to a minimum. The actual amounts have no relation to whatever current market realities are in effect. (When I sold my first hardcover novel, its retail price was $7.95, which is barely more than today's paperbacks.) So let's say you get a publisher to give you $10,000 as an advance against future sales and royalties; for the sake of easy math, let's say you've been offered a 10 percent royalty on the retail price of your novel; and the retail price is $20.

All that boils down to this: you're earning $2 per book sold (.10 × $20 = $2), which means your publisher needs to sell 5,000 copies of your book before you have "earned out" your advance (5,000 × $2 = $10,000).

If you're still with me on the math, you should ask: okay, what next?

In the Black

What's next is that your book is considered *in the black*, and any additional sales are put into a mythical place called a "royalty account" where your publisher will keep track of every copy sold (and not returned). Thereafter you will get a statement several times a year that tells you how many $2 bills you have earned through additional sales.

Easy, right? Well, yes and no. If you were reading the previous paragraphs carefully, you may have noticed and wondered about that amended phrase in parentheses "and not returned."

Now what could that possibly mean? What indeed?

A LIKELY STORY

Your hero has just been informed that he has inherited a vast estate worth millions. But in order to claim it, he must complete a rigorous task or perform a dangerous feat. You decide what it will be and how he succeeds or fails.

Returns

In publishing, *returns* means only everything. You see, there's this odd arrangement in the publishing world that goes far beyond a vendor ordering too much stock and sending a portion of it back to a manufacturer for credit. It's called the return policy, and it allows distributors (the ones who buy mass quantities of books from publishers, warehouse them, and ship them around the country to bookstores) to send books back to the publishers if they don't sell. So you have an interesting situation that ultimately affects you, the writer of the book.

Your book is "sold" to the distributor ... ah, but not really. The distributor sells it to a bookstore or a chain like Barnes & Noble, and they put it on their shelves for sale. Meanwhile, back at your publisher, the initial order from the distributor is logged into your royalty account as *sold copies*. But there's one small problem—your books aren't really sold.

More accurately, they're kind of "on loan" to the distributor and the bookstores to see if they can sell them. If they can't, then your books are returned.

And that's the part of your royalty account that can get a little weird. Many writers over the years have seen royalty statements showing their book has sold enough copies to "earn out" their advance, but they still don't get any additional royalty payments because their publisher holds back the money owed against *possible* returns.

Wow, what does that mean? It depends on the terms of your original contract with the publisher. Most contracts stipulate what percentage of earned sales royalties the publisher is allowed to retain against returns. That percentage can run from 0 all the way to 100 percent. So read carefully before you sign anything.

But Wait ... There's More!

The business of returns in publishing is all about money. Shipping large quantities of books around the country costs a lot of money. Hardcover books weigh a lot, and shipping them costs accordingly. Having known this for many generations, most publishers, distributors, and bookstores do not want to pay the double shipping expense of a delivery and a return if it can be avoided. To keep this at a minimum, all parties try to keep their hardcover printing, ordering, and shipping under close scrutiny so there's a minimum of hardcover returns.

This has worked out pretty well over the years, and if your novel is published in hardcover, your concerns over returns and royalties held against returns should not be overly obsessive. Another good thing about appearing in hardcover is your sale to the libraries, which always buy hardcovers and never return them. Ultimately, whatever copies of your hardcover novel may be left (after all sales and all returns are accounted for) are then "remaindered," which means they are sold at a big discount to bargain outlets, mail-order catalogs, book clubs, or you.

The advantage here is two-fold:

- You will get a royalty on the remainder sales.

- You can buy copies of your own book for pennies on the dollar. This is something you *always* want to do.

TOM'S TIPS

I always buy all my remainders (if they're available) because I do a lot of public speaking and my audiences always want to purchase copies of my books after they've been wowed by my appearance. Figure it out—friends, you buy your books for a dollar and sell them for $20. Hmm. Sounds like a good deal to me. Besides, copies of your books make great gifts, and believe me, they beat the stuffing out of business cards. You give somebody a hardcover copy of your *book,* and they're going to remember you.

Paperbacks Are Different

But you might ask, what happens if you sell your novel as a "mass-market original"? This is another way of saying you sold your novel to a publisher who decided to publish it in paperback (without a hardcover edition first). As you might expect, an entirely different set of parameters exist for original paperback novels, and we need to look at them.

For one thing, the retail price of a paperback is much lower than that of a hardcover, which means you need to sell a *lot* more copies to earn a commensurate royalty check. Also, the return rate on paperback books can be astronomically high.

"Sure," you might be saying. "Paperbacks don't weigh nearly as much as hardcovers, so why is everybody less reluctant to ship them around?"

Good question. But the fact is: publishers and distributors do not want to ship paperbacks back and forth. Primarily because of an absolutely bizarre and essentially absurd business agreement you're going to have a hard time believing. It's called "stripping," and it has nothing to do with taking off your clothes.

A Singular Arrangement

Let me get into this with a hypothetical situation and a question. Let's imagine you're a manufacturer of lawn mowers. You make lawn mowers and you sell-them-but-not-really-sell them to hardware stores (the way publishers "sell" their paperback books). At the end of the season, the hardware stores get to send you *back* all the mowers nobody bought.

Well … not quite.

Let's add a little twist to the business transaction and say that all the hardware stores don't have to ship back the whole mower (because it's so heavy, right?). Let's allow them to just send back the blade or the pull-cord, and trash the rest of the mower, and you'll still give them full credit for their original "purchase" of a lawn mower.

What? You have to be thinking, *That is seriously nuts!* And you're right—it is. No company still in control of their faculties would cut such a deal. To allow a customer to "buy" your product, then mangle or defile it in a manner to render it useless for a resale somewhere else, trash it, and still get a full and complete credit or refund, would be madness.

When Strippers Are Not Entertaining

Yet this exact scenario has been taking place in the book industry for generations. It's called stripping, and for a long time, convenience stores, newsstands, airports, train stations, superstores, and even the distributors themselves have been doing it. For a long time, they stripped the books by tearing off the front covers by the thousands and binding them up in neat little rubber-banded stacks until they were sent back to the publisher for credit. Hey, makes sense to me—what costs less to ship? A thousand books or a thousand front covers?

Some of you may be wondering, *What about the rest of the book?* Well, theoretically, they get destroyed. This in itself is an incredible waste of time and resources. The best-case scenario is that all that paper somehow gets recycled so it can be stripped again, and ad infinitum.

Unfortunately, there is a worst-case scenario in which the stripped books somehow do *not* get destroyed but end up in the hands of people who sell them to unscrupulous outlets that hawk them in "bargain bins" at flea markets, dollar stores, yard sales, and venues of a similar stripe.

> **WORDS OF WISDOM**
>
> If you would be thrilled by watching the galloping advance of a major glacier, you'd be ecstatic watching changes in publishing.
>
> —John D. MacDonald

A few years ago, the stripping policy was altered so the cover and the first 50 or 60 pages were also to be removed from the book. This was done to presumably keep the books off the illegal resale (black) market.

Regardless of how it is accomplished, I think stripping books is one of publishing's biggest mistakes—because of the incredible waste and also for all the opportunities to commit fraud. But I have a feeling it's never going to change. So let's move on.

Other Ways to Get Paid

Aside from your initial advance and subsequent royalties (after returns, remember), several more viable income streams may flow your way. They are not as dependable or automatic, but they are options we should consider.

Foreign Rights

If your novel becomes sufficiently popular, or happens to be in a category (or genre) that appeals to international audiences (like espionage, science fiction, or horror), there's a good chance you can sell your novel to many foreign publishers.

My novels have been published in many languages, including French, German, Japanese, Romanian, Spanish, Portuguese, Italian, and even Finnish. Foreign publishing usually happens through your agent or the agency's network of foreign affiliates selling books in a variety of countries around the world. And as an added bonus, you're not responsible for having your novel translated; the foreign publisher takes care of that.

All you need to do is cash the check when it comes in. The amount of the check can vary widely, depending on many factors: your popularity, the size of the country, the value of its currency, the category in which they will market your novel, and even the skill of your foreign rights agency.

The bottom line is you should never count on foreign rights sales, and always treat them (when they happen) as if you were walking along one day and found a brown paper bag full of money. That way, you're always surprised and you're always happy with whatever you get.

Film, TV, and Video Games

These are situations where a producer, director, or even an actor may want to adapt your novel to the big screen, the small screen, or the CD-ROM. The negotiations and actual details of every "media" deal (which is what these are called) can vary from project to project, and the things you want from such opportunities is beyond the scope of what we're trying to accomplish here. Plenty of books and articles are available on the subject of selling your story to the movies or television. Go find a few and read up if you ever need to.

Book Clubs, Websites, and Other Adaptations

Many book clubs fill certain niche markets—mystery, science fiction, romance, and so on. If your book fits one of those categories, it's quite possible you can get some reprint money for allowing them to produce a "book club edition" of your novel.

The same goes for the burgeoning arena of e-publishing. Websites abound where readers can buy books online and either read them on-screen, download them for later, or print them out. There will probably be more and more of this going on, and you may be able to get paid for it. (I already addressed this in Chapter 16, so this is merely a reminder.)

Your novel could also be adapted as a musical or a stage play, and this can be as lucrative as a feature film if you have a Broadway hit. Your chances of winning the Irish Sweepstakes are probably a whole lot better than your chances of having this happening, but hey, I gotta tell you about the possibility.

> **A LIKELY STORY**
>
> A group of friends on a camping trip wreck their SUV when it slides off a mountain road and they're trapped in a steep-walled canyon. Supplies are limited. Escape may not be possible. What happens?

There's also a limited chance you may be approached by a small press or specialty press who wants to do your novel in a "limited" edition. These are usually small print runs of 250 to 1,000 books, with hand-sewn pages and real cloth bindings, that are numbered and signed by the author. They are books for people who love and collect books.

If your novels become collectible, this is a nice way to preserve your work for generations to come. Some of my books have been done as limited editions, and they are beautiful and prestigious—you should be so lucky.

Odds and Ends

That's the short course on the economics of publishing and what kind of remuneration you can expect from your novel writing. However, there are a few other things (concerning how you get paid, taxes, budgeting, and insurance) that bear mentioning. So before moving on, I want you to have a quick look at them.

Proposals and Partials

You can receive your advance in several ways. If you have turned in a whole, finished book, you will get your entire advance in one check, just the way I described it earlier.

However, you can also sell a novel based on what's called "chapters and outline" or a "proposal." This is not as prevalent as in years past, but it is basically a substantial portion of your novel—enough for an editor to get a good feel for what the finished product will look like. For a partial novel like this, you will get only a part of your advance when you sign the contract. You'll receive the balance when you turn in the final, completed manuscript. This can happen if you've already published a few books and your editor feels confident you can finish what you start.

This isn't a bad arrangement if you end up staying with the same publisher year in and year out.

Money Management

This is just a reminder that, unless you're a really fast typist and a faster writer, you may only write one book a year. That means you will only get paid once a year. For people who are more accustomed to getting paid every two weeks, this kind of adjustment can be, ah, kinda tough.

If the money you make from writing your novel is your major or only source of income, you're going to need to learn some basic money management skills. If you've never held a check in your hand with at least five digits before the decimal point, you might feel an urge to go out and blow a substantial portion of it on a convertible or an 8-foot plasma TV or gold membership at the Beach Club, but that might not be such a good idea.

WORDS OF WISDOM

The profession of novel-writing makes horse-racing seem like a solid, stable business.

—John Steinbeck

You need to learn how to stretch the check across the chasm of many months where you will be earning nothing but gold stars for doing good work.

Just be careful. And never say I didn't warn you.

Insurance

As a self-employed novelist, you won't have anyone (like your publisher, for instance) paying for your health insurance, life insurance, or any other kind of insurance. If your spouse or your "whatever" doesn't have a way of getting it either, you must decide if you want it and, if so, how much you are willing to pay for it.

Disability insurance also might be a wise investment. It's fairly inexpensive, and it could carry you through some rough spots if you have an accident and can't write to your deadline.

Taxes

If you've always worked for someone else, your employer has probably withheld substantial portions of your paycheck before you ever saw it. Well, it's not going to be that way if you write novels. You will get a check for all that's owed you, and it's up to you to do what you want with it.

I'm not going to advise you on the income tax laws of your state or any federal questions of liability, because it would require an entire *Complete Idiot's Guide* of its own. I just want you to be aware of how publishers pay you. What you do after you receive the payment is up to you.

That's about it on the business of writing. This chapter was not supposed to be a complete manual on how to run your economic life, but more of a heads-up about how your existence will be different if you are a self-employed novel writer.

The Least You Need to Know

- Self-employment is very different from what you have probably experienced. It's a good idea to have a plan for how you're going to survive.

- Publishers pay (and *not* pay) you in ways you never could have imagined— advances, royalties, and holds against returns. And they do it for reasons you absolutely would have never imagined.

- You can make additional money from your novel beyond the original advance and royalties by selling the rights to produce your novel in paperback, for book clubs, for visual media, etc.

- You need to learn how to manage your income, which can be described as sporadic at best.

The People of Publishing

Chapter 21

In This Chapter

- Editors and editing
- Literary agents and what they do
- Bookstores, publicists, reviewers, and readers
- Distributors and how they can help you

Okay, you've lasted this long, so it looks like you're in for the long haul. After we finish this chapter on how to deal with the people you're going to meet as a novelist, you will have learned everything I can possibly think of to tell you about writing novels.

There Are Editors ... and Then There Are Editors

The most prominent people in publishing are the editors. Editors serve a variety of purposes and wear a variety of titles. Let's have a look at some of that variety.

The Gatekeeper

When you send your novel to a publishing house, someone called an assistant editor or an associate editor will look at your manuscript. (These titles may be very accurate or, then again, maybe not.)

If your novel was sent in without a query letter, recommendation, or representation (this used to be called "over the transom"), it was most likely carted up from the mailroom and given to someone called a "first reader." In many publishing houses, the first reader is also an assistant editor.

The first reader's job is to be a filtering device, a gatekeeper, a first line of defense against the unpublishable submissions all houses receive on a daily basis. A first reader has a tough job—I speak from experience because I used to be one for a magazine called *Fantastic Stories* when I was just breaking in as a writer. I did it for a few years before burn-out took me down.

It's very demanding to read so many manuscripts that were clearly unprofessional—either in presentation or execution—and I gradually lost the critical ability to recognize what was really good, publishable work. When a first reader encounters so much mediocre to poor writing for an extended period, there is a tendency to ascribe a higher status to any submission that's actually just average. It's that darned relativity thing.

Ten Pages?

This may surprise you, but it's true—the first reader can usually tell within 10 pages whether or not the writer has what it takes. In that amount of space, a lot of things reveal themselves: grammar, setting, character, pacing, dialogue, and many of the rest of the elements we've looked at throughout this book and even again in this chapter.

> **WORDS OF WISDOM**
>
> My definition of a good editor is a man who sends me large checks, praises my work … and has a stranglehold on the publisher and the bank.
>
> —John Cheever

Therefore, your first 10 pages have to be incredibly arresting, polished, and as cleanly professional as you can make them. That way, the first reader will continue on to the next 10, and the next, and the next. If your book is really good, the first reader may get lost in it and read much more than usual. If it's excellent, he or she might read the entire book.

But that's not really your goal at this point. What you really want is for the first reader to separate your crisp, shining wheat from the dull chaff (allow me a little metaphorical riff here, okay?), and pass it along to the next person in the Divine Hierarchy of Publishing.

Now You're Getting Somewhere

If this happens, your submission goes on to meet a person with an even more critical eye and more decision-making power. Depending on the size of the publishing house's staff, your manuscript may go to an associate editor (who is the "real" editor's right-hand man/woman) or maybe right to the desk of The Editor, who is sometimes called the acquisitions editor. This is the editor who makes the ultimate decision to either reject or buy your book.

Bear in mind these people have not been sitting around, thumbs a-twiddlin', waiting for you to send them something good to read. Odds are they already have manuscripts stacked up on their desks, chairs, and every available square inch of shelf space. I've been in hundreds of editors' offices, and they all look just like that.

Even if your submission makes it this far, there's still no way to tell when it's going to get read. So a word of advice: be patient. These things take time. That's not to say that in the fullness of time, you shouldn't inquire about the status of your submission. After 8 to 10 weeks, I would send a polite postcard just checking in. After 3 or 4 months, you should call and ask to speak to someone.

E-mail is also becoming an acceptable way to contact a publisher who has your submission. You may need to call a gatekeeper to get a usable address and/or name, but it may be worth the effort.

Now let's imagine the best of all cases—the editor wants to buy your novel.

> **TOM'S TIPS**
>
> If you sell your novel, my advice to you, after you stop doing the happy dance, is that you arrange to meet with your editor. Even if you are the shy, retiring type (I personally never had that problem), you've got to trust me on this one. You will be far better off if your editor can attach a face and personality to the manuscript. It makes them care about you more—it's human nature. So even if you live thousands of miles from New York or wherever your editor is, get thee to an airport or a train station.

Your editor is going to be the person who shepherds your novel through all the stages before it goes to press. His initial task will be to give your book a thorough reading and make any suggestions for making it better—including your characters, plot and subplots, dialogue, pacing, resolution, and everything else that goes into a novel.

You work closely with your editor on revisions until you are both satisfied and then it goes to another type of editor.

You're Going to Copy *What?*

This person is called the copy editor. Some writers love this person, and some writers want to kill this person.

Here's why.

Where your regular editor's job was to tackle your work in the broadest, most sweeping ways, the copy editor's task is to scrutinize your novel line by excruciating line. This is not as bad as it sounds … and then again it can be.

 WORDS OF WISDOM

No passion in the world is equal to the passion to alter someone else's draft.

—H. G. Wells

The copy editor specifically looks for all the grammatical mistakes, the changes in tense, point of view, punctuation, syntax, spelling, and usage. Copy editors are also good at getting the foreign words and locales right, the facts of infinite variety of esoterica, and all the rest of the details most people don't notice but that can ruin the reading experience for someone who does.

We've all had the experience of reading something we know is wrong, and that seems to blow the credibility and enjoyment right out of the book. Copy editors are supposed to keep that from happening, and most of the time, they do a great job.

In fact, the only time you might have trouble with one is when he or she decides your style or your tone is off and starts rewriting you. Usually, I've seen this happen in dialogue—where you may have people speaking in fragments and ungrammatically. Some copy editors *insist* on making everybody speak like English professors, and that just doesn't always cut it.

So if and when your novel gets copyedited, try to keep things in balance and tell yourself it's all for the best.

Don't Believe All Those Jokes About Agents

Literary agents are also very plentiful in the publishing industry. They are the people who "represent" you and your novel in the marketplace. They send your manuscript to the editors, and they negotiate the terms of the purchase … if there is one. They also take care of the legal details in your agreement with the publisher. Agents are combination talent managers and lawyers.

There are lots of jokes about agents. Most of them are as bad as this one:

> An agent opened the door of his BMW, when suddenly a car came along and hit the door, ripping it off completely. When the police arrived at the scene, the agent was complaining bitterly about the damage to his precious BMW.

> "Officer, look what they've done to my Beeeemer!!!" he whined.

> "It's worse than that," said the policeman. "You kidding me? Your left arm was torn off!?"

> "Oh no …" replied the agent, finally noticing the bloody left shoulder where his arm once was, "Where's my Rolex?!"

Most agents are more considerate than that. Let's see why.

You Can't Get a Degree in It

Literary agents don't attend universities to learn their craft. Most of them have roots in publishing as previous editors, mailroom clerks, sales force reps, reviewers, or even printers or publishers.

Most successful writers have literary agents. But then again, a lot of unsuccessful writers have them, too. That doesn't really mitigate my belief that having an agent is an absolute necessity in the world of modern publishing.

The plain, simple fact is that editors pay far more attention to manuscripts submitted under a literary agency's cover letter than the ones coming in blind and naked from the writers themselves.

You need an agent. How do you get one? And what kind of an agent do you want? Writers' magazines, websites, and annual almanacs and "market encyclopedias" such as the *LMP* provide listings of many of the legitimate literary agencies. Many of them are based in New York because that city has been the traditional seat of publishing power and influence. Plus, it was always easier to take a walk or a subway around town to hand-deliver a manuscript or have an office chat or a lunch with a prospective editor. Agents in Minneapolis can't do that.

> **TRADE TALK**
>
> The most well-known market encyclopedia is the *LMP,* or *Literary Market Place.* This huge annual book is full of every conceivable type of information about the publishing industry. In addition to the names and addresses of all the publishers in the United States, it also contains a comprehensive list of literary agents. You can find it in most big libraries.

Personal contact is very important. Editors get to know agents, and some of them even become friends. If your work gets an agent's attention, he will ensure that some of the editors he knows will get a look at it.

Getting Their Attention

How do you get an agent's attention? Let's review a few strategies you might want to try.

Do the research. Get a comprehensive listing of agents, and start making calls, sending query letters and sample chapters, and writing e-mails. If you have any prior publishing credits, this is time to dress them up and put them on parade.

Get face to face. If you can spend a little time in New York City, do it. Make calls, and tell the receptionists you're in town looking for an agent and you want to make an appointment. There is no substitute for a face-to-face meeting. When agents and editors can connect a face and a personality to the sheet of paper, things begin to happen. If you're shy, get over it.

TOM'S TIPS

If you've had a commission-only job where you had to bug people because you had to try to sell them something, you're ahead of the game. You'll have to sell yourself as well as your work to get an agent. Salesmanship and personality are part of the equation, so get used to it. Taking "no" for an answer is simply not an option. Whether you like it or not—you just became a salesperson.

Go to where they hang out. You should also consider cruising places where agents are going to be found. The world of publishing is full of events where many publishers, editors, and agents convene as an excuse to do a lot of drinking and partying. Book fairs, booksellers' expositions, conventions for fans of genre fiction, awards banquets, and other organizations and "societies" dedicated to the world of books are all good places to start.

You can find listings for many of these events in compendia like the previously mentioned *Literary Market Place, Publishers Weekly* magazine, and a wide range of newsletters devoted to the doings of various genre organizations like the Mystery Writers of America, the Horror Writers Association, the Romance Writers of America, and many others.

If you go to these kind of events, hang out in the bar—you'll find agents who will talk to you. That's how I met my first agent. I was attending a convention of science fiction and fantasy writers, and I was at the bar listening to everybody talk. One guy was saying he'd just moved to New York, hung out his shingle, and was at the convention looking for some new clients so he could get started(!).

You can correctly assume I homed in on him like a JDAM missile and started selling myself. We became pretty good buddies and had a good relationship for years. Another young client my agent picked up right around the same time ended up having a pretty fair career himself. Maybe you've heard of him—his name is Stephen King.

Do you need a specialist? Many agents work with a specific kind of book—fiction or nonfiction; genres like science fiction, mystery, romance, biography, how-to, self-help; etc.

If your novel definitely falls into a readily recognizable category and you plan to keep writing in the same genre, you will probably be happier with an agent who specializes in that particular category. It's a good bet he or she already knows most of the editors in that genre who are looking for good material. Despite their workload, all editors are always looking to develop new writers in the hopes that one of them becomes big and they can claim they "discovered" him.

Talk to other writers. If you immerse yourself in publishing, you will eventually meet other writers. They tend to hang out at the same places where the agents gather. You will probably become friendly with enough of them to get referred to a variety of agents. You'll also get to hear the inside story on who's hot … and who's not.

 A LIKELY STORY

A writer discovers that someone who runs a regional distributorship was a heated rival back in high school. The rival is doing everything he can to destroy the writer's book in the marketplace. What happens?

A Few Final Thoughts

All the previous information should give you an idea about where and how to find an agent. You may change agencies a few times in your career, and that's okay. It's a matter of finding someone who likes your work and with whom you get along personally.

Also remember that any "agent" who wants to charge you a "reading fee" is not an agent. He is a professional reader who will give you a critique that may or may not be worth his fee.

For a long time, agents' commissions were 10 percent of whatever they earned for you. Now they want 15 … what else is new?

Lastly, you should realize that your agent usually becomes a pretty good friend—a confessor and confidant. He can really be the best thing that ever happens to your career.

People You Never Thought About … Until Now

This group we need to know about are a varied and sun-dried lot. They are the people who can really help make your novel a success, and for that reason, you should be as nice as possible to all of them. But don't get the wrong idea. I'm not advocating duplicity or subterfuge … just common sense.

Book City! Book World! Book-a-Rama!

After your book's pub date arrives, you are going to be very eager to see it on the shelves and display tables of every bookstore you enter. You most likely will keep checking on how many copies remain in your neighborhood stores, and you might even cop to turning it face-out if it's on the shelf with just the spine exposed. Don't feel badly. Every writer does it. But there's a lot more you can do with bookstores—whether it's a small, local mom 'n' pop or the latest mega-super-giga-chain store.

First thing is to go into all the bookstores in your area and *make friends* with the owners or managers. Even if you're shy or feel self-conscious about telling them you wrote a book, get over it. Bookstore owners are usually people who like books and love to meet real writers. Many of them are closet-writers and dream of publishing their own books someday, so they'll enjoy meeting you.

TOM'S TIPS

Readings, book discussion groups, and signings are all good ways for you to interface with your local and regional bookstores. Don't expect lines out the door like you may have seen for best-selling "celebrity" writers. The best way to look at it is with a dash of Zen—reminding yourself that even a thousand-mile journey must begin with but a single step.

Why are you doing this? You want the bookstore owners and managers to make sure your book is displayed prominently. Also, you want to be involved in any book or sales "events" the store may plan during its promotional year. Depending on the size of your town or city, the size and type of store, and the target audience, these events could be very big and helpful in introducing you and your book to potential readers.

The thing to remember here is that you should do whatever you can to make your readers notice you and make sure your local stores take care of you. They will ... if they know you're there.

Taking It to Another Level

Do you need a publicist? The idea of paying someone to promote your book may sound like a bad idea, but it can be a big plus if you have the right book and the right person doing the publicity.

However, the honest truth here is that most new writers don't have the money to hire a professional publicist, whose fees are usually *far* more than the average first novel advance (which can be as low as $2,500).

Most publishers have their own publicity department, but their budgets are usually reserved for the books that received the highest advances and require some good old American drum-beating to ensure enough sales to earn back the initial expenditure. So unless they paid you six figures for your novel, don't expect a great deal of effort from your publisher.

This doesn't mean you can't get publicity, but you may need to generate it yourself. For now, I just want to make you aware of publicity and how it fits into the entire picture.

Make some decisions about whether you will hire people or do it yourself, and then do it.

Reviews—They Can Make You or Break You

I can't stress the value of good book reviews enough. Some writers believe to the contrary, but they *can* make a difference. The problem is getting your book reviewed at all. And reviewers who work for the biggest venues often ignore new novels.

There isn't a lot you can do about it, but I do have one idea that can't hurt. Get a list of reviewers from your publisher or editor, which will give you the names and addresses of everybody who receives review copies of their new titles each month.

Then write them a personal note, introducing yourself as a new writer and telling them that you look forward to their reading your novel and sharing their opinions. Keep it short and sweet.

Address the envelope in your own handwriting. That's important because most mail is machine-printed and very cold. Your handwriting makes it personal, and they'll remember your name when your book hits their desk.

WORDS OF WISDOM

The only reason I didn't kill myself after I read the reviews of my first book was because we have two rivers in New York and I couldn't decide which one to jump into.

—Wilfrid Sheed

The People Who Buy Your Book

The most important people in publishing are your readers. These are the people who see your book on the shelf or the display table, see someone else reading it on an airplane, or take a recommendation from a friend who's reading it—and they do the most wonderful thing: they go out and buy your book. These people are your best friends in the world.

And for most of the history of this business, they were the ones you had the least contact with. For many, many years, I spent my time writing with very little feedback from my readership. Every once in a while (several times a year), my publisher would forward a fan letter to me. Normally, I heard nothing and worked in the vacuumlike atmosphere of zero feedback.

But since the advent of the Internet and e-mail, the relationship between writers and readers has become a very interesting one. I receive countless e-mail messages about my books, plus I can track comments and reviews through many websites devoted to discussion groups of books and also several sites with "forums" (I know—the correct Latin is *fora*) and groups of topics where I can log on and chat directly with people who are reading my work.

There's an old idea that you can't know you need something you never had in the first place. Reader feedback is one of those things. I never knew how important and perhaps necessary it was to keep me as sharp and interesting as I could be to my audience.

As you continue to grow as a novelist, never forget there are people out there who part with their cash to read what you wrote. Seek them out. Make yourself accessible to them. Don't fall into that "celebrity" trap—you don't want to distance yourself from your readers. Be nice to them, and they will be more than nice to you.

How You Get Your Book from Here to There

There's one final group of people who have a hand in your fate and your career as a writer of novels. People you probably haven't thought about ... if you knew they existed at all. They are known by many names—*wholesalers*, *distributors*, and on a more local level, *jobbers*. These are the people who order your book in large quantities (well, we can all hope they're large) and move them around the country to a variety of places that sell them at retail price.

> **TRADE TALK**
>
> Whether they're called **wholesalers, distributors,** or **jobbers,** these people get your hardcover into the bookstores (chains and mom 'n' pops) and the libraries (a market many people forget). For your paperbacks, they cover the newsstands, the airports and train stations, the big super stores like Walmart, convenience stores, and every other possible venue for a book.

Sadly, just like the book reviewers, you have very little opportunity to get in touch with distributors and jobbers. So what do you do? Again, I would recommend sending out personal letters to whomever you can locate who may have any chance of handling, shipping, or displaying your book.

Don't forget that these people have gotten into the habit of moving books around from trucks to boxes to shelves and back again, and they think about their product about as much as if it were a can of peas. If they are somehow reminded that each book they handle is a product of years of worry and doubt, of bravado and dreams, it will mean a lot more to them.

> **TOM'S TIPS**
>
> Track down the local jobbers in your town, county, the major cities, and even the whole state. Spend a few days driving around and introducing yourself to the people who put your book on the shelves. Bring coffee and donuts. Bring a smile. Let them connect your face with your name on your book. It will mean so much to them. They will remember you and your book, and they will take care of you—that is, give you longer and better shelf space and life. Louis L'Amour did this when he was young and unknown, and he always swore that being friends with his distributors made him a best-selling writer.

The Least You Need to Know

- Editors can help you make your novel better. A good editor asks questions that will make you think and explain why you wrote what you wrote.

- It's almost essential to have a literary agent who's connected to the publishing industry and knows plenty of editors willing to read your book.

- Booksellers and publicists want to see your book do well. If you have the time and the money, you should seriously think about investing in signings, tours, and a personal publicity campaign.

- It is important to be aware of the other people who have some influence over the fate of your novel. Reviewers, librarians, and distributors are all people you should take the time to get to know.

Glossary

abbreviations   Shortened versions of words—used in vernacular and informal styles. Some strict grammarians and stylists abhor abbreviating anything. Ignore them.

about the author   There's one in the back of this book where you get to find out all kinds of cool stuff about me. These are usually written in the third person, even though they're almost *always* written by the author.

abstract   A distillation of a book, story, or lecture to its salient points. You will also see it called a *précis* or *summary*.

acquisitions editor   The person at a publishing house who reviews submitted material and decides how worthy of publication it might be. Some of them are also involved in shepherding it into production.

advance   A portion of your writing fee paid to you up front, usually before you've turned in the project. It's paid in *advance* of you (a) finishing the project or (b) the publication date. Hence the name. But it also means an *advance* payment against the expected royalties the publisher thinks your book will earn. The amount varies depending on so many factors. As a beginning writer, you'll probably take whatever they offer with a big smile … and you should.

agent   A person who makes his living by marketing manuscripts to publishing houses. Agents usually charge a commission that can range from 10 to 15 percent, and I've heard some who are asking 20 percent (but they better be the best of the best). A good agent will get you a much better deal than you can, and they will be able to establish you and sell you in lots of foreign countries. *Caveat:* some people who will charge you a reading fee also call themselves "agents," but they are not.

all rights   If you grant these to the publication buying your work, it means they own the right to publish where and when they choose as often as they want—throughout the universe. In other words, you can never resell the work again. Good thing to keep in mind here: *never sell all rights.*

American Booksellers Association (ABA)   A nonprofit trade organization devoted to meeting the needs of its members—independently owned bookstores with store-front locations.

anthology   A collection of short stories, novelettes, or novellas written by various authors, compiled in one book or journal according to a particular theme … or not.

appendix   What you're looking at now. Appendixes are stuff added to the back of a book to make it more informative (or at least *bigger*).

argument   Aside from what we do when we're mad, it's also a type of writing when you make an assertion or take an opinionated stance on something that's usually controversial. It's always a good idea to present your argument with reasoned evidence.

attachments   Files that are inserted as extra stuff in e-mail, or any photos, graphs, or illustrations that accompany a manuscript. You usually use attachments for a nonfiction book, so don't do this with your fiction novel.

audience   The people you're writing for. It's very important that you understand who they are.

audiobook   Digital versions of books, often read by the author or an actor and recorded on CD or saved as an audio file.

autobiography   The writer's life story written into a book.

back matter   The section after the main body of the text. This is also not really for novels. But just so you know, it's things like endnotes, the index, bibliography, appendixes, and the about the author page.

backlist   A publishing buzzword for titles publishers have done that are still in print but aren't part of the "new" stuff coming out during the current season.

bar code   A label consisting of stripes and bars printed on the back cover of a book used universally in the book industry for automated ordering and inventory systems.

binding   The process of holding all the pages together in a single bound book. They can be sewn, glued, or spiraled.

bio   Abbreviation for biographical stuff (usually brief) about the author.

biography   An in-depth examination of the life of someone other than the writer telling his own life story.

blank verse   Poetry that doesn't rhyme.

blueline   This is what you get just before your book is published. It's a "proof" of all the pages (sometimes in cheesy blue ink) exactly the way they'll look when bound. With the advent of the digital age, they may soon be obsolete.

blurb   A brief, very positive review of your book or you. These appear on the front or back cover and should be written by the most famous or credible people you can find.

boilerplate   A contract written in industry-standard language. You hire an agent so he or she can make changes to the boilerplate, which can be better for you, especially financially.

book   A bound publication of 49 or more pages that is not a magazine or periodical.

BookExpo America (BEA)   Formerly called the American Booksellers Association Convention and Trade Exhibit (ABA), this is usually a huge expo where publishers hawk their newest offerings. It's a great place to get lots of free books.

bookmark   Computer-speak for the saved address or a website you might want to visit again. Or then again, it could still be a little piece of cardboard you stick between your book pages to mark your spot.

Books In Print   A gigantic book, maintained by R. R. Bowker, that lists books in print or about to be printed. It's based on the ISBN numbers assigned by each publisher.

brainstorming   Heavy-duty thinking about what you plan to write. Everybody does this differently, but it seems to help.

byline   The name of the person who wrote the piece you're reading.

call number   This is one of those terms that only makes sense if you're doing research in a library—the old-fashioned way. The number can be based on either the Library of Congress system or the Dewey decimal system. If you don't understand it, go ask the librarian.

camera-ready   When everything on your book is done and it's ready for the printing press—texts, pictures, cover layout, whatever.

Cataloging in Publication (CIP)   The bibliographic information supplied by the Library of Congress and printed on the copyright page of your book.

chapbook   A small booklet of poetry, journal entries, or stories. These are often done by small presses.

chronological order   A way of telling your story, in the exact time sequence in which everything occurred. Also called "linear order."

clean copy   A manuscript that looks nice—no cross-outs, errors, coffee rings, or fingerprints.

cliché   An expression that's been used so much, it has lost its power to communicate well. "Clear as a bell" is one of thousands of examples. Avoid using these phrases.

clips   Published examples of your writing some publishers want you to include with your proposal. They can be photocopies of the originally published works. They're also referred to as "tear sheets" by old-timers who've been around before photocopying machines, when you actually had to rip out pages from your personal copies of your published work. Technology *is* grand, isn't it?

closing scene   This is one of the most important parts of your story. It's the last chance to make your point and leave the reader with a valid emotional sense of completion.

colloquial   Conversational dialogue. It suggests an informal way of communicating, the way people really talk to one another, rather than in some formal or idealized way.

column inch   Buzzword for the amount of space in 1 inch of typesetting for newspapers. You probably will never need to know or employ this, but knowing it makes you smarter.

commercial novels   A general (and sometime pejorative) term referring to novels designed to appeal to a large audience. Academics disdain commercial fiction for reasons known only to their narrow, pointy little heads. Commercial novels are purchased by editors who tend to specialize in specific categories such as thrillers, romance, mystery, science fiction, western, etc. *See also* genre.

contributor's copies (C.C.)   When you sell your writing, you want these. They are the concrete proof you were published, and you can drag them out to show your grandchildren. Always be sure your contract stipulates that you get *lots* of them—books, magazines, whatever. Small magazines sometimes offer to pay in copies instead of cash—not a great idea for you.

copyedit   An editing run-through of your novel manuscript that checks for grammar, spelling, punctuation, and typos. Sometimes a copy editor will also check other details, such as organization and clarity.

copyright All beginning writers fret over this concept because they're worried about their work being stolen. By U.S. law, anything you write is automatically copyrighted as soon as you write it. But when your work is published, it should be accompanied by the standard notice, Copyright © DATE by AUTHOR'S NAME.

cover art The original artwork, illustration, or graphic design of your book's dust jacket.

cover illustration Cover art used on a paperback.

cover letter A *very* succinct letter included with your manuscript as part of a submission packet that introduces you and your manuscript to the editor. *Never* more than one page, it's basically used to list any prior publication credits you have, so do it fast and then get out of Dodge.

creative nonfiction Articles or essays written in the first person. This used to be called the "new journalism," but it's old now.

credits A list of your publications or other writing qualifications. Your *bona fides*. Despite what you might hear elsewhere, editors do tend to pay more attention to writers who have been previously published.

curriculum vitae (CV) A short, one-page resumé or a lengthy detailed list of education, experience, and credits.

curtain line The line at the end of a chapter that makes the reader want to keep reading. It's the thing that creates a "page-turner."

deadline The last, drop-dead date your novel is due. *Never* miss a deadline if you want your editor to keep being your editor.

dialogue Capturing what your characters are saying and surrounding it with quotation marks.

digital rights management (DRM) The process of developing effective methods to protect creative material and intellectual property that's been converted to digital formats.

distributor A company that buys books from a publisher or other distributors and resells them to retail accounts. It also provides services to publishers, such as warehousing, fulfillment, and marketing to bookstores.

draft Usually seen following the word *rough*. It's generally an early version of a story, outline, or chapter of a novel. Early drafts work on plot and pacing rather than style and grammar.

dramatic arc A narrative journey of discovery that carries your reader from the first to the last page. Arcs state the problem to be solved and work toward the resolution. You can actually have more than one dramatic arc in your novel. It's probably better that way.

dramatic narrative The kind of story that makes a good novel. It uses dramatic tension to keep the reader involved.

dummy Usually a hand-drawn approximation of what a page will look like in print. These are most often used for books with lots of illustrations.

e-book or **electronic book** A book published in electronic format, usually appearing on a website or contained on a CD-ROM that can be downloaded to computers or a portable reader.

e-publishing An umbrella term used to cover any type of nonpaper publication such as CD-ROM, DVD, PDF files, or any other digital format.

e-zine A magazine published online, as a downloadable file, or distributed through e-mail.

editing This is what makes your writing better. Either your editors will help you, or you will eventually learn to do it yourself. It is more than just checking for grammar, logic, and factual errors. It's also looking for subtle ways to improve the narrative.

editing service A company that will copyedit, revise, or even rewrite your book. Some are very good. Others are a scam. Try to find ones with references from well-known writers' organizations.

editor The person on a publisher's staff who reads and edits submissions.

editorial An article, typically concise and expressing an opinion or point of view. These are usually staff-written, although that's not a requirement.

electronic rights Permission to have your writing appear on the web. Be sure you understand what you're granting if/when you agree to sell such rights. The actual meaning and execution of electronic rights are still being settled by lawyers.

electronic submission A manuscript sent to a publisher by e-mail or on CD. It can be a story or an entire book manuscript that's been created with word-processing software. This is the preferred way publishers now want to receive submissions already accepted for publication.

elite A unit of measurement. Elite is a fixed-width type that provides 12 characters per linear inch.

ellipsis Spaced periods (three or four) to indicate an omission from a quoted passage ... like this. They can also be used in a stylistic way to indicate a pause in dialogue or narrative.

em dash A punctuation mark used to signal that a pause longer than that of a comma but not as long as that of a period will follow. You can also use it as a formatting and layout device.

entry point Where your story starts; the opening scene. This is an important choice. Once you've started your narrative, you may find you have to go back and change it. Revisions are part of the writing process.

epilogue Additional text at the end of the book, providing your reader with additional information. Some writers use them as "wrap-up" chapters.

experimental fiction A loosely used term that usually describes fiction innovative in content or style. Sometimes it's used to excuse bad writing.

fair use A portion of the copyright law that allows small passages from copyrighted material to be used without the owner's permission, as in a book review.

fanzine Usually refers to a publication produced by speculative fiction (science fiction) fans that features fan-written articles, reviews, opinions, and even stories about characters from popular published stories.

fee The amount of money you receive for your writing. Different types of writing projects may require different fees. Short fiction for magazines and anthologies is usually paid by the word, but novels are paid through an agreed-upon advance.

final draft The final version of your manuscript after all other proofing, editing, and revising has been done.

first electronic rights Similar to the first rights, except that it refers specifically to your work appearing on the web or some other electronic media.

first North American rights Again, similar to the first rights, but the rights are more specifically nailed down to Canada, the United States, and Mexico. The rest of the world still belongs to you.

first rights or **first American serial rights** This is the permission you grant to allow your work to be published for the first time ... but only *one* time. After it appears, you still retain all additional rights to sell for any other appearance, reprint, or use.

first-person point of view   A narrative style in which the story is told by one character who refers to himself as *I*.

flash fiction   Fiction under 500 words.

flat fee   This is also called "work-for-hire." It applies mainly to magazine writing, although some book publishers try to get new writers to agree to such a setup. It means you retain no rights and you get no royalties. The rule here is *never* agree to it.

follow-up   A brief note to check on the status of a submission or query.

font   The style of letter used in typesetting.

foreign rights   Rights you grant or sell that allow your novel to be printed and sold in other countries. This is a great source of additional income.

format   The layout, or the way your manuscript looks, defined by the margins, spacing, font, etc. Standards include using an easy-to-read font such as Courier 12-point (I prefer Times New Roman), inclusion of proper contact information, double-spacing between lines, indention of paragraphs, 1-inch margins all around, and unjustified right margins.

formatting   The act of creating a format.

formulaic fiction   Fiction that follows a familiar formula. The evil scientist who tries to take over the world and is destroyed by his own creation is a very old formula. The "odd man" who rebels against his oppressive society is another.

four-color process   Using four colors (magenta, cyan, yellow, and black) to produce pictures in a range of colors. This is what CMYK is all about. (The *k* stands for "black.")

freelancer   Someone who works for himself. Writers, editors, and artists are often freelancers.

front matter   The pages in your book that appear before the body of text—title pages, copyright info, dedication, acknowledgments, and table of contents.

frontlist   These are the new books being featured each new publishing "season" and are usually found in the *front* of the marketing catalogue.

galley or **galley proof**   The prepublication copy of your book that you get to check one last time for errors. By the time you get galleys, you might be pretty sick of seeing your book! This is also what is sent to reviewers so they have enough time to do a decent review.

genre Also called a category, this is a specific "type" of literature, distinguished by its form or content. Science fiction, romance, erotica, gothic, mystery, and western are all genres.

geographic links Spatial references that place the reader in the story. Usually you want to depict places universally identifiable to the reader.

ghost writer This is the real writer of a book but whose credit has been attributed to someone else who doesn't have the time or talent to do it himself. Sports figures, celebrities, and politicians often employ a ghost writer when they "write" a book.

go-ahead A reply from an editor telling you to write what you proposed in your initial contact with the publisher.

gothic novel A genre that tells a story involving a pretty young woman, a castle or mansion, a menace, and a hero. This is one of the most well-known genres because it's considered the oldest form of the novel.

graphics The nontyped parts of a book such as drawings, illustrations, photographs, charts, etc., that are used to enhance the content of a book. Novels don't have much of this stuff.

guidelines (GL) The set of instructions an editor or publisher gives out to writers that makes the act of submitting material more uniform and tailored to the particular market.

haiku A 3-line, 17-syllable poetic form traditionally about nature. Originally Japanese, but you probably figured that out.

hard copy A printout of a manuscript.

hardcover A book that's bound with hard cloth over cardboard attached to a sewn or glued binding of pages and covered with a paper dust jacket.

heroic myth A reference to some of civilization's earliest examples of epic storytelling. The heroes in these tales—Hercules, Gilgamesh, Ulysses, or Aeneas—encountered great challenges and hardships and overcame them all.

historical fiction Fiction set in the past. Lots of research makes these successful.

hook A narrative trick that "hooks" a reader's attention in the first paragraph and keeps him reading.

hypertext Words in an electronic document that are linked to sites, pages, illustrations, or other text. This is an interesting and useful technique to use when it's not overdone, but it's not used much, if at all, in novels. Although someday that may change.

idiomatic   Particular to a certain language or cultural usage. For example, "get your goat" when it means make you angry, not "fetch a farm animal."

Index to Periodicals   A huge set of thick books that lists every legitimate magazine published.

informal   Pertains to your style. It generally means loose and relaxed so the writing isn't stuffy or distancing. This book is written in an informal style. The intent of being informal is to make the writing as accessible as possible. It's easier to get across an idea or point when you don't have to worry about proper usage.

institutional sales   Buzzword for books sold to libraries and schools.

interactive fiction   Something that has yet to catch on in a big way. These stories let the reader have a choice in what happens in the narrative.

International Reply Coupons (IRC)   These are often mentioned in guidelines. They're used whenever you send a manuscript to a foreign country. Include IRCs with your SASE in place of stamps.

International Standard Book Number (ISBN)   A 13-digit identification number code uniquely assigned to every book and obtained from the R. R. Bowker company.

Internet   A vast and largely unexplainable network of computers at hundreds of thousands of locations all around the world. I have no idea how it works. But it does.

jobber   A type of distributor, usually a tough little guy who smokes cigars and doesn't read, who gets books (mostly paperbacks) into the airports, grocery stores, drug stores, and so on.

journal   Notes you make to yourself for story ideas, memories, feelings, opinions, etc. If you get *really* famous someday, someone might want to publish your journal.

kicker   A newspaper/journalism buzzword for a short, snappy ending.

kill fee   A portion of the negotiated fee originally agreed to be paid to you if an editor buys your work and then decides not to publish it. It can range from 25 to 100 percent of the agreed-upon fee. Contracts sometimes specify the percentage in the event of a cancellation.

lead   A newspaper/journalism buzzword for the beginning of an article, a story, or a feature.

lead time   How much time the publisher needs to get a story or book submitted and finally into print.

Library of Congress The national library of the United States located in Washington, D.C. They claim to have a copy of every book published in the United States. They also have a numbering system (LOC numbers) to help catalog this vast collection.

list price The sales price printed on your book or the retail sales price.

literary fiction A general category for nonformulaic, intelligent, and serious fiction. Literary fiction is also called mainstream fiction. It is often dull, pretentious, and unreadable, but it can also be great. Just like commercial fiction.

***Literary Market Place* (*LMP*)** A huge annual book full of every conceivable type of information about the publishing industry.

little/literary A term that can refer to a small magazine or press that purports to give "literary" writers a place to get published … with no real zeal for making a profit. This is seen in some circles as noble.

logline A one-sentence description of a screenplay or TV play. Those insipid, annoying little summaries in *TV Guide* are good examples.

logo An identification mark an individual, business, or organization employs as a recognizable and unique symbol. Publishers put them on the spines of their books.

main character or **protagonist** The person in your novel through whom most of the narrative is experienced or told. It is the person we learn to care about the most. Novels have lots of supporting characters, too.

manuscript Originally a paper written by hand, it now means any set of pages submitted for publication in typewritten or word-processing form. Publishers will not read handwritten submissions.

marketing plan A bookselling plan that considers budget, target audience, distribution, promotion, and schedule.

markets Places where you can sell what you write.

mass market The term used to describe the small, pocket-size paperback edition of your book. These books end up in the racks at airports, grocery stores, and drug stores.

mass-market publishers Publishers who produce paperback books inexpensively in large quantities. These books are designed to sell fast and in volume. They do not get reviewed.

media kit   Also called a "press kit," this contains reviews, blurbs, biographical data, maybe even pictures about your book and you. This is supposed to make people want to read your book.

memoir   A narrative of a writer's (or fictional narrator's) family history or personal background.

microfilm   The only way to preserve crumbling documents such as newspapers before the advent of digital scanning and storage. It is a reel of photograph (positive) film you thread into a reader, a simple projector that displays the images on a screen.

mid-list   A publishing buzzword that refers to books that aren't best-sellers.

monograph   Academese for a scholarly article usually written in the driest, stuffiest, and somnambulistic style imaginable.

mood cues   Transition cues that move your reader to the next scene. They can take the form of a sudden idea, a revelation or an epiphany, an outburst, an attack, a retreat, an exit, or any other emotional or rational decision from within your character.

multiple submissions   Submitting more than one piece of work at a time to an editor. You should check to see if it's okay before you do it.

narrative   Your story. Or any kind of writing that tells a series of events and reactions to them in classical story form.

net price   Sometimes called "wholesale price," this is what's left for the publisher from the sale of your book after discounts to distributors or book stores. Do not allow your royalty to be based on the net price. Industry standard is based on the list price.

New Age   A type of group category that includes occult and UFO phenomena as well as alternative health, mystical religion, and psychology.

novel   A fiction book for adults that's usually a minimum of 60,000 words. Most commercial fiction is at least twice that word count.

novelization   Usually a paperback novel based on an original screenplay (which means not based on prior material such as a novel) of a popular movie. Also called a movie "tie-in."

novella   A *very* long short story that's more than 1,500 words but less than 40,000.

novellete   A long short story that's more than 7,500 words but less than 15,000.

on acceptance   This is the best way to get paid for your work. When the editor accepts your story, the publisher sends you a check.

on publication   This is not the best way to get paid for your work. When your story is finally published, the publisher sends you a check. You want to be paid on acceptance.

on spec   This means "on speculation," and it's something you write because you are very much interested in writing it, but do not have a publisher waiting to pay you for it. You write and worry about selling it later.

one-time rights   When your publisher buys the nonexclusive rights to publish your work only once. You can sell the work to other publishers simultaneously.

out of print   This is when your book is no longer available to order from the publisher. They've stopped selling it. Gone. Finished. Time to resell it to another publisher.

outline   A mapped-out plan for your story. Some writers do a scene-by-scene outline. Others just do a rough synopsis of the plots. There's no one correct way to write an outline or use it after it's written.

over the transom   Any submission of *unsolicited* material sent to an editorial office. This dates back to a time when offices often had transoms, and people still knew what they were. (I do, but that's not because I'm all that old … rather because I'm smart.)

page rate   When a publication pays by the page instead of per word.

paraphrase   To rewrite a passage in different words but retain the original meaning.

parody   A flimsy and obvious imitation of a well-known book intended to be funny and clever. Sometimes parodies work, and sometimes they're plainly bad.

passive voice   A way of describing action in which the subject *receives* the action instead of performing it. Everyone says to avoid passive voice. (So how come we even keep it around?)

pen name or **pseudonym**   Not the writer's legal name. This is employed when the writer doesn't want his identity known.

periodicals   Magazines, journals, and newspapers. It's from the word *periodic*, which means "at regular periods."

permissions   A fee collected from anyone who wants to reprint part or all of your book, such as for inclusion in a textbook, a special limited edition, and so on. Your publisher handles permissions for you and usually splits the proceeds 50/50.

pica   A printer's measure of type equaling 12 points. (Points are measures of space across a page.)

plagiarism   Stealing someone else's work, usually word-for-word, and publishing it as your own work.

podcast   A digital audio program produced in segments and offered online as a download to personal, portable digital playback devices.

point of view (POV)   The decision you make when writing fiction that allows you to tell your story through either one central character, or many, or even an omniscient one.

potboiler   An old publishing term. A fast-and-dirty project to bring in some cash or "keep the pot boiling." Depending on how facile you are, this can be a story, an article, or even a book.

précis   The reduction of material to its key points; also called a summary or abstract.

preface   An opening section of a book that usually explains why the book was written, what it is about, or how to use it.

pretentious language   Artificial or stilted expressions that more often obscure meaning than communicate it. Avoid this if you want your readers to get what you're saying as clearly as possible. In other words: eschew obfuscation.

print-on-demand (POD) publishing   Contracting printers to produce very small numbers of books as needed—such as on monthly orders from the marketplace. Some say this is the wave of the future, and all books will one day be POD. I'm not so sure they're right.

process   Professors and teachers talk about "process" a lot, so you might see it mentioned somewhere with odd allusions to some semi-mystical connection to creativity. It is largely crapola. This word can mean a lot of things, but here I mean to refer specifically to writing *methods*, the processes by which writings are generated. To some extent, it also implies that writers use a good, full set of strategies, with different stages for planning, drafting, revising, and editing.

proofreader   The person who checks your manuscript to make certain the copy is correct and verified before final printing.

proofreading symbols   A special "shorthand" notation intended to call attention to typographical and other errors. To take a look at some proofreading marks, visit www.utexas.edu/visualguidelines/proofreaders.html.

proposal   After you've written a few books and generated some sales numbers, you can sometimes sell your next book with one of these. It's usually 60 or 70 pages of the actual book, plus a chapter-by-chapter outline of the rest. If your editor likes it, you can get a contract, a partial advance, and the balance when you turn in the completed manuscript.

prospective narrative   One of the two main types of narrative, this describes a story as it happens, as it is taking place. The writer watches and reports the story as it develops. (The opposite is *retrospective narrative*.)

pub date   *See* publication date.

public domain   Any work that has never been copyrighted, or work whose copyright has expired.

publication date   The date set for when the book will become available to the buying public.

publicity   The way you hype your book. Hopefully, it is through free advertising outlets such as press releases.

publisher   The person or company responsible for the entire process of producing books. This includes overseeing the writing, editing, design, production, printing, and marketing of the book.

quotation marks   The punctuation marks for dialogue. This is how you tell your reader somebody is talking.

reader   A dedicated person who reads the "slush pile" (the unsolicited manuscripts) for an editor. This person is a screener, a gatekeeper.

reading fee   What you would pay an editing service for their time spent in reading your manuscript. You can usually get friends or relatives to do it for free.

record of submission   A way of keeping track of all the places and people to whom you've pitched your book ideas or stories.

redundancy   Saying the same thing more than once, usually dressed up in new verbiage.

rejection slip   Every writer's recurring nightmare. A rejection slip can consist of anything from a scrawled "NO" on a returned manuscript to a multipage letter telling you exactly where and how you went wrong writing your manuscript. Unless you're this generation's Asimov or Sheldon, you'll get rejected often before you start selling regularly. Different writers deal with rejection slips in different ways; some toss them, some use them for wallpaper or scrap paper, and some keep them in scrapbooks. I've done all of these things.

reprints   Stories or novels you sell more than once. When the rights to your work revert back to you within several years of original publication, you can get it published again.

repro   Basically, it's just short for reproduction.

response time (RT)   Generally, the turnaround time required to hear back from a publisher based on when the manuscript was submitted.

retrospective narrative   Reconstruction of a story that has already happened.

review   A critical evaluation of a book, which can help or hinder its sales. Good reviews in the right places are like gold.

review copy   A free copy given away to be reviewed. If you like getting free books, call yourself a book reviewer.

revise, revising, or revision   Making major changes to your manuscript rather than just tweaking and tinkering in the editing process.

rights   The "intellectual property" rights you can sell to a publisher or editor. Some of the types covered elsewhere in this book and glossary are *all rights, worldwide rights, electronic rights, first serial rights, one-time rights,* and *reprint rights.*

royalties   This is how you make money on your book. It's the percentage of the sales price earned from each copy sold. These are charged against the advance until it is earned out. For books in print, this may vary from 7 to 15 percent; for e-books, royalties of 25 to 50 percent are common.

royalty publisher   A publisher who pays the author in dollars instead of copies.

sci fi   Along with SF, this is the pop culture abbreviation for science fiction.

second rights   The rights you sell to a publication for your work that has already been published somewhere else. It's a reprint right.

second-person point of view   A style where the writing speaks directly to the reader, using *you.*

self-addressed stamped envelope (SASE)   Including one of these will get your manuscript and/or rejection slip back to you in the event of rejection. If you don't include one, don't expect to get anything back.

self-publishing   A great trick if you can make it work. You publish your own books, cutting out the middlemen and maximizing your income. Computers have made this easier to attempt.

sense impressions   Emphasis on sight, hearing, taste, smell, and touch provided by description that pulls the reader more completely into your story.

short short story   Fiction under 1,000 words.

short story   Fiction under 10,000 words but usually less than 7,000 for most markets. In science fiction, it's less than 7,500 words.

sidebar   A short addition to a piece of writing. This book is full of them. Many times, they get a different look or design, as in this book.

simultaneous submission   When you send off a story, book proposal, or manuscript to more than one editor at a time. Traditionally, this has been frowned upon by editors, but life is far too short to let your work sit in offices for many months before it's even *looked* at. My advice is send your stuff everywhere, don't tell anybody you're doing it, and accept the best offer you get. Everybody else falls into the you-snooze-you-lose category.

slang   Nonstandard language usually connected to a time or locale. Depending on what you're writing, slang can be effective or silly.

slug line   A line in a screenplay describing a new scene; or, in journalism, the identifying tag for a story.

slush pile   The mailbags full of *unsolicited* manuscripts sent to a publisher. Now they can be e-files sent through e-mail. Every publisher gets slush pile submissions, and they are read, but sometimes slowly.

speculative fiction   The term sometimes used for sophisticated science fiction. It also covers any kind of fiction dealing with realities other than our own.

spine   The binding on the side of a book.

story-boarding   A filmmaker's practice of mapping out a plot in a series of pictures.

subsidiary rights   The sales of your book by your agent or publisher to other outlets such as movie studios, foreign publishers, book clubs, or magazines. The idea here is to retain all these rights in your original contract with your publisher.

subsidy publisher   A publisher who expects/demands their writers to pay for the publication of their books. You should only use a publisher of this type if you have a solid way of selling your book. *See also* vanity publishing.

subtext   Kind of a literary concept. The story within the story. If you talk like this at the right kind of parties, they will all think you're really smart.

surrealism   A way of looking at the world in ways it never was. It's a juxtaposition of recognizable images in places that aren't part of our reality.

symbolism   When one object or idea represents another.

synopsis   What you can include with a proposal after the sample chapters. It's a summary that can be from one paragraph to several pages long. I've done one much longer, depending on what the editor is looking for. The synopsis is not really the same as an outline, as it rarely carries elements such as chapter headings.

tear sheets   An older word for clips or samples of your writing. Since the invention of photocopiers, writers have avoided mutilating copies of their work.

temporal links   Time references that place readers in the scene. Sometimes as easy as just putting a time/date as a subheader under the chapter name.

terms   The arrangements for publication of a particular work, made between you and an editor or a publisher. These include types of rights purchased, when and how much you'll get paid, expected date of publication, and other similar items. These will be outlined in your contract or agreement.

third-person point of view   This is the one most writers use. The narrative describes the action by using *he, she, it, they*, and so on.

title   The name of your book. Most people are surprised to learn titles can't be copyrighted. There are a lot of books called *The End of the Line*, *Time's Up*, and other clever handles like that.

transition cues   Phrases or changes in your narrative that set up or prepare the readers for a change.

trim   The final size of your book after the printer or bindery has "trimmed" off the excess paper. Standard hardcover trims are 6×9 and 5.5×8.5 inches.

typesetting   A term that originally referred to the manual setting of type made out of lead. They were locked up in wooden frames and sent to the printing presses. Now it's all done on a computer screen, and it's almost unimaginable it was ever done by hand … and backward.

unsolicited manuscript Any writing—an article, a story, or a book—sent to an editor who didn't specifically ask for it. Also called the *slush pile*.

vanity publishing Books published at the total expense of the author—either through an independent "publisher" who is actually just a glorified printer, or by the author himself and the aid of a printer.

website A location or Internet address where you find information on just about anything. Most writers have websites and are learning how to use them to increase their sales.

wholesaler Another name for a distributor of your books.

withdrawal letter A letter you write to a publisher when you've grown tired of waiting for a decision on your manuscript or you've sold it somewhere else. If you've sent a few notes checking on the status of your manuscript and have heard zippo, it's time to yank it.

word count The number of words in your manuscript. It's easy to get a very accurate count these days with any word-processing program. On a typewritten page, you can do it one of the old-fashioned ways: (a) count every single word, or (b) count the number of words in 10 margin-to-margin lines, divide by 10, multiply your answer by the number of lines on a page, and multiply again by the number of pages. It should be close enough.

word of mouth A kind of advertising that happens when people start telling each other about a great new book they just read.

wordiness New writers have to really watch this. It's easy to use 10 words to express what 5 or 6 will do.

work for hire You get paid for a piece of writing, and that is the end of it. You cannot ever make another penny off the piece; in fact, you don't even own it. Don't sell your work like this. Ever.

works cited A list of books, articles, websites, interviews, or whatever that informs a reader of where you acquired your research information. Novelists don't need this—they're supposed to make up everything. (Just kidding.)

writer's block This is one of those things that happens once in a while when writers claim they *cannot* write. It's never happened to me, so I'm not one to say much about it. Deadlines and grocery bills have a way of keeping me writing.

young adult (YA) fiction The category of fiction for young adults, ages 12 to 18. YA novels usually run from 20,000 to 45,000 words. It's a good place to sell books.

Lee Child

Many readers and fans of Lee Child's work would be surprised to learn he was born in 1954 in Coventry, England. His novels are primarily set in the United States, and he writes with such an intimate knowledge of American geography and culture (to say nothing of his tight, ultra-clean style) that he simply *must* be American.

After college, he attended law school in Sheffield, England, and took a part-time job in the theater. He so much enjoyed the experience, he joined Granada Television in Manchester for what turned out to be an 18-year career as a presentation director during British TV's "golden age." During his tenure, his company made *Brideshead Revisited*, *The Jewel in the Crown*, *Prime Suspect*, and *Cracker*.

After a corporate downsizing is 1995, Lee found himself unemployed and in search of a new career. He decided to write a novel, which eventually became *Killing Floor*, about a character named Jack Reacher. The book became the first of a series involving Reacher and has achieved best-seller status.

Lee has three homes—an apartment in Manhattan, a country house in the south of France, and whatever airplane cabin he happens to be in while traveling between the two. Lee spends his spare time reading; listening to music; and watching the Yankees, Aston Villa, or Marseilles soccer. He is married with a grown-up daughter. He is tall and slim, despite an appalling diet and a refusal to exercise.

When did you realize you wanted to be a writer?

Writing has two halves—the mental and the physical. I had always done the mental stuff—the daydreaming, the "doing narrative" ... I started doing the physical side when I needed a job.

At what age did you attempt to write your first novel?

I was almost 40.

What was it about (theme, genre, etc.)?

It was "Killing Floor"—the first Jack Reacher novel. It was a thriller, a suspense novel, a crime novel, a Western.

Did you ever take any writing classes? Or specific instruction (seminar, workshop, etc.) to learn the craft of writing a novel?

No, I'm allergic to classroom situations.

Is writing the only "job" you've ever had? If not, what else did you do careerwise, and how did it help or hinder your writing?

I worked exclusively in entertainment—theater, and then television. Both indirectly helped enormously, in terms of understanding deadlines, and most of all in understanding that the audience is king.

How do you feel about the distinctions often expressed about "commercial" versus "literary" novels?

I think commercial novels are far, far harder to write.

What misconceptions, if any, did you have about the writing and publishing field when you were first getting started?

I underestimated two things: how patient publishers were prepared to be, in terms of slowly building a career; and how nice everyone in the business would be.

How have things (technology, society, culture, literature) changed since you got started?

In lots of ways—the pace at which people expect to consume things has accelerated. We have to write accordingly now. The economics of the book business have deteriorated badly—for instance my 1997 hardcover was $24 and my 2009 hardcover was $27—a 12% increase where other prices have at least doubled.

It is often said that if you can write a good short story, you can write anything. Do you agree?

No, but I take the point that a good short story writer has a unique skill. It's harder than it looks.

Do you write many short stories?

I have written maybe ten or a dozen, mostly as contributions to anthologies edited by friends.

What specific writers influenced, inspired, and, therefore, instructed you?

Alsitair MacLean, John D. MacDonald, Robert B. Parker.

When you are not reading fiction, what do you like to read?

Everything—history, current affairs, politics, technology … anything at all. It's the only real training for being a writer—read everything.

How would you describe your own "style"?

Accessible, unpretentious, clear, vernacular, authentic.

I *know* this is the question we always get, but aspiring novelists really *do* need to know: where do you get your ideas?

From reading and thinking.

How long, on the average, does it take you to go from initial idea to finished draft (ready to submit)?

Seven months.

Can you describe your writing process for us—do you develop character profiles and outlines for your novels before writing them, or do you let your characters/ideas develop as you write?

I let things develop as I write.

Do you ever encounter "writer's block," and if so, how do you overcome it?

No. Writing is certainly creative and exciting and wonderful and somewhat transcendent, but at heart it's a job. Do nurses get nurses' block? Do truck drivers? Obviously writers and nurses and truck drivers have days when they really don't feel like doing it … but you get up and go to work, and within a few minutes habit and muscle memory have things running smoothing.

How did you get past the initial barriers of criticism and rejection?

I worked in theater and television, so I was used to differing opinions. Sticks and stones may break my bones, etc, and you can only please most of the people most of the time.

What are the best and worst aspects of writing for a living, in your opinion?

There are no bad aspects. It's all good. You're getting paid to make up stories.

Can writing *well* be taught to someone who does not?

No, I don't think so. We can't even define it, let alone teach it. It's there or it isn't.

In relationship to sheer talent, how important would you rate discipline and time management to being a successful novelist?

It's hard to separate them—it's a three-legged stool. The non-talent factors are at least 90% of the game.

If you were to give an aspiring novelist *one* piece of advice, what would you tell them?

Ignore my advice. To even get to the starting line, a book has to be living, breathing, organic, alive … i.e. the product of one mind and one mind only. To say, "I really want to do (A), but Lee Child says do (B), and Stephen King says do (C), and my MFA professor said do (D)," leads to a committee decision without the vital spark of integrity a book needs. You can't guarantee success, but you can guarantee failure, simply by over-thinking.

Janet Evanovich

Janet Evanovich is *The New York Times* #1 best-selling author of the *Stephanie Plum* series. Her latest novel, *Finger Lickin' Fifteen*, appeared in 2009.

When did you realize you wanted to be a writer?

I decided I wanted to try writing somewhere in my early 30s. I thought it would be fun to write a novel, sell it to the movies, and get lots of money.

What was your first book about (theme, genre, etc.)?

My first book was about a fairy who was expelled from a fairy forest in Ireland and shipped off to America.

Did you ever take any writing classes? Or specific instruction (seminar, workshop, etc.) to learn the craft of writing a novel?

I took a couple creative writing courses as an adult. They were all pretty worthless. After I published my first novel, I joined Romance Writers of America and I found some of the conference classes to be helpful.

Is writing the only "job" you've ever had? If not, what else did you do career-wise, and how did it help or hinder your writing?

I've never exactly had a career. I worked as a customer service rep for an insurance company and a hospital supply company (think colostomy bags). I was a waitress (disaster). I did telephone soliciting. I was a file clerk. I sold used cars for half a day.

How do you feel about the distinctions often expressed about "commercial" versus "literary" novels?

I think the distinction is bogus.

What misconceptions, if any, did you have about the writing and publishing field when you were first getting started?

I thought it was going to be easy. I thought you stayed home and wrote books.

How have things (technology, society, culture, literature) changed since you got started?

The frontlist has replaced a lot of the midlist. Eccentric, reclusive authors are barely tolerated (it's actually easier to be dead). The computer has replaced the electric typewriter.

It is often said that if you can write a good short story, you can write anything. Do you agree?

No.

Do you write many short stories?

I did one for a Mary Higgins Clark anthology. I probably won't do another one. It's not cost-effective.

What specific writers influenced, inspired, and, therefore, instructed you?

Robert B. Parker and Carl Barks.

When you are not reading fiction, what do you like to read?

Catalogues.

How would you describe your own "style"?

Jersey girl cooked down to a tasty reduction sauce.

I *know* this is the question we always get, but aspiring novelists really *do* need to know: where do you get your ideas?

Movies, newspapers, television, and past history.

How long, on the average, does it take you to go from initial idea to finished draft (ready to submit)?

Four months.

Can you describe your writing process for us—do you develop character profiles and outlines for your novels before writing them, or do you let your characters and ideas develop as you write?

I develop a small outline, maybe two or three pages, so I understand the plot line. Really it's a timeline of action. I don't feel compelled to stick to it totally but I usually stay pretty close.

Do you ever encounter "writer's block," and if so, how do you overcome it?

I don't believe in writer's block. I show up for work every day and I put my time in. Some days I only write a paragraph or two but I never leave with a blank screen.

How did you get past the initial barriers of criticism and rejection?

I took responsibility for the failure of my product, and I never doubted that I could learn to make it better.

What are the best and worst aspects of writing for a living, in your opinion?

The best aspect of writing is the pleasure of approaching the computer fresh each morning with new ideas, a cup of coffee, and the cat. The worst part of writing is the end of the day and the end of the book when you realize you've not done enough and never will.

Can writing *well* be taught to someone who does not?

Some parts of writing can be taught—pacing, for instance. The music of a sentence probably can't be taught.

In relationship to sheer talent, how important would you rate discipline and time management to being a successful novelist?

They are essential.

If you were to give an aspiring novelist *one* piece of advice, what would you tell her?

Never hold anything back for the next book. Always go for it. And be brave.

Heather Graham

New York Times and *USA Today* best-selling author Heather Graham majored in theater arts at the University of South Florida. After a stint of several years in dinner theater, back-up vocals, and bartending, she stayed home after the birth of her third child and began to write, working on short horror stories and romances. After some trial and error, she sold her first book, *When Next We Love*, in 1982. Since then, she has written *more than 100* novels and novellas, including category, romantic suspense, historical romance, vampire fiction, time travel, occult, and Christmas holiday fare.

She wrote the launch books for the Dell's Ecstasy Supreme line, Silhouette's Shadows, and for Harlequin's mainstream fiction imprint, Mira Books. Her work has been translated into 20 languages.

She lives in Florida with her husband, Dennis, and still loves to have fun with her five children—even though they're all grown up now.

When did you realize you wanted to be a writer?

I didn't know that I wanted to be a writer until I was suddenly home with three small children, and was no longer working out of the house. I realized immediately that I had no talent for doing anything creative in the home design or management arena, but I had spent my life loving to read. Because of a strange quirk in high school— I had gotten it in my head to write an essay about the political situation at the time—I had gotten a partial scholarship in mass communication, so I had a vague idea of what I wanted to do. I had purchased *Writer's Digest Writer's Market*, and I still suggest it as an invaluable tool. I loved mystery/horror and such classic gothic romance authors such as Anya Seton and Victoria Holt, so I started sending off romances and short horror stories. I was in my early twenties at the time.

At what age did you attempt to write your first novel?

My first short story was about the vampires in a high school that only showed their true colors on Halloween. I attempted my first novel around the age of 20.

What was it about (theme, genre, etc.)?

My first novel was about a rock group that had split up to get back ten years later— when one of their number had been murdered.

Did you ever take any writing classes? Or specific instruction (seminar, workshop, etc.) to learn the craft of writing a novel?

When I was in high school, I had an amazing teacher named James Parrot for a creative writing class. He was an amazing man—I still credit him for the love I feel for what I do—this many years later! We wrote and filmed a project in his class about an evil teacher, and he was the evil teacher, of course. In college, I majored in theater arts, and loved playwriting. Nowadays, I still attend lectures by friends and other authors. No matter how long you're in this field, you'll never learn all that is out there!

Is writing the only "job" you've ever had? If not, what else did you do career-wise, and how did it help or hinder your writing?

When I left college, I went into dinner theater in South Florida. I loved it. I did some commercial work, and also loved it, but the pay was non-union and minimal. I bartended, sang back up for local entertainers, and was actually a singing, tap-dancing barbecue rib waitress. And still, with the three children, it cost more to go to work than I was making! Since I didn't seem to have any other talents—including the ability to keep a neat and livable house!—I was desperate to find my niche in the world. At first, while the rejections poured in, I decided that my education had been such that I would be experienced with rejection. As the years have gone by, I've realized that my college years and my first work experience were invaluable. I can speak at the drop of a hat, and now, with several colleagues, we put on dinner theater and other events for charity, and I like to think we add a lot of fun and a light touch that creates a great conference/learning experience for others.

How do you feel about the distinctions often expressed about "commercial" versus "literary" novels?

I'm not so sure that we know the actual difference between literary fiction and commercial fiction right now. The late and amazing Kate Duffy once put that in to perspective when she had taken a group of us out. One author said, "Hey, we're not trying to write Shakespeare." Kate said, "Actually, Shakespeare was the commercial fiction of his day. Just like Dickens." I think the biggest mistake many authors make is believing that they must be more "literary." It can probably be done, and done well by a very talented person, but the best books are written by authors who love what they're writing, be it sci-fi, mystery, romance—or the great American novel.

What misconceptions, if any, did you have about the writing and publishing field when you were first getting started?

When I started writing—and this is ridiculous, I know, I'd certainly spent enough time in bookstores—I didn't even realize just how books fell into genres. I thought you just wrote a book!

How have things (technology, society, culture, literature) changed since you got started?

Since I started—wow! The whole industry has changed. I fought against using a computer, and now I can't imagine life without one. I remember when a friend, Sally Schoeneweiss, first told me I need a web page and wanted to make one for me. I thought, hey, sure—but please don't be disappointed if that doesn't take off! Ah, what did I know? Now of course, we're changing again—"E" everything is out there. Only the future will show where that will take us!

It is often said that if you can write a good short story, you can write anything. Do you agree?

Writing a short story is one of the hardest forms of writing—so much must be conveyed in a minimum of space. But short stories and books require different disciplines. One demands precision with words while the other demands concentration and the ability to follow through with a story in a manner that keeps a reader turning page after page—after page.

Do you write many short stories?

I love short stories. I hadn't done many in a long time until just a few years ago. This year and last year, I wrote several, one for Dark Delicacies, and a few for International Thriller Writers. I am "thrilled," I must say, to participate. Changing around keeps the mind sharp, I believe. We always need to challenge ourselves.

What specific writers influenced, inspired, and, therefore, instructed you?

So many authors influence me! I will always be a reader at heart. But a few of the books I believe have totally withstood time are those written by Poe, DeFoe, du Maurier, and Dickens—there are more I'm sure. A few of my favorite all time books/ stories are *The Fall of the House of Usher, The Tell Tale Heart, Treasure Island, Rebecca,* and *A Tale of Two Cities.* Also, a brilliant book—*Killer Angels,* by Michael Shaara. In *Killer Angels,* I think we see the American Civil War (the War of Northern Aggression where I'm from!) in an amazing light. It's about people, why they believed the way they did, and how heartbreaking it was for men and women when their families were divided. There's a scene in which General Armistead, CSA, a friend of General Hancock, USA, looks forward to getting together with his old friend for dinner. Armistead is a leader during Pickett's Charge at Gettysburg, and is mortally wounded at his friend's line. While dying he tells one of the soldiers (paraphrased,) "Please convey my regrets to General Hancock. General Armistead will not be able to join him for dinner." I have seldom cried so much over a book! I admired Shaara's ability to show the personalities of the men, their strengths and weaknesses, on both sides of the tragic conflict.

When you are not reading fiction, what do you like to read?

When I'm not reading fiction, I love books about history and biographies. People influence history, and it's fascinating to find out about those who came before us, and how they shaped the world, be it in a large arena, or perhaps their immediate neighborhood. I find the Civil War fascinating and if I could sit down and speak to a few ghosts, I'd love to have a chance to chat with Lincoln and Lee, and the lives of women in their era fascinate me as well, especially Varina Davis, wife of the one and only President of the Confederate States of America. There were correlations in both presidential families—one being the heartbreak of losing their own young children in the midst of the trauma and tragedy of war.

How would you describe your own "style"?

If I have a style, it's because I try to do what I have so loved in others—create a place so real others want to see it, and people who are so real others want to know them, have dinner with them—or, in the case of villains, string them up and rip off their flesh!

I *know* this is the question we always get, but aspiring novelists really *do* need to know: where do you get your ideas?

My ideas come from everything around me. My kids! I've done books that include Little League, ballroom dance, rock bands, graphic art, modeling, and I make use of their friends as well. One of Shayne's friends is a Miami-Dade police officer, and he sighs every time he sees me coming, but he's great. I live in South Florida, where there is always some insanity to be found in the newspaper. I'm working on books set in Key West now, and the stories down there actually surpass anything I might invent!

How long, on the average, does it take you to go from initial idea to finished draft (ready to submit)?

From initial idea to submission could be six months to a year—all the way to years and years. I once wrote a book about a Civil War soldier who went through a haze of black powder to find himself in the midst of a twenty-first century re-enactment. He kidnaps the heroine because he's convinced she's a spy. It was sent back when I wrote it, but five years later my editor called and asked for it—they used it to start one of the company's new lines.

Can you describe your writing process for us—do you develop character profiles and outlines for your novels before writing them, or do you let your characters/ideas develop as you write?

Sometimes I start work by imagining a character—and sometimes because of a place, or an event. This sounds clichéd, but it's absolutely true—it's being somewhere and thinking, *Oh, my God! What if?* I write almost every day, but this is equally important—don't stop living. That's what we're all writing about, really. People—and the lives they're leading. (Even the dead ones these days!)

Do you ever encounter "writer's block," and if so, how do you overcome it?

I am very grateful for my schedule (and FPL, the mortgage company, etc.) because I've never actually had writer's block. Nora Roberts once said that it was possible to fix a bad page but a blank page was a *blank* page. There's tremendous truth in that.

How did you get past the initial barriers of criticism and rejection?

Ah, here I am grateful for treading the boards as a theater person. You learn quickly that you just go on and on after every rejection or criticism. Criticism is good—it helps us grow. But there's the trick—learning first that we're in a field that is incredibly subjective, and then learning how to take what helps you and embrace it, and just shake off the insults that won't help you in any way.

What are the best and worst aspects of writing for a living, in your opinion?

I'm not sure there is a worst aspect to writing for a living. Certainly, I get rewrites that make me walk around the house calling an editor a stupid dickhead—but most of the time, I sit back and discover that their comments were right on and I thank God that they made me go back. Age has its benefits. Any "bad" aspect can just be something that slips off the shoulders. And I love my editors. Of course, they mostly still like me, because they have the same philosophy—and they know I don't really think they're dickheads!

Can writing *well* be taught to someone who does not?

Writing is something that we can hone and improve, and especially the techniques of writing. I don't really know if it can be taught and learned. Most people trying to learn to improve and publish their work do love books and they are readers, so there's the start. I do know that you could give me a zillion art classes and I'd still be horrible at so much as drawing a stick figure, but I don't have a passion for art. Maybe that's what's most important—if the passion is there, then, yes, of course, many things can be learned.

In relationship to sheer talent, how important would you rate discipline and time management to being a successful novelist?

Ah, success can be counted so many ways! I know writers who are English language enthusiasts first, and they've done well. I know story-tellers who are not as adept at language who are also successful. In fiction, however, I think the story must come first. A really great book happens when there is a fantastic story that is really well written. Writing does take discipline. Tenacity. If you really love books and do work on craft, tenacity and discipline are the virtues that will get a writer through. A very good friend—and good writer, story-teller—spent ten years being rejected. She meant to make it happen, and she did!

If you were to give an aspiring novelist *one* piece of advice, what would you tell them?

Oh, lord! One piece of advice. Okay, think of all this as one piece. First, read. Never forget to read, because loving to read is what made you want to write. While you're reading, work. Always work. Don't make excuses. Dedicate an hour, a day, certain hours to your work, no matter what your job, and no matter how many children you have! While you're reading and working, don't forget to live. Life is what gives us people, places—and stories.

Also, never say, "Wow, that was horrible. I know I can write that!" Always remember that you want to write a story equal to the best that's out there. Seriously—why would you want to write something that's just a touch above "horrible"?

Stephen Hunter

Stephen Hunter was born in 1946 and lives in Baltimore, Maryland. He wrote for *The Baltimore Sun* from 1971 to 1996 and then went to work for *The Washington Post*. He graduated from Northwestern University in 1968 and then spent 2 years (1969–1970) in the U.S. Army as a ceremonial soldier in the Old Guard (3rd Infantry) in Washington, D.C.

He won the prestigious American Society of Newspaper Editors (ASNE) 1998 Distinguished Writing Award in the criticism category. He has been nominated for the Pulitzer prize many times and was a finalist in 1995 and 1996. In 2003, he won the Pulitzer for his "authoritative film criticism that is both intellectually rewarding and a pleasure to read."

He is also the author of many novels, including *The Master Sniper*, *The Second Saladin*, *The Spanish Gambit*, *Target*, *The Day Before Midnight*, *Point of Impact*, *Dirty White Boys*, *Black Light*, *Time to Hunt*, *Hot Springs*, and *Pale Horse Coming*. He also wrote two nonfiction books, *Violent Screen* and *The Beatles Literary Anthology*.

When did you realize you wanted to be a writer?

I never *didn't* realize I wanted to be a writer. I knew from an extremely early age that this is what I had to do. My first manifestations were for drawing. I had a vivid imagination for drawing but I realize now that the drawings, the finished product, weren't the point—the process was the point. I was drawing, I was fantasizing, I was basically telling a story. The finished drawing was gibberish because the story was changing as it went along. So that was my first idea of storytelling. I was an imaginative kid powerfully attracted to stories from the very, very beginning.

At what age did you attempt to write your first novel?

Age nine. I dictated it to my mother, who grew bored very quickly. And she typed very quickly. After she left in a huff, I typed three more paragraphs. It was the '50s—what can I say? Six paragraphs … at age nine … that's not bad.

I loved to read. I was really affected by a series of books by R. Stanley Bowen, who wrote boys' adventure novels during World War II. I discovered them in the 1950s. There were two series: One was Dave Dawson and the Royal Air Force; the other was Red Randall and the American Army Air Force. I read all the ones I could get my hands on. I think it probably had to do more with my style than Hemingway and Faulkner. I mean they sank so deep in. I'm just a pathetic imitation R. Stanley Bowen. It was about an American teenager flying Spitfires and shooting down Nazis, and I loved it.

What was it about (theme, genre, etc.)?

It was Steve Hunter's version of Dave Dawson and the Royal Air Force. My hero was probably named something like Jack Jones or Bill Bailey. The first and the last names had to have matching initials. I don't know why.

Did you ever take any writing classes? Or specific instruction (seminar, workshop, etc.) to learn the craft of writing a novel?

Yes. I was identified very early in my life as a writer. I was very lucky to have a great education. You got a great education in the '50s, and very early on I was a total utter loser. I was a crappy athlete, I wasn't tough, I wasn't particularly attractive. I was a baby who cried a lot, whose feelings were really sensitively hurt, but whenever we had to write a story, *my* story was one of the stories read. The teachers back then were smart enough to recognize talent, and to encourage talent, and you know—they invented my life. God bless them. I don't know where I'd be. I'd be selling shoes at Sears in Schenectady if it weren't for those teachers who said to me: "You're special. You can be somebody. This is what you're good at; and nobody else in here is as good at that as you are." And that just followed me through my entire education. That was a constant from the third grade through college. I was always identified for that gift and it became the foundation of my identity from a very early age.

Is writing the only "job" you've ever had? If not, what else did you do career-wise, and how did it help or hinder your writing?

No, I was a soldier for two years, a gardener for four years, a newspaper copy reader in college and a book review editor. I didn't get a job as a writer until I'd been in the newspaper business for 10 years and that actually probably helped me. Having edited people for so long I realized I burned out on it. I didn't care about other people. I just built up this intensely narcissistic overdrive. I had to stop being involved in other peoples' writing and that was it. I had to be involved in my own writing. That's sort of a reflection of the blind, cool narcissism of the writing profession. We all are suffering from narcissistic personality disorder. I mean, the very act is somewhat arrogant. I mean, oh gosh, what I do is so important, you should make room for it in your pathetic and nothing little lives.

How do you feel about the distinctions often expressed about "commercial" versus "literary" novels?

I could do a number here. But the truth is, for what I do, it's probably not wise to think or brood too much on that. There are certain things you can't change; they are just there. They're part of the fabric of the culture, so I'm just going to concentrate on what I do, and do it as well as I can do it. What someone else wants to call it, however they want to categorize it, that's nothing I can control. I just try to pay no attention to it. I think a lot of what you do when you reach a certain point in your career is tune stuff out. You've just got to concentrate on your work, and not be worried about outside influences. It's just better to keep yourself pure and simple.

What misconceptions, if any, did you have about the writing and publishing field when you were first getting started?

I thought it would be more noble. There was a very strange difference from journalism. I mean, what I learned, coming into it from the newspaper business, was that in the newsroom, we have absurd ideas about our own "sanctity." What I mean by that is we would never talk about selling, we would never talk about advertisers, never talk about the crass aspect of merchandising a newspaper. But when you get into the publishing industry (if you finally manage to get into it) you realize that's all they ever talk about. They don't care about literature or anything. They just have to figure out how to sell this stuff. You learn how important the sales force is. It's a market-driven unit of the economy.

How have things (technology, society, culture, literature) changed since you got started?

I feel that my career has encompassed the arc of the information revolution. I started working in ball-point pen on yellow legal pad, and now I sit at a blue screen tapping away. I've gone from legal pad to typewriter to electric typewriter to primitive computer to sophisticated computer.

However, I'm still stuck in the early '90s; I'm way behind everyone else. My computer is nothing but a dedicated typing machine. I'm not Internet-connected. I don't have e-mail at home. I just know that if I get e-mail and the Internet in here, I'm finished. I have benefited from the great changes. When I started out, I always felt that one of my great advantages over anyone who is competing in this great field (particularly in the entry level), was that I could do the work. I mean, the business of taking a manuscript through four or five drafts was an enormous burden of physical labor because you had to retype it. You typed it; it was all done on the energy of your forearms.

When that changed, we all moved to computers and suddenly the physical energy of writing was lessened by about 70 percent—which meant that a lot more lazy people could finish books. I think most talented people are lazy so I really feared those people. If there are too many of them, I'm out of business. It turned out they were just as lazy with the computer as they were with a typewriter.

It is often said that if you can write a good short story, you can write anything. Do you agree?

No! I don't agree. I think that literary talents are very specific and people can't always be that multi-talented. It's like a sport. I always compare a literary talent or writing talent to athletic talent. You can be a pretty good athlete, but you're really an outstanding basketball player. You couldn't play professional tennis or you couldn't play professional football, but in this one area of basketball you have very specific talent. It meshes perfectly with your physical package and your intellectual package. I think that's true of writing. People are naturally fiction writers or nonfiction writers. People are naturally dramatists, or prose writers, or they're poets.

They're all subtly different from each other. I think short story writers and novelists are very different. Short story writers have a lot of trouble with novels because they understand the microworld of the word and the sentence. Somehow they don't have a natural talent for understanding the rhythm of a larger story spread out over 600 pages. Whereas a novelist has a lot of room and it's very hard to be that incisive to get something into a few pages. I'm not a good short story writer. Every short story I write is just too short; I can feel it fighting to become a novel.

Do you write many short stories?

I have no interest in writing short stories.

What specific writers influenced, inspired, and, therefore, instructed you?

Hemingway is where my idea of a novelist came from. As obsolete as that image is, I still can't escape it. It's like faith, you know you may see through it but in some real basic level you still believe. I love John Le Carre, the elegance of his writing. I went through a period when I read and was influenced by writers, but I'm out of that now. I read very little. I don't read my competitors, my colleagues. I don't read much fiction. I've retreated into my own little world and I'm just interested in that. I'm kind of hermetically sealed off, because I tend to be a mimic—if I come across something I like, I steal it. I don't want to be caught stealing too much.

When you are not reading fiction, what do you like to read?

I don't read many books. When I do read books, I read biography and history almost exclusively; I find nonfiction more interesting. I just don't read a lot of fiction anymore. I have an incredibly busy schedule. Plus, being both a film critic and a novelist, I probably get enough of stories. I'm a great believer in the need for stories, so much so that narrative is almost like a drug to me. But I get enough, so I don't read much fiction.

I *know* this is the question we always get, but aspiring novelists really *do* need to know: where do you get your ideas?

The trick isn't getting the idea—the trick is discriminating between good ideas and bad ideas. I get a lot of ideas. Ideas are always popping into my head because I suspect I have a kind of a "story brain." It's always conjuring up possibilities, but only one out of a hundred is powerful and resonant enough for me to somehow develop. If I have a good idea, it carries with it a charge of energy that's very, very intense. I consider myself lazy. Look, I've written 12 novels in 22 years while working full-time for a newspaper as a writer. I'm lazy as hell, and I couldn't do this much work if the ideas weren't provocative. I don't have the discipline or the will to do it as a conscious effort. The only way I can do it is if the ideas generate the energy, and they take over my imagination so powerfully that I have to work on it.

How long, on the average, does it take you to go from initial idea to finished draft (ready to submit)?

I don't submit at this point in my career. I'm lucky enough that I can sell books on my reputation. So what I submit is an outline. It's not that every outline is accepted.

I've had several outlines that they've said to me: "You know, I don't think this is going to work. Try something else."

But I'm not in a position anymore where I would write a book on spec. The last book I wrote on spec was *Dirty White Boys*. I just knew I'd have trouble selling it, and it did cost me a publisher and an agent who didn't want anything to do with it. Actually, it may have been some subtle, psychological gaming going on there inside my own mind, because I profited from leaving that agent and that publisher. And yet, had I made a decision to say you're fired and I'm through with you, I just couldn't have done that. I'm not ambitious enough to hurt people to advance myself. So my subconscious found a way to make these changes happen without me having to be a bastard—a very peculiar thing that happened in my career.

The time from start to finish is getting shorter. It took a year to go from final manuscript to actual physical book. But now it can be done in five to six months, so that also means that the pressure on us to produce books faster has grown; and I've been asked on several occasions in my life, *Pale Horse Coming* as an example, where the idea of that book was to do it very quickly. And in fact, the book is the way it is in part *because* it was done very quickly—in seven months. *Dirty White Boys* was also done in seven months. For a number of years, the first 5 or 6 books were all the same—they took 19 months to write. *Point of Impact* took about three years. It would *not* work. I had to take it apart and start over several times. I lost contact with it. I gave up on it. If it weren't for a very gifted editor who believed in it simply on the basis of the fact that one of the characters had the same name as her son, the book would have been my Waterloo. That would have been the book that finished me as a writer. But I stuck with it, and subsequently it's done very well in the market. And now the books take about a year. Part of that is because I'm not doing the laborious re-transcribing of chapters.

Can you describe your writing process for us—do you develop character profiles and outlines for your novels before writing them, or do you let your characters and ideas develop as you write?

I very much believe in outlines. I had so much trouble with *Point of Impact* because I didn't really have a very good outline. I drifted randomly across the landscape for two years and I learned that the last place I want to be is figuring out what happens next at 4 A.M. So now I outline very, very exhaustibly.

I hear this all the time when writers say: "Oh, I don't want to know how it comes out; I just trust myself to figure out how it comes out." Boy, I want to know where the commas are. I want to know where the semicolons are before I start. I usually have a destination in mind. One of the things that keeps me writing is the fact I'm trying to get to a scene that I can't wait to write. But I always put that off and reward myself by getting in the time. Although invariably, when I do get there, I'm never in a good mood because I've put too much pressure on myself, and it doesn't come out as well as I'd hope it would. Nevertheless, that "treat" of getting there sort of drives you.

Do you ever encounter "writer's block," and if so, how do you overcome it?

I've never really had it. I don't have time for it. I think one of the reasons is the newspaper job, and that keeps me supple. I have to write three or four pieces a week so I never lose steam. It's not like those reflexes go sour or get stale.

How did you get past the initial barriers of criticism and rejection?

Like everyone else: poorly. Like everyone else, I've had reviews from idiots that I felt were "so unfair to my sensitiveness," and the only lesson I've had in this business is that you're in it for the long term and you can't get too upset. It's baseball; it's not football. It's a long season and you're going to have slumps and you're going to make errors and you're going to get bad breaks. But over the long haul, your talent is going to express itself at its own level. And that's what keeps you going.

What are the best and worst aspects of writing for a living, in your opinion?

The best aspect is that you feel tired at the end of the day but you feel you've done good work, enjoying and embracing the accomplishment instead of being obsessed with the outcome.

The worst aspect is the temptation to become bitter simply because careers are so whimsical. Maybe you'll be lucky; maybe you won't. Maybe you'll get that big review and maybe you won't. And maybe someone who seems to be much less talented will have a much better career than you. I think that if you're going to do this, you have to find some way to get yourself through the paranoia and the bitterness of the process. I read Hemingway's biography and learned something interesting. As much as he'd accomplished, he ended up angry, bitter, and alone. So that's the pitfall. I will consider myself a success if, at the age of 75, I'm not bitter over someone getting what I think I deserved myself. You know that way lay horror and destruction.

Can writing *well* be taught to someone who does not?

I don't think so. It's talent. The only way to find out if you have that talent is to write. But it's very much like a sports talent. I could not hit a major league curve ball. It's not in my genes. It doesn't matter how much I want to or how hard I work on it. I don't have the hand-eye coordination, acuity of vision, and the courage to face a major league curve ball. I could not do it. It doesn't matter how much I want it. You know, it just isn't going to happen.

The smartest thing you can do as a writer is to be honest with yourself about the level of your talent and understand what is in your reach and what is not in your reach. When I started out in the newspaper business I was surrounded by great writers. Everyone was going to be a great novelist. I just wanted to write some thrillers. The years have passed and I've written 13 thrillers, made a fair amount of money and had a lot of fun, and none of those people have written their great novels. I understood what I could do. I understood that I had a definite narrative gift to do a certain kind of book pretty well and I focused on that. That was my target and it just so happened that it was a popular genre for my kind of book. It was, and still remains, sort of a significant commercial entity. What I wanted to be was a professional writer, and I had no sort of vaporous illusions of being Dostoyevsky. If my books have any merit, they acquired that merit honestly by the fruit of labor—as opposed to a function of my great genius, of which I have absolutely none.

In relationship to sheer talent, how important would you rate discipline and time management to being a successful novelist?

It's 50 percent. The two most important words you write in a book are: The End. I don't know why people give up. If you can't finish the thing, you lose. You're finished; it doesn't matter how much talent you have. It just doesn't matter. I always hear the story of Robert Stone's agent pulling out crumpled-up pages from a wastebasket, pressing them and submitting them, and getting a contract after he had quit the biz. Maybe so, but that's the exception. The reality is: You have to work hard. You have to work regularly and if you can't teach yourself how to, then you're going to fail no matter how talented you are. So many talented people aren't closers. They're not finishers, and their lives become nothingness. They live the bitter lives because they expected so much and did so little. Us grinds and dorks, hey, we put the hours in at the computer and they just dreamed. Somehow we ended up so much better off than they did.

If you were to give an aspiring novelist *one* piece of advice, what would you tell them?

Know your own talent, your own voice, and your own genre, and work specifically toward that as a goal. Be sensible about what is possible. Don't think you're Dostoyevsky just because you want to be Dostoyevsky. You have to treat it as a profession at some point and treat yourself as a journeyman—as opposed to treating yourself as a gift to the human race from God. And maybe in doing that you will become that gift. You're sure not going to get it any other way.

Lisa Jackson

Lisa Jackson is the author of more than a dozen *New York Times* best-sellers, including the number-one ranked *Fatal Burn*. In 2009 alone she had four national best-sellers: the hardcover *Malice*, the paperback originals *Chosen to Die* and *Wicked Game*, as well as the reprint edition of *Lost Souls*. Her latest novel is *Without Mercy*.

It's been common knowledge for some time that Lisa has been killing people everywhere from Savannah, New Orleans, and Baton Rouge to Los Angeles, San Francisco, the Pacific Northwest, and, now, Montana. It's been worth it. Her readers come back again and again, her novels are fixtures in bookstores and on national best-seller lists, and it all means that Lisa gets to do what she loves best—sit back down, open her mind to possibilities, and spin another complex tale of suspense and relationships.

When did you realize you wanted to be a writer?

I had always thought about being writer, even in grade school and throughout high school and college. However that dream had always seemed a tad unrealistic. I'm a pragmatist at heart, I think.

At what age did you attempt to write your first novel?

I wasn't quite thirty, I guess when my sister, author Nancy Bush, came up with the idea of writing romance novels. I thought she was crazy as we were mystery buffs and had never paid much attention to romance, but we decided to give it a whirl. We wrote that first book, *Stormy Surrender*, together, with another friend and it was rejected all over New York. Nancy sold her next solo effort right out of the gate, but it took me another eighteen months, I think. My first book on my own was rejected as were the next two or three. I finally struck gold with *A Twist of Fate* for Silhouette Special Edition.

What was it about (theme, genre, etc.)?

Stormy Surrender was a contemporary (at the time) romance novel.

Did you ever take any writing classes? Or specific instruction (seminar, workshop, etc.) to learn the craft of writing a novel?

Only in college and that was just the basic stuff: Writing 101. I did take a couple of workshops over the years, but nothing that I think was really all that helpful.

Is writing the only "job" you've ever had? If not, what else did you do career-wise, and how did it help or hinder your writing?

Oh, no. I've done everything from work in a cannery and sell corn dogs as a kid, to working in banking and investments as an adult. I was actually babysitting (so I could stay at home with my toddler and baby) before I took a stab at writing. I believe that every human, emotional experience adds to your depth as a writer. My first book was set around the investment world and an embezzler, so I drew on my knowledge of the banking industry. Over the years I've plumbed my knowledge of growing up in a very small town and added that flavor to my books.

How do you feel about the distinctions often expressed about "commercial" versus "literary" novels?

I just write what I like to read. I don't care about any labeling.

What misconceptions, if any, did you have about the writing and publishing field when you were first getting started?

I was pretty naive. Just went for it. There were "rules" to the kind of category books I was writing—guidelines that I had to kind of ignore. At the time, suspense in a romance novel wasn't wanted; so I had to tone that down. Funny how things change.

How have things (technology, society, culture, literature) changed since you got started?

Everything's changed. I write on a laptop not a standard typewriter. DNA makes trapping a culprit more precise. Cell phones are everywhere. Technology has exploded. What about the Internet? For quick reference and research? For sending my manuscript via e-mail? In culture and society women and minorities have newer, broader roles. The last thirty years have shown us major changes. As I mentioned, currently suspense is "hot," so when once I was told to tamp it down, now, finally I can ramp it up!

It is often said that if you can write a good short story, you can write anything. Do you agree?

Absolutely. A short story teaches the writer to write an entire tale concisely—beginning, middle and end. The writer is forced to plot tightly and to show characterization in a flash.

Do you write many short stories?

Ha! No. My synopses for my works are nearly short stories and I have contributed to anthologies, but I usually stick to the big books.

What specific writers influenced, inspired, and, therefore, instructed you?

Well, I loved Daphne DuMaurier and Charlotte Brontë, as a kid. Then moved on to Mary Stewart, Walter Farley and Agatha Christie. As an adult, Stephen King, Dick Francis, Sue Grafton, Michael Connolly, Harlan Coben, Steve Martini, Sue Monk Kidd, Sandra Brown, Tami Hoag and Patricia Cornwell, are favorites, though, to be truthful, I read a lot of books by different authors, whatever the buzz is about. These authors I do love, but there are books by William Lashner, Nelson DeMille, Anita Diamant, Khaled Hosseini, Ira Levin and Chris Bohjalian and William Peter Blatty that will always be on my keeper shelf.

When you are not reading fiction, what do you like to read?

The newspaper. Magazines that range from *National Geographic* to *People*. I don't read a lot of non-fiction books except for research, and usually then only in bits and pieces. The exception would be *Sea Biscuit*, by Laura Hillenbrand, I guess. That was a truly compelling and fascinating book.

How would you describe your own "style"?

Huh. *Style?* Hmm. I write romantic suspense, the kind I like to read. *Style?* Hmmm. I've never really thought about it, but I do get into a rhythm when I write. *Style?* Wow? Do I have one? I suppose. Dunno.

I *know* this is the question we always get, but aspiring novelists really *do* need to know: where do you get your ideas?

From life. Trust me, truth *is* stranger than fiction. Just read the newspaper or watch television or read articles on the Internet, or listen to a colleague. Really, I couldn't make some of this stuff up!

How long, on the average, does it take you to go from initial idea to finished draft (ready to submit)?

It varies. I write in stages. First an idea, then a synopsis and finally, maybe a book! Sometimes ideas never flourish. They die before I get started. Other times they come to fruition long after conception, but if I were to guess (and it varies book to book) it probably takes me around six months from onset to "The End." Sometimes less, sometimes more.

Can you describe your writing process for us—do you develop character profiles and outlines for your novels before writing them, or do you let your characters/ideas develop as you write?

I write from a detailed synopsis, which can be from 20 to 75 pages, depending. The characters are listed and placed in a roster, where I add notes, but it's not a form profile. When the detailed synopsis is approved by my editor, I try to follow it and the characters kind of tell their own back-stories as I write. Invariably, I wander, new characters come to play, new twists form, but I basically know where I'm going when I sit down to write page one. The synopsis sometimes takes me a month or two to put together. The book then *should* flow, but often times it doesn't.

Do you ever encounter "writer's block," and if so, how do you overcome it?

Absolutely. For me, a real block is usually from an outside force, family issues, something that doesn't have anything to do with the book. If that's the case I just have to work through whatever's going on in my real life until it's solved or I can deal with it. However, if the blockage starts within the pages and an unforeseen snag becomes a brick wall, I know the problem isn't the scene that I'm drafting, but something prior. I usually have to go far back to resolve that issue in the plot, then rewrite the pages that lead to the blocked scene. However, if the problem isn't one of plot or character or motivation, sometimes it's the scene itself. Since I write in the third person point of view, I sometimes will rewrite the blocked scene from a different angle, from someone else's viewpoint. New eyes may or may not allow a different insight to the scene and help it flow. However, if the problem is earlier in the book this "quick fix" won't work.

How did you get past the initial barriers of criticism and rejection?

I developed a thick skin … and I'm still developing it. I don't think of criticism and rejection as barriers, but more as part of the learning process. Even so, I don't believe my reviews either good or bad. I don't read them much either, especially anonymous reviews. I just try to write the best story I can. I realize not everyone's going to love it.

What are the best and worst aspects of writing for a living, in your opinion?

The best: freedom. I can work my own hours, at my own pace, around my family's schedule and I get paid for doing what I love. How incredible is that? The worst? It seems as if I'm ALWAYS working. If not at the computer, then mulling something over, or jotting notes, or coming across a new story idea.

Can writing *well* be taught to someone who does not?

Hmmm. Probably, but writing *well* isn't always the answer. The answer is to write/tell a good story. It's not about English and grammar. It's about story-telling, connecting with the readers, getting them immersed in the story making them want to turn to the next page!

In relationship to sheer talent, how important would you rate discipline and time management to being a successful novelist?

Pretty damned high. So what if you're talented but you can't sit your butt down and write? So what if you can write an incredible sentence if it isn't going anywhere? First and foremost the book has to be written and that does take discipline and time management. That said, let's be honest, not everyone who wants to write a book will be able to. A person can write and rewrite and polish and spell check 'til he's blue in the face, but if the sentences aren't interesting and the story's boring, it's not going to get published. Writing a book is a blend of talent, dedication and hard work.

If you were to give an aspiring novelist *one* piece of advice, what would you tell them?

A) Don't give up your day job.

B) Finish the damned book.

That's *two*, isn't it? Well, they're both equally important.

Dean Koontz

It seems almost silly to write an introduction to a writer as well known and loved as Dean Koontz. He's written close to 100 books, he's had more than a dozen #1 *New York Times* Bestsellers in hardcover, and his books have been translated into 38 languages. Without question, he exhibits a dedication to his craft that's rarely seen in any creative arena. Although born in Pennsylvania, he has made his home with his wife, Gerda, in California for many years.

When did you realize you wanted to be a writer?

When [I] was eight, I wrote stories on tablet paper, drew covers, and taped them onto booklets that I sold to relatives for a nickel. The previous seven years, I was a dreadful slacker. As a senior in college, when I won a prize in an *Atlantic Monthly* competition, I knew I was going to be a writer. I desperately wanted to avoid having to learn plumbing or another honest trade.

At what age did you attempt to write your first novel?

When I [was] 20 and still in college. It was something to do when I wasn't playing pinochle.

What was it about (theme, genre, etc.)?

It was a science-fiction novel about the nature of identity and the inseparability of body and soul. It never sold.

Did you ever take any writing classes? Or specific instruction (seminar, workshop, etc.) to learn the craft of writing a novel?

As an English major, I had a few classes in creative writing. Subsequently, I had to unlearn most of what I was taught. Writing is learned by reading, by writing, and by listening to your intuition, which is the voice of the soul.

Is writing the only "job" you've ever had? If not, what else did you do careerwise, and how did it help or hinder your writing?

In high school, I worked as a stock clerk in a supermarket and, for a couple of summers as a uniformed "ranger" in a state park, though I was really a glorified front-desk clerk at the campground. After that, I taught school for two and a half years while writing in the evenings and on weekends. Gerda, my wife, offered to support us for five years, to give me a chance to build a writing career. "If you can't make it in five years," she said, "you'll never make it." I tried to get her to commit to seven years, but she has some Sicilian blood and so wins every negotiation. Without her faith in me, no career would have been possible.

How do you feel about the distinctions often expressed about "commercial" versus "literary" novels?

The distinction was largely fostered by academics following the explosive growth of the university system after World War II. Prior to that, someone like John P. Marquand could win the Pulitzer for a realistic novel and still publish Mr. Moto mysteries under his name without diminishing his reputation. The purpose of the academics in this enterprise was entirely political: an attempt—and quite successful— to establish a class system in literature that facilitated their control of writers as well as subjects and philosophies and techniques that they determined to be permissible material. This inevitably led to the political correctness that now infects and makes worthless most contemporary literature. Most commercial or genre writing is indeed terrible, but so is most mainstream or literary writing. True art can be found in any form of writing.

What misconceptions, if any, did you have about the writing and publishing field when you were first getting started?

That there was a community of writers without envy, with higher ethical standards than the rest of the world. That most publishers wanted writers to stretch themselves and challenge readers. That an agent was your partner, always with your best interest at heart. That all critics always read the books they reviewed and had deep insights into things like subtext or pattern of metaphor.

How have things (technology, society, culture, literature) changed since you got started?

Change is continuous, and none of it really matters. The only thing that matters is what doesn't change, which is the Truth.

It is often said that if you can write a good short story, you can write anything. Do you agree?

No.

Do you write many short stories?

No.

What specific writers influenced, inspired, and, therefore, instructed you?

In the order I read them: Robert Heinlein, Ray Bradbury, Theodore Sturgeon, Roger Zelazny, John D. MacDonald, Charles Dickens, Flannery O'Connor, Walker Percy, St. Thomas Aquinas, T. S. Eliot, C. S. Lewis, Joseph Conrad, Dostoevsky, G. K. Chesterton, Philip Rieff.

When you are not reading fiction, what do you like to read?

Through my forties, I read about 200 novels a year. These days, I read about a dozen novels, half of which I have read before, social theorists like Rieff of whom there are few as profound, cultural observers like Thomas Sowell, and poetry.

How would you describe your own "style"?

A writer who spends a lot of time talking about his style is often a writer who is defensive [or] misunderstands his role. When you talk too much about your style, you're sticking a knife in your work and letting the mystery bleed out of it. A reader can't be stirred by a sense of the ineffable if you blow away the mist with babble.

I *know* this is the question we always get, but aspiring novelists really *do* need to know: where do you get your ideas?

The imagination is a muscle. The more you use it, the better it performs. And the richer your intellectual diet, the better your ideas. If you watch a lot of zombie movies, you'll generate stories at the zombie-movie level. Maybe that's what you want to do, which is fine. But to get noticed in the sea of zombie books, you might have to write something that no one else is writing. I love T. S. Eliot's *Four Quartets*. I've read it hundreds of times, and lines in it have inspired five of my most recent twelve novels. C. S. Lewis' *The Abolition of Man* was the inspiration behind my decision to play with Frankenstein and re-imagine it for this age of smiling fascism. Reading a lot of quantum mechanics led me to write *From the Corner of His Eye*, to explore the way human relationships reflect what quantum mechanics tells us about the systems of the physical universe, especially what Richard Feynman called "spooky effects at a distance." If that book has a spiritual godfather, it's Feynman.

How long, on average, does it take you to go from initial idea to finished draft (ready to submit)?

Sometimes an idea percolates for years before it's fully brewed and ready to be poured. With other projects, the idea hits me and I have to start writing *right then*. Once I start writing, a book can take anywhere from four or five months to a year, partly depending on length, but sometimes depending on the complexity of the story even though it is of average length. I get up at 5:30 or 6:00 in the morning, walk the dog, and get to my desk by 7:00 or at the latest 7:30. I work straight through until dinner and never eat lunch. 50 hours is my minimum work week. Toward the end of a book, I become so immersed in the story, I can for a month or more spend 70 or 80 hours a week at the keyboard. So in four or five months I put in a lot of time.

Can you describe your writing process? Do you develop character profiles and outlines for your novels before writing them, or do you let the characters/ideas develop as you write?

I stopped outlining with *Strangers*, and the work immediately got better. I begin with a couple of characters who intrigue me and a premise, a story hook, that strikes me as irresistible. When I give the characters free will, as God gave it to me, amazing things occur, and the story goes places I would have never thought to take it in an outline. The characters become real to me, and I follow them with increasing fascination. This allows … for a more organic story line and, usually, lots of surprises. Character profiles are useless to me. Their decisions and actions make them who they are, and they become deeper than I would have imagined them if I had worked up a profile on each.

Do you ever encounter "writer's block," and if so, how do you overcome it?

All writer's block has the same source: self-doubt. I have more self-doubt than any writer I know. I beat myself up every day at the keyboard. To avoid being blocked, I overcome the doubt by revising each page 10, 20, 30 times, whatever, until I can't make it any better, and only then do I move on to the next page. At the end of each chapter, I print out and pencil changes because you see things on the printed page you don't see on a screen. When I reach the last page, the entire script is in a state of high polish, and I have staved off writer's block. In other words, if you *use* your self-doubt to revise, you keep moving, and the block cannot establish. The only time in my life I've been unable to write was immediately after the death of our beloved golden retriever, Trixie. I was in the middle of *The Darkest Evening of the Year*, which was a book filled with goldens, and in my grief, I couldn't get out a word for five weeks. I finally realized that I could write the book if I did it in the spirit of a tribute to Trixie. Then it flew.

How did you get past the initial barriers of criticism and rejection?

Criticism and rejection are nothing more than other people's opinions. Except for my wife's opinion, I don't care what anyone thinks of my work. To care is to give other people power over you. And as C. S. Lewis said, if ever the people who despise your work and its world view were suddenly to praise you, *that's* when you'd know you'd gone terribly astray. Praise that you take too seriously can be as destructive as unfair criticism. I've seen good writers who when praised for certain aspects of their work, subsequently emphasize those aspects at the expense of other qualities of their writing, thereafter producing distorted fiction less rounded, less impressive than what they did previously.

Besides, writing talent is an unearned grace. Because we're born with [it], we have no reason to take pride in it, only *to a limited degree* in the craft with which we develop it and the purposes to which we put it. I am grateful for this talent and for the life it has given me, and though I've had 90% good reviews over the years, I don't do it for praise or awards. I don't do it for money, either, much of which we've given away. It is the writing itself, the process, that is the reward. I love our challenging, complex, and musical language, and working with it is a joy. I'm delighted by the infinite possibilities of storytelling; it's at once hard work and play. When I'm creating at my peak, when I'm transported and in a flow state, I feel a connection to that higher power from which my talent came, and writing is then almost a form of prayer. The process is emotionally, intellectually, and spiritually rewarding, which is why I keep going from project to project without much delay between. Only the writing matters, not what happens after the book is written.

What are the best and worst aspects of writing for a living?

Being your own boss, being free to follow your inspiration where it leads you, not only in your work but in your life, is a priceless boon. The worst is publishers' and others' resistance to new ideas and new approaches, which never quite entirely ends no matter how successful those new ideas and approaches prove to be. With Bantam, I'm in the best relationship I've ever known in publishing, and I have no complaints. But it was a long road getting here.

Can writing *well* be taught to someone who does not?

If they have talent, if they have an underlying appreciation for the musicality of language—yes. If they lack those things—no. For the most part, we teach ourselves to write, and that's how it ought to be. Writing fiction is arguably the most intimate of all the arts. Music and painting can speak to us deeply and emotionally but not with the complexity of language. Furthermore, the composer needs musicians to interpret him for the listener. Uniquely among the arts, the painter needs the art historian/critic to interpret him for the viewer. The writer needs only the reader. Such an intimate art can not be created in a communal atmosphere. The writer must continuously test himself and push himself in an ambience that allows no distraction, which means in solitude. Writing classes and seminars nearly always become stages, where writers find themselves performing for one another. Writing is not a performing art. It is the art of revelation: revelation inspired by the seductive rhythms of language the dream-deep reach of storytelling.

In relationship to sheer talent, how important would you rate discipline and time management to being a successful writer?

Many talented people have no discipline whatsoever. You can be brilliant but directionless, in which case the brilliance is of little consequence. To have a worthwhile career, you have to be able to put in long hours at the keyboard. Discipline and diligence are evidence not just of a writer who's a good businessman, but of a writer who is committed to his vision both as an artist and a craftsman.

If you were to give *one* piece of advice to aspiring writers, what would you tell them?

Don't scope the market with the hope of writing what is wanted, and avoid buying into the intellectual fashions of your time, for they will look foolish in years to come. The novelists and playwrights who were Stalinists during the 1920s, 30s, and 40s, and who allowed their Stalinism to color their work, are unreadable now, and the writers themselves appear naïve at best. For some reason, writers have a desire to be seen as intellectuals, although the history of intellectualism is packed full of monsters and fools. Think for yourself, hold fast to your common sense, identify the enduring truths that intellectuals routinely strive to deny, and your work will be human and humane, rather than ideological. Because the great majority of fiction is always consciously or unconsciously slavish in its service to intellectual fashion, you will stand out as different from others, and your work will find an audience.

Kat Martin

Currently living in Missoula, Montana, Kat Martin is the best-selling author of more than 40 historical and contemporary romance novels. Before she started writing in 1985, Kat was a real estate broker. During that time, she met her husband, Larry Martin, also a writer.

Kat is a graduate of the University of California at Santa Barbara, where she majored in anthropology and history. Her early works were historical romances, but she has since found an enthusiastic audience for her romantic suspense novels.

When did you realize you wanted to be a writer?

It was mostly by accident. I was helping my husband with his grammar in a novel he had written—his first attempt—and discovered I loved the work. I thought, "Maybe I should try this myself." And so I did.

At what age did you attempt to write your first novel?

I didn't start writing until I was in my late thirties.

What was it about (theme, genre, etc.)?

It was a romance. I loved reading romance novels and I was by nature an extremely romantic person. I still am.

Did you ever take any writing classes? Or specific instruction (seminar, workshop, etc.) to learn the craft of writing a novel?

My husband and I took classes for a year from a teacher at UCLA who gave private lessons in the evenings, a hundred mile drive for us. I also took classes in Fresno the following year, an hour ride each way on the train. I've always been a big believer in seminars, workshops and conferences.

Is writing the only "job" you've ever had? If not, what else did you do career-wise, and how did it help or hinder your writing?

Are you kidding? I've been working since I was sixteen. In high school, I did cleaning at Sprouse-Ritz drug store. I worked as a clerk at J.C. Penney's. After college, I worked in the title business, Title Insurance and Security Title. Then I went into real estate. I did that for the next thirteen years. I think all of those jobs helped me as a writer. The experiences I had in each job, things that happened that I can use in my books. Selling real estate demands self-discipline. So does being a writer. If you are writing for a living, it's your business. The more you understand that, the better off you are.

How do you feel about the distinctions often expressed about "commercial" versus "literary" novels?

I could be honest and say it's a bunch of bull. A happy ending makes a book less literary? A book has to be boring in order to be a literary achievement? I think it's simply that some writers would rather write for themselves than for readers. And of course there is a certain snobbery that goes with the label "literary author." And having said that, there are always exceptions. There are some great literary works out there.

What misconceptions, if any, did you have about the writing and publishing field when you were first getting started?

I knew so little about publishing I had no idea what to expect. I knew it would take me some time to become successful, but that was my goal from the start. I thought perhaps three or four years of very hard work and I would be making a good living. Boy, was I wrong! It has taken me years to achieve financial stability as a writer.

How have things (technology, society, culture, literature) changed since you got started?

Technology has certainly changed, though I started on a computer, not a typewriter as did some of my friends. Society and culture are radically different, but being a writer, I tend to live in my own, much more insulated world and block out what I see as society's long slide downhill. As for literature, it changes constantly. Looking back a hundred years you can see how language usage has changed. Still, a writer has his own style no matter when he writes and that seems to last through the years.

It is often said that if you can write a good short story, you can write anything. Do you agree?

In theory, yes. I think if you can write a short story that captures a reader's attention and hold it, you can use those skills as a basis for writing longer fiction. But there is a lot that has to be learned.

Do you write many short stories?

The first thing I ever wrote (fifth grade) was a short story. I got an A. Perhaps that was an indicator of the future. Currently, I have a novella on the market, a small hardcover called *The Christmas Clock*. Professionally, I've only written one other short story. It was published in an anthology.

What specific writers influenced, inspired, and, therefore, instructed you?

I have always read a lot. Wilbur Smith was an early favorite. I loved Herman Wouk's *Winds of War* series. I read Kathleen Woodiwiss, the goddess of Romance novels. I read, re-read, and practically memorized Dean Koontz's *How to Write Best-Selling Fiction*, a wonderful book that unfortunately is now out of print.

When you are not reading fiction, what do you like to read?

I belong to a readers group, which provides me with a variety of book choices. A favorite non-fiction book is *Undaunted Courage*, the story of Lewis and Clark. *The Color of Water* was a really interesting book. I read books for research, but that is mostly just necessary for my job.

How would you describe your own "style"?

Fast-paced and plot-oriented. As Elmore Leonard is reported to have said, I try to leave out the parts people skip. I love it when readers say they couldn't stop turning the pages.

I *know* this is the question we always get, but aspiring novelists really *do* need to know: where do you get your ideas?

I'm not one hundred percent convinced that people who ask that question should be writers. Or if they want to be, maybe they should write something other than commercial fiction. I started with dozens of story ideas. I've written most of them, and constantly think of new ones. I'll see a movie and think how much better it would have been if only … I read a newspaper headline and think what an interesting story that would make. I admit after forty-five novels, coming up with fresh ideas is a little harder than it used to be. I always try to write down an idea when it hits me so that I can look at it later.

How long, on the average, does it take you to go from initial idea to finished draft (ready to submit)?

As I said, the initial idea might be several years old. From start to finish, six months. But that is now and not when I started. It took me eighteen months to write my first book. A year each for a number of books thereafter. I like pressing myself to write faster. I think it helps keep me focused.

Can you describe your writing process for us? Do you develop character profiles and outlines for your novels before writing them, or do you let your characters/ideas develop as you write?

I learned from an author friend, Fern Michaels, to do character outlines. I find them invaluable as the book progresses. There are little things you forget that are there in the profile—like after you come back from vacation and you can't remember the color of the characters eyes! Same with plot. The better I know the story, the easier it is to write. Knowing the ending is particularly important, even if the middle wanders. You need to be sure you can resolve the conflict.

Do you ever encounter "writer's block," and if so, how do you overcome it?

I tell myself I don't get writer's block—I can't afford it. The truth is it lurks there for me the same as anyone else. Doing more research is a good way to get past it. Often I talk to my husband, who is also a writer, and we kick plot problems around. Usually that works.

How did you get past the initial barrier of criticism and rejection?

I sort of closed my mind to it, though it bothers me greatly even now. I'm a commercial writer. I write for a living. I have to charge forward. I have to believe in myself even if other people don't. Once an editor told me a book I had written, a contemporary, which I had never written before, was so bad it was "unpublishable." I believed in the book. I sold it elsewhere. It was published and later nominated for a Rita Award, very high praise in the world of romance fiction.

What are the best and worst aspects of writing for a living?

Financial insecurity is definitely on the bad side. Never knowing if your contract will be renewed. And the isolation. I used to sell real estate. It was really fun. Writing is challenging and fulfilling, but it is lonely. On the plus side is finishing a book, knowing you have actually completed a novel. And getting letters from readers who have enjoyed the book makes all the hard work worthwhile.

Can writing *well* be taught to someone who does not?

Writing can definitely be taught to someone. There is an endless amount that can be learned, and practicing what you have studied will make you better. Can you be taught to write really well? I would think there would have to be an element of talent involved, as well.

In relationship to sheer talent, how important would you rate discipline and time management to being a successful writer?

I'd give talent a 5 and discipline and time management a 10. Most people would disagree. And undoubtedly there are people so talented they get away with very little self-discipline. But for most of us, sitting down and doing the work when we would rather be snow-skiing or just watching TV is the most important thing.

If you were to give an aspiring novelist one piece of advice, what would you tell them?

Don't give up. That would be my advice. Persist against all odds. Do what you love and don't give up until you reach your goal and achieve your dream.

Richard Matheson

Richard Matheson was born in New Jersey in 1926, and he has lived and worked in California since 1951. Ray Bradbury called Matheson "one of the most important writers of the twentieth century," and his work has inspired many other notable authors. Stephen King cites Matheson as "the author who influenced me most as a writer," and Dean Koontz says, "We're all a lot richer to have Richard Matheson among us."

Even if you've never heard of him, you've almost certainly seen some of his work. In addition to novels in the mystery, science fiction, horror, fantasy, and western genres, Matheson has been a prolific film and television script writer. He wrote the script for some of the most memorable episodes of *The Twilight Zone*, including "Nightmare at 20,000 Feet" (you remember—William Shatner sees a gremlin on the wing of the plane …), "The Invaders," and "Little Girl Lost." He also wrote episodes of *Have Gun, Will Travel*; *Night Gallery*; and *Star Trek* (among them "The Enemy Within," in which Kirk is split into good and evil halves).

Several of Matheson's novels and stories have been made into films, including *The Shrinking Man* (filmed as *The Incredible Shrinking Man* in 1957), *I Am Legend* (filmed three times, once as *The Last Man on Earth* starring Vincent Price in 1964, again as *The Omega Man* starring Charlton Heston in 1971, and most recently with Will Smith), and *Bid Time Return* (filmed as *Somewhere in Time* starring Christopher Reeve and Jane Seymour in 1980). Matheson also wrote the scripts for Stephen Spielberg's first feature film, *Duel*; the TV movie *The Night Stalker*, which drew a record 75 million viewers on its first broadcast; and several of Roger Corman's Edgar Allan Poe films, including *House of Usher* (1960), *The Pit and the Pendulum* (1961), and *The Raven* (1963).

Throughout a career spanning five decades, Matheson has won numerable prestigious awards, including the World Fantasy Convention's Life Achievement Award, the Bram Stoker Award for Life Achievement, the Hugo Award, the Edgar Allan Poe Award, the Golden Spur Award, and the Writer's Guild Award.

When did you realize you wanted to be a writer?

I was just a kid when I had little poems and stories published in the *Brooklyn Eagle;* I must have been seven or so. A true writer always knows; it draws him in inevitably. I think it's a part of creativity. Coming out of the Depression the only thing I could afford was typewriter and paper. I would have written music if I had had a family who had a grand piano and the wherewithal to do that. I might have done that. I've acted and would have pursued that if there had been any possibility. But I chose the most practical route and I think it's the most rewarding route anyway.

At what age did you attempt to write your first novel?

Fourteen.

What was it about (theme, genre, etc.)?

That was something that a Danielle Steel person would write back then. I was a Christian Scientist at the time and I got this idea about a young woman who had fallen down a flight of stairs, smacked her head, and never aged no matter how many years went by. I called it *The Years Stood Still.* It had all kinds of characters, multiple locations and times: Africa, World War I. It was kind of crazy trying to write authoritatively about England and World War I. At that age you're too stupid to know that you don't know anything. After that, I always did research.

Did you ever take any writing classes? Or specific instruction (seminar, workshop, etc.) to learn the craft of writing a novel?

I took writing classes at the University of Missouri. I don't think you can teach writing. The best value of a writing class is that you are forced to write material and then sit with various people in the class who read it and analyze it and that's all there is to it. You can't teach writing, though.

Is writing the only "job" you've ever had? If not, what else did you do careerwise, and how did it help or hinder your writing?

Like all writers, I have had every kind of job. When I got out of the Army I worked in a place called Petty and Wherry (I don't know why I remember that name). They sold huge wheels that you would have on machinery, and I used to pack them and send them out. All through high school I worked at a place called Merritt Farms, a cheese store in New York. I don't think they exist anymore. I learned how to make packages. I can still make a package for mailing. I learned how to tear string without a knife. That was a great accomplishment. I got to the point where I could whack off a piece of cheese for a pound—and get exactly a pound! That's probably a greater accomplishment than all the books I've written.

How do you feel about the distinctions often expressed about "commercial" versus "literary" novels?

I remember the little religious statement from college—there are three types of story: the literary, the glossy, and the pulp. I came to the conclusion that there are only good stories and bad stories. I've read better stories in pulp magazines than I read in literary magazines.

In literary magazines, plot doesn't seem to be one of their central interests and that carries into movies today. I heard about a producer saying "I don't care about story anymore." They're just so interested in effect.

Story is everything. That's what holds the audience.

What misconceptions, if any, did you have about the writing and publishing field when you were first getting started?

None. I knew nothing about it so I just figured if I wrote something worthwhile somebody would buy it. Fortunately, the first short story I published was unique enough so that an agent approached me and asked if he could handle me.

I wrote a novel, a huge one; I don't know, it was about 700 to 800 pages. My agent, the one above, said this is unpublishable, and I had no confidence in my work back then and I believed him so it got stuck in a drawer. This same agent, when I wrote *A Stir of Echoes*, he said, again, this is unpublishable; you're writing about things that are not interesting. I got so ticked off that I contacted Don Congden and he sold *A Stir of Echoes* and this first agent said well obviously Congden did a massive re-write. I did nothing.

I wish I had Harlan Ellison's chutzpah—I would have done the same thing with *Come Figures, Come Shadows*. It was just the beginning. It was going to be a huge novel and I wrote just part of Part One, but I got discouraged by an editor who said "Only Matheson could or would write this novel." So I put that away, too.

Do you think an agent is necessary to a novelist these days?

Sure, sure. To send stuff out, and wait, and wait. Then you get it back and it's rejected. You know, an agent is absolutely necessary.

It is often said that if you can write a good short story, you can write anything. Do you agree?

Not necessarily. The novel is quite a long drink of water to be involved in and people always say the short story is the most difficult form. I suppose it is. To my knowledge, I never really mastered the form. I wrote short stories for a number of years. I probably have 85 of them. They were all well-plotted and some of them had a sociological aspect. But I never really felt that I mastered the short story by any means at all.

I never knew what science fiction was. I never read it in my life up to that point. When I wrote "When I Met a Woman" people said: "Oh, that's about a mutant." I asked what a mutant was. There were about 50 to 60 science fiction magazines in the market. So I thought—my mother raised a practical boy—I guess I'll try writing science fiction.

As every writer does, they write a story where the couple, as they try to escape, turn out to be Adam and Eve. That's *de riguer* for writing a first science fiction tale, I think.

Do you write many short stories?

Not any more. But I have written hundreds.

What specific writers influenced, inspired, and, therefore, instructed you?

Ray Bradbury—he wrote me a letter when I had just a couple of stories published. There was a story in *Galaxy* called "Third from the Sun." He said that he had finished a story himself about a couple escaping from a bad regime, and in his story they were going to the past. In my story they were going to another planet; but he said it even had the same scene where the wife wonders if they should lock the front door. He was very encouraging. I think he always had been to young writers. He was an inspiration to all of us. He himself has commented that when he first started out he was terrible. He worked and worked and worked.

A good story will always last.

I *know* this is the question we always get, but aspiring novelists really *do* need to know: where do you get your ideas?

Initially, when I read science fiction—I had to take a crash course because I knew nothing about it—without thinking, I automatically became imitative and derivative. Actually, I was a very ardent moviegoer as a kid and I think most of my ideas came from the movies.

I saw Bela Lugosi's *Dracula* and I thought to myself: Well, if one vampire is scary, what if the world was full of vampires? That became *I Am Legend*.

Then I saw a comedy where Ray Milland put on Aldo Ray's hat, and Aldo Ray's head was so much bigger that the hat went down and over his ears, which provided a laugh in the movies. But to me it provided an idea—what if a guy put on his own hat and that hat was too big? *Shrinking Man*.

Actually, most of the ideas I had, the good ones, came from poor movies. If you see a good movie, you're absorbed by it. If you see a lousy movie, you're distracted.

How long, on the average, does it take you to go from initial idea to finished draft (ready to submit)?

Putting it together was probably more time-consuming. The writing of it took two to three months. I would write up to the point where I was writing twenty pages a day. That decreases more and more as the years go by. But if you write ten pages a day, in three months you have a novel.

Do you ever encounter "writer's block," and if so, how do you overcome it?

I never did. Fortunately, I don't even know what it is. But when you have four children and a wife to support, you know writer's block becomes untenable. So I just went on writing every day. I used to write six days a week, leaving one day off for my family. My wife got me down to five days.

How did you get past the initial barriers of criticism and rejection?

You have to be stubborn. For the last I don't know how many years, I always wrote the entire novel figuring that even if some people didn't like it, someone would publish it.

What are the best and worst aspects of writing for a living, in your opinion? What do you think is the hardest part of being a writer?

The ability to just write day after day after day. I'm not disciplined at all, but I found that compulsion served adequately. I wanted to write these things. I've never written anything that I wasn't interested in.

In relationship to sheer talent, how important would you rate discipline and time management to being a successful novelist?

Very important. The difference between being a working writer and a dreamer is the discipline to write down what you think about. A lot tougher to do than you can imagine.

If you were to give an aspiring novelist *one* piece of advice, what would you tell them?

It's a fallacy that you should write what you know about. You should write what interests you.

David Morrell

David Morrell is the award-winning author of *First Blood*, the novel in which Rambo was created. He was born in 1943 in Kitchener, Ontario, Canada. In 1960, at the age of 17, he became a fan of the classic television series *Route 66*, about two young men in a Corvette traveling the United States in search of America and themselves. Stirling Silliphant's scripts so impressed Morrell that he decided to become a writer.

In 1966, the work of another writer, Hemingway scholar Philip Young, prompted Morrell to move to the United States, where he studied with Young at Penn State and received his M.A. and Ph.D. in American literature. There, he also met the distinguished fiction writer William Tenn (real name Philip Klass), who taught Morrell the basics of fiction writing. The result was *First Blood*, a novel about a returned Vietnam veteran suffering from post-traumatic stress disorder who comes into conflict with a small-town police chief and fights his own version of the Vietnam War.

That "father" of all modern action novels was published in 1972 while Morrell was a professor in the English department at the University of Iowa. He taught there from 1970 to 1986, simultaneously writing other novels, many of them national best-sellers, such as *The Brotherhood of the Rose* (the basis for a highly rated NBC miniseries starring Robert Mitchum). Eventually wearying of two professions, he gave up his tenure to write full-time.

Shortly afterward, his 15-year-old son Matthew was diagnosed with a rare form of bone cancer and died in 1987, a loss that still haunts not only Morrell's life but his work, as in his memoir about Matthew, *Fireflies*, and his novel *Desperate Measures*, whose main character has lost a son.

"The mild-mannered professor with the bloody-minded visions," as one reviewer called him, Morrell is the author of 28 books, including such novels of international intrigue as *The Fifth Profession*, *Assumed Identity*, and *Extreme Denial* (set in Santa Fe, New Mexico, where he now lives with his wife, Donna). His most recent publications are the dark-suspense thrillers *Creepers* and *Scavengers*.

Morrell is the co-president of the International Thriller Writers organization (internationalthrillerwriters.com). Noted for his research, Morrell is a graduate of the National Outdoor Leadership School for wilderness survival as well as the G. Gordon Liddy Academy of Corporate Security. He is also an honorary lifetime member of the Special Operations Association and the Association of Former Intelligence Officers. He has been trained in firearms, hostage negotiation, assuming identities, executive protection, and antiterrorist driving, among numerous other action skills that he describes in his novels. With 18 million copies in print, his work has been translated into 26 languages.

When did you realize you wanted to be a writer?

I made the absolute decision to be a writer when I was 17 and the classic TV series *Route 66* premiered. The mixture of action and ideas in the scripts by Stirling Silliphant so excited me that I wrote a letter to him and said that I wanted to be him.

At what age did you attempt to write your first novel?

I started my first novel *First Blood* when I was 25. I was in graduate school at the time. In a way, my education made me a late starter.

What was it about (theme, genre, etc.)?

First Blood is the novel that introduced the character of Rambo. The novel is about a troubled Vietnam veteran who comes into conflict with a small town police chief and fights a miniature version of the Vietnam War.

Did you ever take any writing classes? Or specific instruction (seminar, workshop, etc.) to learn the craft of writing a novel?

In undergraduate school, I took a fiction writing class. Later when I was in graduate school at Penn State, I studied with the first true professional writer I had ever met. His pen name is William Tenn. His real name is Philip Klass. My conversations with him were invaluable.

Is writing the only "job" you've ever had? If not, what else did you do career-wise, and how did it help or hinder your writing?

For 16 years, I was a professor of American literature at the University of Iowa. Writing and teaching were a good match, but eventually I got tired of working 7 days a week, so I resigned my tenured professorship, one of the few people who has ever done that.

How do you feel about the distinctions often expressed about "commercial" versus "literary" novels?

The only distinction I care about is whether a story is well written and well told. To me, all fiction can be fit into a genre. "Literary" is too often a synonym for "difficult to understand."

What misconceptions, if any, did you have about the writing and publishing field when you were first getting started?

I was perhaps naïve about letting my fiction speak for itself instead of seeking out publicity opportunities.

How have things (technology, society, culture, literature) changed since you got started?

Computer word processing has made revising a pleasure rather than a manual chore. I used to hate typing the final draft of my books, praying that I wouldn't make a typo and need to start the page anew. I have arthritis in my fingers from the damage to my fingers in those years.

It is often said that if you can write a good short story, you can write anything. Do you agree?

Short stories and novels require two different skills. Compression versus expansion. I know a lot of writers who are skilled at one form but not the other.

Do you write many short stories?

I've written around 70 short stories, some of which have won prizes. They are very time consuming. Thirty pages might take me five weeks. By contrast, I normally write thirty pages of a novel in just one week.

What specific writers influenced, inspired, and, therefore, instructed you?

Stirling Silliphant's scripts for *Route 66*. Ernest Hemingway (my MA thesis is about his style). James M. Cain (*The Postman Always Rings Twice*). The great British suspense writer Geoffrey Household (*Rogue Male*). Believe it or not, Henry James, especially his theories about the first person. I used to teach a seminar about him at the University of Iowa.

When you are not reading fiction, what do you like to read?

I don't read fiction when I'm working on a project. I find that another writer's fiction style can be like the flu and contaminate me. I read a lot of non-fiction, especially about history.

How would you describe your own "style"?

Direct sentences that use concrete words and take the sense of sight for granted, using the other senses as much as possible. I talk about this at length in my writing book, *The Successful Novelist*.

I *know* this is the question we always get, but aspiring novelists really *do* need to know: where do you get your ideas?

Day dreams.

How long, on the average, does it take you to go from initial idea to finished draft (ready to submit)?

A year. The research often takes a lot of time also. I'm like a method actor. I immerse myself in a topic. For *The Shimmer*, whose main character is a private pilot, I took flight training and received my pilot's license.

Can you describe your writing process for us—do you develop character profiles and outlines for your novels before writing them, or do you let your characters/ideas develop as you write?

At the start of each project, I write a letter to myself in which I answer the question, "Why is this project worth a year of my life?" I then analyze the theme and situations as if I were having a conversation with myself. This document can be 30 or 40 pages long when I'm finished.

Do you ever encounter "writer's block," and if so, how do you overcome it?

I had writer's block twice. It has two causes. Either the story has been ill conceived and refuses to move forward, or else something in the subject matter makes my subconscious uncomfortable.

How did you get past the initial barriers of criticism and rejection?

The start of my career was charmed. I sent the manuscript of *First Blood* to an agent, who sold it in six weeks. I never experienced the rejection that can discourage a writer.

What are the best and worst aspects of writing for a living, in your opinion?

Being self-employed as a writer isn't for everyone. You need to enjoy living by your wits all day every day.

Can writing *well* be taught to someone who does not?

I can teach someone to write prose that avoids the common mistakes. I can't teach anyone what to write *about*.

In relationship to sheer talent, how important would you rate discipline and time management to being a successful novelist?

The key elements of a successful career are talent, determination, discipline, and luck.

If you were to give an aspiring novelist *one* piece of advice, what would you tell them?

Follow your light. Be a first-rate version of yourself and not a second-rate version of another writer.

Peter Straub

Peter Straub was born in Milwaukee, Wisconsin. He lived in Ireland and England for a decade, and now he lives in New York City.

Straub is the author of sixteen novels (including two collaborations with Stephen King), two collections of poetry, and two collections of shorter fiction. He has won four Bram Stoker Awards, two World Fantasy Awards, a British Fantasy Award, and an International Horror Guild Award. In 1998, he was named Grand Master at the World Horror Convention.

His newest novel, *A Dark Matter*, appeared in 2010.

When did you realize you wanted to be a writer?

The best answer I can give to that question is the following. Early one evening in the mid-1950s, I was watching an episode of *Father Knows Best* in which the son, Bud, who was played by a doomed little actor named Billy Gray, had to prepare a homework assignment. He put the implements on the table, and for about a second and a half, there was a shot of a perfectly sharpened pencil arrayed slantwise atop a pad of clean white lined paper. I gasped; I thought it was one of the most moving, most beautiful, most spectacular things I had ever seen in my life. I must have been about 12. It was like a religious experience.

At what age did you attempt to write your first novel?

I must have been 24—it was the second year of my marriage, and the second year of my teaching job (the only job I ever had, and after one more year, I quit).

What was it about (theme, genre, etc.)?

It was mainly about the vanity of the infant author, his absolute cluelessness, and how very many books he had read. It was in the form of a diary, and the diarist referred to everyone by his or her first initials.

Did you ever take any writing classes? Or specific instruction (seminar, workshop, etc.) to learn the craft of writing a novel?

When I was a second-semester freshman at the University of Wisconsin, I took a creative writing course. I didn't learn a thing, but it was pretty enjoyable. There was a stunning young woman who sat in the first row. We all called her "the big Indian," but she wasn't an Indian, and she wasn't all that big.

Is writing the only "job" you've ever had? If not, what else did you do career-wise, and how did it help or hinder your writing?

As I said earlier, I had a teaching job. From 1966 to 1969, I taught English to prep-school boys at the University School of Milwaukee. I wasn't capable of writing anything worthwhile in those days, but if I had been, the job would have been a tremendous interference.

How do you feel about the distinctions often expressed about "commercial" versus "literary" novels?

I think this distinction is sometimes valid, as in the case of James Patterson, and sometimes not, as in the case of Robert Stone.

What misconceptions, if any, did you have about the writing and publishing field when you were first getting started?

Well, I knew nothing at all, so I hardly had any misconceptions. I just waited to see what would happen. After my first novel was accepted, for about ten minutes I thought, "Oh wow, this means I'm going to be rich and famous," but that went away in a hurry. I must have been infected by *Youngblood Hawke*.

It is often said that if you can write a good short story, you can write anything. Do you agree?

Not at all. Remember Katherine Anne Porter? Short stories require a different set of muscles than those involved in writing a novel.

Do you write many short stories?

I wish I did. Actually, I wish I wrote more novellas. I probably write one or two short stories a year.

What specific writers influenced, inspired, and, therefore, instructed you?

This is a long, long list, so I'll give you the short form. Thomas Wolfe, Sinclair Lewis, John O'Hara, Ernest Hemingway, F. Scott Fitzgerald, William Faulkner,

Raymond Chandler, Henry James, John Ashbery, Stephen King, Donald Harington, Paul Scott.

When you are not reading fiction, what do you like to read?

Biographies and autobiographies of writers, poetry, Eve Sedgwick, books about jazz.

How would you describe your own "style"?

I'd say my style is more or less orderly, with occasional manic breakdowns. I like to find the really right word, which is often an unexpected word.

I *know* this is the question we always get, but aspiring novelists really *do* need to know: where do you get your ideas?

I don't think anybody knows the answer to that question. Ideas turn up by themselves, sometimes perfectly attired, sometimes in rags. The longer you sit at your desk, the more ideas you get. All ideas are not equal, however. Some must be turned away at the door and sent off to tempt some other, less fastidious writer.

How long, on the average, does it take you to go from initial idea to finished draft (ready to submit)?

This varies wildly. On the average, though, it takes from about a year and a half to two years.

Can you describe your writing process for us—do you develop character profiles and outlines for your novels before writing them, or do you let your characters and ideas develop as you write?

This also varies from book to book. I like to begin with as much material as possible in hand—that is, a good knowledge of the characters, and a reasonably accurate idea of what happens in the first third of the book. Very often, the book grabs the wheel and drives itself somewhere previously unknown, not even guessed at.

Do you ever encounter "writer's block," and if so, how do you overcome it?

I hate the whole idea of writer's block. I don't believe in it. It should never be mentioned in respectable company.

How did you get past the initial barriers of criticism and rejection?

What criticism and rejection? I have no idea what you are talking about.

What are the best and worst aspects of writing for a living, in your opinion?

The best aspects of writing for a living: Your time is your own, you have no boss and no competition, you can do exactly what you wish to do. The worst aspects of writing for a living: You are absolutely alone all of the time, you might as well be in solitary confinement; and this condition leads to dizzying mood swings and a tendency to apply fantasy to everyday life.

Can writing *well* be taught to someone who does not?

No. It would be an unbelievably horrible task, like committing surgery on an infant puppy.

In relationship to sheer talent, how important would you rate discipline and time management to being a successful novelist?

These things are pretty important. If you can't make yourself sit at your desk for hour after hour and day after day, you'll never get anything done. In fact, you'd turn out to be the kind of louse who goes around saying he has "writer's block."

If you were to give an aspiring novelist *one* piece of advice, what would you tell them?

I'd say—start reading like a demon at the age of six and never stop.

Whitley Strieber

Whitley Strieber is the author of 74 books and 300 short stories. He has published 20 of the books and 30 of the stories. He has also written 10 film scripts, 9 of which have been turned into digital files and stored in a computer. One was made into a movie.

Mr. Strieber is a Grand Knight of the Teutoberger Wald, the ancient order of the descendants of the German Cherusii tribe who defeated the legions of the Roman general Varus in the Teutoberger forest in 9 A.D. He is also a member of the Sons of the American Revolution and has danced in the Follies Bergere.

Mr. Strieber is noted for his extensive collection of phasmids and is a member of the board of the British Stick Insect Foundation. He is also a leader in the campaign to link the phasmid protection organization to Ducks Unlimited and is the creator of the signature recipe for phasmid soup.

For many years, Mr. Strieber performed onstage with a 6-foot-tall ventriloquist's dummy called Robert A. Fredricks. Their act ended in 1976, after Mr. Fredricks was broken up in a fight.

Mr. Strieber was captured and eaten by aliens in December of 1985. Despite this, he can be found on his website, unknowncountry.com. With 20 million hits a month, it is the largest website of its kind in the world. It's also the only one of its kind.

When did you realize you wanted to be a writer?

Age six. I stole my mom's highball and drank it, then wrote a story called "The Moon Come Up Over the Valley." There was no moon. There was no valley. This was my introduction to the concept of fiction.

At what age did you attempt to write your first novel?

I finished my first novel at the age of 17. It was called *Little Paradise*. It has never been published.

What was it about (theme, genre, etc.)?

It was about the inner journey of an angst-ridden late adolescent attempting without much success to attune his hormonal being to civilized society. In other words, it was about me at the age of 17.

Did you ever take any writing classes? Or specific instruction (seminar, workshop, etc.) to learn the craft of writing a novel?

I took a writing course at the University of Texas that was fairly pointless. But then I discovered Dick Humphries at Columbia. He was one of the very few truly great writing teachers. His brilliant innovation was to have students discuss work in seminar, but without reference to the author. So work got discussed objectively. He gave me a Cornell Woolrich fellowship, which enabled me to attend the course for a very productive year.

As a teenager, I was greatly helped by Bro. Martin McMurtry at my high school, Central Catholic in San Antonio. He used to give me his own stories to read and critique, which made me feel very much like a fellow writer. And he encouraged me to believe that I could write.

I do not think that there is any general craft to writing a novel. There are no rules. If you write something a couple of hundred pages long that is, in general, untrue, then you are a novelist. Novelistic styles are as individual as faces. The important thing is to let your voice come through with complete clarity and honesty. However you accomplish that is up to you. If the method you hit upon happens to draw readers, then you can publish your work. If not, then it becomes a part of your spirit.

Is writing the only "job" you've ever had? If not, what else did you do career-wise, and how did it help or hinder your writing?

I worked as an advertising executive from 1970 until 1978 when I sold *The Wolfen*. I enjoyed my work a great deal. Mostly, it involved lunching with clients and having a good time, with a modicum of marketing thrown in. I was not a copywriter but an account executive. My work involved delivering the capabilities of the agency to the client, finding and fulfilling their advertising needs. I wrote after work and on weekends. There were seven failed novels, many tries at getting an agent, many rejections from publishers. I still have these novels, and some of them are damned odd. My first reading by a member of the public came when an agent who had intensely disliked one of my efforts rejected it by tossing it in a mailbox without a wrapper. A postman gathered up the heap of pages and found my address on the title page. He brought it to me on his day off, a Saturday. He and his wife had read it and they thought it was just great. It was called *Catherine's Bounty*. My wife said to me: "See, you're a writer, this proves it." Well, sort of.

How do you feel about the distinctions often expressed about "commercial" versus "literary" novels?

This distinction means nothing to me and little more to the culture at large. It's a social thing. Novels either last or they don't because of the characters they portray. If they happen to attract a large audience, they're called commercial. If not, then they're literary. Anthony Powell's twelve novel sequence *A Dance to the Music of Time* is going to be immortal, not because it pretends to linguistic innovation, but because it portrays characters to sublime perfection. It's a breathtaking achievement. On the other hand, "commercial" novelist Stephen King's creation of *Misery Chastain* is a fabulous achievement, also.

As we in our culture have become more and more able to see ourselves as individuals, to identify an "I" within that is more than a reflection of our place in our social context, the novel has taken on more and more meaning for us. Reading a good novel is a constant process of comparison—we are comparing our moral predicament to the moral predicament of the characters. Novels that matter enable practically anybody to say, "yes, this situation has meaning to me." It's why *Don Quixote* and *Ulysses* will always and forever be remembered, and *Mrs. McIntosh My Darling*, for all its bravado and courage, will slip into the past.

As far as commercial versus literary is concerned, if a novel isn't entertaining, it's not a novel but something else, perhaps a moral statement or what I believe they now call a "text." All good novels betray a similar nervousness and humility: They are, like Molly Bloom, deceptively eager to entertain.

What misconceptions, if any, did you have about the writing and publishing field when you were first getting started?

I had all the misconceptions. I was basically a bum looking for a way to live in a nice house and still be a bum. I thought writing novels would enable me to do that. Type it out, send it in, get a check back. Neat.

Not so neat. When I actually began to write, I found my whole being involved. I found myself digging into myself in truly terrifying ways. My novels became a kind of occult journey into my own dark heart. What had seemed at seventeen like a lark became a phenomenal and terrible spiritual undertaking that I could not and cannot resist.

As far as the marketing end goes, I just write what I want to write and hope that somebody will publish it. I am really, really interested in conveying enormous amounts of significant content in very simple ways. I'm interested in the elegance and universality of language, and its potential to touch souls with unexpectedly intense gentleness. For this reason, because it seems so simple, my own work is pretty much dismissed by this age that prizes a sort of baroque innovation in its prose. Important fiction must not contain ordinary metaphors, for example. But I am interested in ordinary metaphors, in charging them with new and unexpected energy. A book like *The Forbidden Zone* is considered a piece of irrelevant trivia. However, it is anything but. It was a great success as literature. I guess I'm misunderstood, poor widdle me! (Do you pay by the word or by the whine?)

How have things (technology, society, culture, literature) changed since you got started?

Cars get better gas mileage. The computer has made it easy to steal votes. Lots of people who used to smoke no longer do so. Television is no longer fun. Music is dead. Mick Jagger, oddly enough, is not. *Soul Mountain* has been published. Turtles now get cancer, but flowers still don't.

It is often said that if you can write a good short story, you can write anything. Do you agree?

If you can write a good first sentence, you can write anything.

Do you write many short stories?

I love to write short stories, but I keep them mostly to myself. I published a book of my stories called *Evenings with Demons, Stories from Thirty Years*. It was a private publication, though. My stories are the treasure of my soul, and I don't want to expose them to critics who are only interested in punishing me for having written *Communion*. Either I am to be ignored or panned, that is my fate for having committed to paper an ancient and terrible truth about the human condition.

What specific writers influenced, inspired, and, therefore, instructed you?

The writers I love the most are legion. I read *Finnegan's Wake* aloud to myself when I was twenty and remained drunk on the words for years. Faulkner is my god. Anthony Powell is my god. Peter Straub is my god. Gunter Grass is my god. Julian Green is my god. Gao Xinjiang is my god. Marcel Proust is my god. Fyodor Dostoyevsky is my god. Malcolm Lowry is my god. Thomas Wolf is my god. Beneath the black foam of immediate life, rides a great ocean of perfect souls.

When you are not reading fiction, what do you like to read?

Right now I am reading Moustafa Gadalla's *The Egyptian Mystics* and the newest book by Laurence Gardner, *Lost Science of the Sacred Ark*. They are in the process of recovering the mystical and alchemical secrets of ancient Egypt. When we recover what we lost there, we will recover our lost humanity and replace the smart bombs with compassionate souls. I also like to read about close encounters, especially the simple stories of ordinary people, because it is out of these stories, now scorned by the high, that a new world will be born. Can you imagine how absurd Marcus Aurelius would have thought the stories of a Jewish revolutionary come back from the dead that were being whispered by his slaves behind the backstairs? It's the same with the tales of alien abduction. They are really stories of the future. Do I think, therefore, that aliens are real and that these stories will some day be prized for their historical moment? I have no idea. I'm not even much interested. I am writing about the spirit of the culture, its zeitgeist, not the bricks and stones of alien office buildings on some distant planet, where they plan tours to Earth, to suck at the souls of the holy.

I read to find a ladder to heaven, basically.

How would you describe your own "style"?

It's like riding a bicycle, to achieve a style. Actually, for me, the word *style* is more important than the word *voice*. I am interested in the power of juxtaposition more than I am the flavor of my sentences. That makes me more or less minor, but I like being minor. You can find out much more, because when you are major, everybody hides their sins from you. People feel free to bully me, to tell me to my face that they think my work is junk, to laugh at me and to pretend never to have heard of me. How, if I was a great voice, could I ever get the chance to see into the secret world of my oppressors? Recently a critic reviewed my book, *Confirmation*, in some newspaper. He said that the publisher, St. Martin's Press, should be "punished" for having published it. The interesting thing was, this review was not published until five years after the book came out. You know you are doing something right when people carry their hatred of you that far.

I *know* this is the question we always get, but aspiring novelists really *do* need to know: where do you get your ideas?

All good ideas come out of desperation. It is not a matter of cobbling together a clever concept, but of being frantic to write something down. I shared the same editor as Jacqueline Susann. She wrote with that frantic dedication, the same desperation that gripped Marcel Proust and Malcolm Lowry. He reported that she could not understand why she was not respected. Well, neither could I. Her prose is a gaggle, her stories are a mess, but those characters, my God, they are brilliant, and, in the end, that's what matters in a novel. As far as planning goes, I am working on a novel right now. I have no plan at all. I have no idea where it will go. I don't even know what it's about. But the characters do. They're over there on the other side of the room plotting; I can hear them. They're whispering about how to do me in.

How long, on the average, does it take you to go from initial idea to finished draft (ready to submit)?

Anywhere from twenty or thirty years to a couple of weeks. I had my book *The Path* gestating in me for thirty years. The novel *Catherine's Bounty* was there for ten years. *The Wolfen* was written in a month. *Communion* was a year of bloody agony and absolute terror. *Lilith's Dream* had been floating around I don't know how long.

I come across ideas kind of by accident. I'll start thinking about a character whose life has interested me for years. Then all of a sudden, there are pages that start coming out. I'm not big on control.

Can you describe the writing process for us—do you develop character profiles and outlines for your novels before writing them, or do you let your characters and ideas develop as you write?

I write outlines in order to deceive editors into buying my stuff. They are a separate prose form that has nothing to do with my work. If my characters aren't surprising me, I'm in trouble.

Do you ever encounter "writer's block," and if so, how do you overcome it?

I don't believe that this exists.

How did you get past the initial barriers of criticism and rejection?

I didn't. You just keep going, one step at a time, like a soldier on the battlefield.

What are the best and worst aspects of writing for a living, in your opinion?

Economically, the best thing is getting a check for a million bucks. The worst is going bankrupt. I've done both.

Spiritually, the best thing is discovering the actual potential of human beings. When you do that, there is a sense of escaping from a web you did not know had captured you.

Intellectually, the best thing is being interested. The worst is when you are not. I've never written anything that didn't absolutely fascinate me, but I have tried and it's soul hell.

Can writing *well* be taught to someone who does not?

No.

In relationship to sheer talent, how important would you rate discipline and time management to being a successful novelist?

Discipline and time management are absolutely crucial. When it's going well, I can do 10 pages in a day. Twenty, when I'm white hot. But usually I am not white hot. Usually, I am struggling. The morning, the empty page, the awful sense that my career is over. Day after day. The key for me is to sit there all day, no matter what.

If you were to give an aspiring novelist *one* piece of advice, what would you tell them?

Give up immediately. Only crazy people in here.

Index

CHECK OUT THESE BEST-SELLERS

More than 450 titles available at booksellers and online retailers everywhere!

978-1-59257-115-4

978-1-59257-900-6

978-1-59257-855-9

978-1-59257-222-9

978-1-59257-957-0

978-1-59257-785-9

978-1-59257-471-1

978-1-59257-483-4

978-1-59257-883-2

978-1-59257-966-2

978-1-59257-908-2

978-1-59257-786-6

978-1-59257-954-9

978-1-59257-437-7

978-1-59257-888-7